ENDOSULFAN : GLOBAL CONSPIRACY AND A KERALA FRAUD STORY

ENDOSULFAN
Global Conspiracy and a Kerala Fraud Story

Kalathil Ramakrishnan

GenNext Publication

ISBN : 978-93-8022-240-0

Price : ₹ 450

First Published, 2015

Published by,

genNext Publication
23, Main Ansari Road, Darya Ganj
New Delhi-110002
Ph. : 23242060, 23261060
Fax : 011-23285914
E-mail: gennext@hotmail.com
Website : www.gyanbooks.com

Laser Typesetting : Quick Media, Delhi
Printed at : G. Print Process, Delhi

Cataloging in Publication Data—DK
Courtesy: D.K. Agencies (P) Ltd. <docinfo@dkagencies.com>

Ramakrishnan, Kalathil, author.
Endosulfan : global conspiracy and a Kerala fraud story / Kalathil Ramakrishnan.
pages cm
Includes bibliographical references (pages) and index.
ISBN 9789380222400

1. Endosulfan—India—Kasaragod (District) 2. Rural health—India—Kasaragod (District) 3. Cashew nut industry—India—Kasaragod (District) 4. Cashew nut—Diseases and pests—Control—India—Kasaragod (District) 5. Agriculture and state—India—Kasaragod (District) 6. Pesticides—Government policy—India—Kasaragod (District) 7. Pesticides—Law and legislation—India—Kasaragod (District) I. Title.
DDC 632.9517095483 23

Contents

Preface and Acknowledgements

It was described as a man-made tragedy next only to the Bhopal gas disaster in its magnitude, sweep and sufferings of the affected people. Most of the media and even the National Human Rights Commission compared the endosulfan fake tragedy of Kasargod to the Bhopal gas leak disaster. The media ran the campaign in India and abroad. The internet and the social network sites played it up taking the news to every nook and corner of the world. Finally, it turned out to be a huge man-made fraud, unparalleled in the media history. In other words, a mountain was eventually reduced to a molehill.

However, after a decade of the controversy the Kerala Government now finds itself in a pathetic situation. Having encouraged the green activists to conduct agitation against endosulfan, it finds itself in a piquant situation in the face of compelling demand by the agitators to rehabilitate the so-called victims. First, it does not have the money to undertake the massive rehabilitation. Second, no help is forthcoming from the Union Government. The government is helpless and it cannot tell the people that everything was a fraud fearing severe backlash from anti-endosulfan activists.

Nevertheless, writing a book on the 'endosulfan tragedy' of Kasargod with a view to denying all that the media and the government machinery as well as the Non-Governmental Organisations, NGOs, have been propagating for nearly a decade is rather a difficult task; it is almost like swimming against the tide. The entire media in the country and the government have been working round the clock to pin down the cause of the diseases to the aerial spraying of endosulfan in the cashew estates owned by the Plantation Corporation of Kerala in Kasargod district of North Kerala. I believe that a gigantic task is, therefore, devolved on me to initiate the whole unlearning process.

Endosulfan is an abominable word in Kasargod. Because of strident media campaign across the country, particularly in Kerala the pesticide is associated with cross bones and a skull–a symbol of danger and death. True, endosulfan, a whipping boy of the media, was conditioned in the minds of the people with a skull and cross bones. Besides, there is also another logo—the large, pitiable head of a girl who died of hydrocephalus—taken by a media photographer. But nobody cared whether the little girl crying with excruciating pain was really a victim of endosulfan. It is said that camera would not lie, but an isolated and stand-alone shot taken from anywhere can be a campaign material if it was used on thousand occasions. It would linger on for long in popular imagination which cannot be wished away.

Internationally, a controversy is going on that endosulfan is an endocrine disruptor and it would cause cancer and a host of other diseases. There are innumerable studies that one can see in the internet that endosulfan is harmful to human beings. There are also studies which are projected in the same internet that endosulfan is not harmful in tropical countries and that studies conducted in cold regions would not be applicable in the entire globe where climates vary and pests are different. There are people who believe that the entire storm on endosulfan was unleashed to market the branded pesticides manufactured in European Union countries in tropical countries including India and China where endosulfan–a generic and non-patented insecticide—was being used for the past 40 years.

Endosulfan was formulated in the early 50s and had been in continuous use in several European countries for more than fifty years. But there had been no hue and cry on the reported ill-effects of endosulfan on human beings while the pesticide was being produced by European Union countries. All the trouble started when the EU lost its predominance in the production of endosulfan conceding grounds to other tropical countries including India.

However, what had happened in Kasargod was crucial.

Whether endosulfan spray had caused all the alleged diseases in Kasargod villages is still being debated about. While some studies blamed endosulfan for the diseases, other studies had exonerated the pesticide from the odium.

Meanwhile, science has become the casualty. There can only be one scientific truth relating to the cardinal issue whether endosulfan had caused havoc in Kasargod or not. There cannot be a science which keeps one in perpetual doubt.

Crores of rupees have been pumped in by the anti-endosulfan lobby across the world to influence the media and for the propaganda. The anti-endosulfan lobby is powerful; the relentless and well-orchestrated propaganda unleashed by the media and the Non-Governmental Organisations influenced even the judicial system. But only a few know that what the media and the government in Kerala have been saying on the endosulfan issue all along was a string of lies. There are two kinds of truths; the truth which is pleasing to hear. Another type of truth is unpleasant to hear; and in this book I am presenting the unpleasant truth. Those who honestly believed or were brainwashed into believing that endosulfan spray was responsible for all strange diseases in the area may be a little bit disappointed after reading this book.

As a journalist who visited the suspected victims of endosulfan, I had doubted the integrity of the anti-endosulfan agitators at the very beginning. I knew that what they have been saying all along was contrary to truth and it was all meant to serve the interests of some powerful Non-Governmental Organisations getting foreign money.

The health department of the state could have arrived at the truth long ago by comparing the statistical data relating to the mortality and morbidity state of the sprayed area. There is national average for each disease and it was a proven fact that the diseases in Kasargod district were well below the national average. Still, there are clusters of diseases in some areas and Enmakaje was one such a cluster village. The diseases may be due to local factors or because of adverse environmental factors. The causes of the diseases may be due to anthropological reasons or because of genetic causes. But the people lost the opportunity to know the real causes responsible for the cluster of diseases in Enmakaje as the anti-endosulfan activists branded the pesticide spray as the prime suspect.

In the height of the controversy, the possibility of natural diseases and natural deaths were ignored and instead every death and every disease was attributed to the use of the pesticide. It was also the classic example of the media failure in reporting the real facts about endosulfan spray. Had the media approached the whole issue in an independent and dispassionate way, there would not have been any need to write a book like this to bring out the truth.

What I intend in this book is not to protect and bail out a pesticide. If it had wreaked havoc on unsuspecting people, it should be banned. But there should be a fair trial. In the case of endosulfan, the culprit was first nabbed and pronounced guilty by the media and environmental NGOs and then began the trial. There was also the global conspiracy against endosulfan spearheaded by the European Union at the Persistent Organic Pollutants Review Committee, POPRC, meet in Geneva known as the Stockholm convention. But the main issue is what really happened in Kasargod– whether it had actually caused the alleged diseases there.

All pesticides are poison. Pesticides are formulated to kill pests. In Kerala, people took the common rat poison to kill themselves in the past. Taking poison or pesticide is still the practice to commit suicide in Kerala, especially among farmers.

Aerial spraying of a pesticide should not have been allowed in a populated area. The people coming under direct contact with the spray would feel uncomfortable. Besides, it is the denial of their right to have access to clean air.

When the anti-endosulfan agitation was at its peak in Kasargod, there had been demands from green activists that India should ban all pesticides. It is a well-known fact that without pesticides, about 30 per cent of agriculture would be lost which would put the global food security of billions of people at risk. But pesticide use should be monitored and should be in constant review as suggested by Prof. Ivan Kennedy of the faculty of Agriculture and Environmental Chemistry at University of Sydney in Australia.

I had preserved copious notes of my field visit to various exposed villages from the very beginning of the endosulfan controversy. I kept the files not with the intention that one day I would be writing a book on the endosulfan controversy. Such an idea was far from my mind in those not too remote days when I visited the sprayed areas on several occasions. But when I started writing in September 2012 all those old field notes and scribbling proved very helpful for me to write the book.

I had collected copies of judgments on endosulfan as well as various documents concerning the issue. It was all meant to guide myself to write fairly good reports for the English paper I was working. Some of my friends had sent me the reports of various commissions which probed the endosulfan issue.

The studies conducted by Dr K.M. Sreekumar and Dr K. D. Prathapan of the Kerala Agricultural University had helped me to get a clear idea of the scientific aspects of the issue. It goes to the credit of their scientific acumen for exposing the whole untruth. They unveiled the fraud based on their strong conviction in scientific truth. The scientist duo had taken much effort, even in the face of risk to their academic career, to unravel the whole truth.

M. Gangadharan Nair, secretary of the Plantation Corporation Protection Council–on whose head and shoulders endosulfan had fallen while filling it in helicopter tank-helped me greatly in unearthing the past misdeeds of the anti-endosulfan activists in the sprayed area. My sons Rahul Ram and Praphul Ram helped me by making valuable suggestions to improve the book. Many of my friends in the field of journalism had encouraged me by giving various suggestions and providing me with ideas.

Finally, I submit the book to the readers hoping that they would find it a welcome change from the often repeated version that they had been reading from newspapers and from watching the television. Contradictory views on any subject and its discussion by the people would help strengthen democracy. But on the contrary, juggernauting all opposite views on an issue contained the seeds of social fascism.

In fact, a major chunk of the media and social activists have been following an obstinate line of thinking on the endosulfan issue. But Indian democracy is robust and it can accommodate opposite views in its stride no matter what the media has been propagating all along. There are other means of communication than the mainstream media. There are people in every walk of life—in bureaucracy, police, the media and the judiciary who follow a conscientious path. These people, though limited in number, make Indian democracy a vibrant and dynamic entity. There are three things which cannot be hidden–the Sun, Moon and the Truth, says a Buddhist proverb. A time will come when all lies are destined to be exposed; I feel that the time has come to expose the untruth.

The dissemination of untruth reached its zenith when a group of members of the Rajya Sabha demanded country-wide bad on endosulfan recently. A CPM member introduced a bill in the Rajya Sabha on August 8, 2014 demanding total ban on endosulfan by the Union Government. The Union Minister of Agriculture assured the members that the ban would be considered and the member withdrew the bill.

The Supreme Court had imposed ad-interim ban on endosulfan on May 13, 2011 and consequently all production of endosulfan stopped throughout the country. The pesticide is no longer produced in India. It is a joke that the member wanted another ban on endosulfan when the ad-interim ban on endosulfan has not been lifted by the apex court so far even after three years of its temporary ban.

Even as I conclude this book, comes the latest disability data in the country released by the Census Commissioner of India. The census was taken in 2011. This confirmed the 2011 data that the percentage of the physically and mentally challenged continued to be less in Kasargod than in other districts of Kerala. This exposes the whole absurd drama being played by anti-endosulfan activists across the country.

Kalathil Ramakrishnan
Kasargod,
August 12, 2014

1

INTRODUCTION: IT ALL HAPPENED IN THIS WISE

Way back in the early 80s, a helicopter went around the cashew plantations located to the east of Kasaragod district of Kerala in South India. The cashew estat[illegible] Plantation Corporation of Kerala (PCK), a c[illegible] the government. The helicopter sprayed e[illegible] year, to combat the menace of the mosquito [illegible] havoc with the cashew plantations.

Children who watched the helicopte[illegible] them were unconscious of the dangers [illegible] a flying machine hovering above their hea[illegible] they enjoyed the spray dripping their ha[illegible] They were also joined by the elders expe[illegible] seeing a flying machine for the first t[illegible] continued for twenty long years. Endo[illegible] sprayed in the months of December as wel[illegible] January, twice a year. The same helicopte[illegible] for Alakkode estate of the PCK and the Ce[illegible] Aralam in Kannur district for aerial spray[illegible] cashew plantations. Strangely, no dise[illegible] in Aralam farm as well in the Alakkode [illegible] estates of the PCK though the aerial spra[illegible] there for a long period. There was also hu[illegible] Alakkode and Alampakkam estates of the PC[illegible] there were several families of tribes living [illegible] plantation.

1

INTRODUCTION : IT ALL HAPPENED IN THIS WISE

Way back in the early 80s, a helicopter would whirl around the cashew plantations located to the east of Kasargod district of Kerala in South India. The cashew estates belonged to the Plantation Corporation of Kerala, PCK, a company owned by the government. The helicopter sprayed endosulfan, twice a year, to contain the menace of tea mosquito bugs that wreaked havoc with the cashew plantations.

Children who watched the helicopter hovering above them were in a boisterous mood. In scores of villages where a flying machine clattering above their heads was a rare sight, they enjoyed the spray clapping their hands and shouting. They were also joined by the elders expressing sheer joy of seeing a flying machine for the first time. The scenario continued for twenty long years. Endosulfan would be sprayed at the end of December as well as at the end of January, twice a year. The same helicopter would then leave for Alakkode estate of the PCK and the Central-State farm in Aralam in Kannur district for aerial spray of endosulfan on cashew plantations there. Strangely, no diseases were noticed in Aralam farm as well in the Alakkode and Mannarkkat estates of the PCK though the aerial spray was conducted there for a long period. There was also human habitation in Alakkode and Mannarkkat estates of the PCK. In Aralam farm there were several families of tribes living amidst the cashew plantations.

The PCK once owned 5,450 hectares of cashew plantations spread over five divisions in the district. In some estates cashew trees were slashed following the endosulfan controversy. Now the PCK has planted rubber saplings replacing the old cashew nut trees. But even then the PCK was maintaining cashew plantations in some estates. In addition to the Kasargod estates, the PCK has 540 hectares of plantations in Mannarkkat in Palakkad district.

However, in early 1977 the PCK management noted serious damages to the plantations due to the attack of tea mosquito bugs and that the quantity of raw nuts was on the decline. The attack of tea mosquito bugs started before the flowering of cashew trees causing heavy fall in the yield of raw nuts. The attack of tea mosquito bugs continued for the succeeding year also. Perturbed, the PCK management was finally compelled to find a solution to the problem which threatened its very existence.

It first approached the Central Plantation Crops Research Institute, CPCRI, in Puthur in Karnataka which was conducting research on cashew crops. Alternatively, the PCK got in touch with the Kerala Agriculture University in Mannuthi for a solution to the severe problem caused by the tea mosquito bugs. After several experiments, the CPCRI advised aerial spray of endosulfan since it was found to be both effective and economical in containing the menace of tea mosquito bugs.

The Directorate of Plant Protection, Quarantine and Storage, under the Ministry of Agriculture of the Union Government granted approval for aerial spray of the pesticide. The Directorate also gave a list of approved pesticides for the aerial spray. In 1978, the PCK again sought the advice of the officials concerned. The Directorate of Cashew Development, Kochi, under the Ministry of Agriculture forwarded a list of chemicals recommended by the All India Coordinated Cashew Improvement Project and the National Research Centre for Cashew in Puthur in Karnataka that can be used for spraying to control tea mosquito bugs. One of the selected insecticides in Kerala was endosulfan. The Kerala Agricultural University also recommended the use of endosulfan after the scientists conducted the trial of the aerial spray in the PCK estates.

It was in Aadhoor in Kasargod division that the aerial spraying of endosulfan started on an experimental basis in 1979. Endosulfan was aerially sprayed in Kasargod division from 1981 to 2000 and from 1984 to 2001 in Cheemeni division. The aerial spray was conducted in Mannarkkat estate of the PCK in Palakkad district for fifteen years. On an average, only a small quantity of 1.37 litre of endosulfan was sprayed per hectare in the PCK estates in Kasargod.

The aerial spraying was conducted with the prior sanction of the then District Collector, Kasargod. Endosulfan was supplied through Krishi Bhavan's (farm outlets) to cashew farmers who were also facing the same problem. The PCK as well as private estate owners sprayed endosulfan to combat the tea mosquito bugs. The pesticide was used by farmers in paddy fields and also for vegetable cultivation.

The spraying, thus, continued for nearly two decades. But in 2000, local environmental activists and some organisations cleverly linked the already existing diseases in the villages with the spraying of the pesticide. They swore to themselves that the spraying would be stopped whatever may be the consequences, challenging the PCK staff. They said that strange diseases were stalking the villages solely because of the aerial spray. In some estates they demonstrated before the helicopter stationed at the PCK estate.

They informed the media linking the diseases with the aerial spray of endosulfan. Among the activists, Dr Mohan Kumar, a local physician wrote an article in the Delhi-based Down-to-Earth magazine which has connections with the Centre for Science and Environment, CSE, a Delhi-based NGO which later conducted a study in Padre Village with institutional support from the Swedish International Agency,

SIDA, New Delhi. He linked all the diseases with the spraying of endosulfan claiming that all types of cancer and cases of mental retardation were the direct result of the spraying of the pesticide. Dr. Mohan Kumar, together with Sree Padre, another local activist, tipped off the information to the media.

They informed the reporters of English newspapers in Kasargod and Mangalore which first broke the story on the strange and unusual diseases in Padre village. It was a newsbreak and then the local Malayalam and Kannada papers followed in hot pursuit publishing the version of the local anti-endosulfan activists. Although journalists pointedly asked Sree Padre whether the diseases were caused by the aerial spraying of endosulfan, he said he was not sure and replied that there was no scientific evidence. So everything was in the realm of conjecture and there was no scientific proof at a time when the media and the activists first put the blame on endosulfan spraying for the strange diseases in the area.

Because of the prolonged media campaign against endosulfan triggered by some Environmental NGOs, the government both at the Centre and in the State appointed various commissions to probe into the issue. Though some committees blamed endosulfan, some others absolved the pesticide from the guilt. But no committees enquired whether all the diseases started with the aerial spray of endosulfan or such diseases had prevailed in the villages before the pesticide spray. Further, no probe committee collected the details about the percentage of diseases in other non-sprayed districts as per the disability census report of 2001 and compared it with the percentage of diseases in the sprayed area in Kasargod district.

However, the Left Democratic Front, LDF, and the United Democratic Front, UDF, ministry in Kerala which ruled the State alternately committed a scam with the government ultimately forced to give lakhs of rupees as compensation to the bogus victims of endosulfan following a strident campaign unleashed by anti-endosulfan activists. Both the LDF and the

UDF governments caved in before the continued threat, agitation and demand of the anti-pesticide activists for compensation to the alleged victims who happened to be the creation of the media, NGOs and government machinery.

Obviously, the whole endosulfan controversy was a scandal perpetrated by some NGOs supported by a section of government officials and political leaders. Both the Central and State governments as well as scientific institutions were taken for a ride by some NGOs and local anti-pesticide activists for well over a decade. The Union Government incurred a huge amount of money to conduct studies by its various agencies. The State Government also incurred loss on the salary and travelling allowances of the officials who otherwise would have been working in other departments. Several government vehicles were pressed into service to ferry the officials to the sprayed villages to study the issue.

All the diseases for which the activists pinned the blame on endosulfan spray had been there in the village of Padre for several generations. For instance, the villagers used to pray at Jhadadhari shrine, a primordial deity in Padre beseeching the divine power to bestow them with healthy babies. The Jhadadhari was a tribal deity in a sacred grove in Enmakaje surrounded by an abundance of flora and fauna which were on the vanishing trail in the populated areas. This myth has enormous social significance which could prove that deformed babies used to be born in the villages for generations.

These diseases were common not only in the sprayed areas but also in the non-sprayed region. There were acute diseases in Paivelige and Mogral Puthur villages in the district where endosulfan was not used. There were similar diseases across the border in Karnataka also. But the health department of Karnataka conducted a study and ruled out the possibility of its causes due to the aerial spraying of endosulfan in the adjacent villages of Kasargod. Strangely, there were no diseases among the people who lived directly under the sprayed area. There were no diseases among the workers of the Plantation Corporation either who directly sprayed endosulfan or helped preparing the pesticide compound for aerial spray. The diseases were also found in villages located far away from the plantations of the PCK as well as in the non-sprayed areas.

Media persons across the country published reports linking the aerial spray of endosulfan with various diseases in the sprayed area by playing up the issue. But the media which compared the incident with the Bhopal gas tragedy never cared to investigate whether the diseases were actually caused by the pesticide spray. It was a classic example of the media failure. The NGOs fighting the pesticide influenced every institution including the media urging them not to publish any adverse reports against them.

The Communist Party of India (Marxist), CPM, and the Communist Party of India, CPI, were initially against the anti-endosulfan movement. But all political parties including the Bharatiya Janata Party, BJP, later demanded compensation to the suspected victims. The agitation was joined by various vested interests and NGOs who collected lakhs of rupees from abroad ostensibly for the endosulfan victims. When the agitation was at its peak, there were as many as 20 Environmental NGOs collecting money from abroad.

But the study conducted by the Centre for Science and Environment, CSE, a Delhi-based NGO in the village of Padre in February, 2001 proved to be a shot in the arm for the anti-endosulfan activists. The study was sponsored by the Swedish International Agency, SIDA. The CSE study said that there was heavy endosulfan residues in water, soil and blood samples collected from the village of Padre. The CSE findings were later ridiculed by scientists as bogus and a mockery of scientific principles since it showed high pesticide residues in human blood far above the deadly level. Meanwhile, the CSE study was played up internationally through internet and the social media network resulting in the phasing out of endosulfan in some developed countries. The pesticide industry alleged that the endosulfan residue tests conducted by various government laboratories used wrong methods in analysing the pesticide and blood plasma samples taken from the alleged victims of the pesticide spray.

The agitation and the scare mongering were supported by all political parties and social organisations quite oblivious of the fact that it was all funded and sponsored by the European Union. Political parties made use of the opportunity to activate their cadres in rural areas. They also enrolled people hit by silly diseases in the endosulfan list as part of their vote bank politics. People with no diseases or having silly or ordinary diseases were enrolled in the endosulfan list. Political parties also used the opportunity to expand their base in rural areas. Gradually, it became a burning issue with political parties and NGOs demanding ban on endosulfan. The Kerala High Court imposed a temporary ban on endosulfan in the state based on a report by the Kerala State Pollution Control Board.

The people of 11 *grama panchayats* were isolated by the people following the strident campaign by anti-endosulfan activists. Many newly married couples opted for abortion since they feared that deformed children would be born to them. The campaign also hit marriage alliances as nobody from outside was willing to marry the girls in the sprayed area. Some of the families moved out of the district after selling out their homesteads at throw away prices. But the land mafia which supported the agitation purchased their land at cheap prices.

Several committees probed the endosulfan issue and prominent among them were the National Institute of Occupational Health, NIOH, and the Frederick Institute of Plant Protection and Toxicology, FIPPAT. However, the FIPPAT found no link between the endosulfan exposure and the diseases. The study conducted by the Kerala Agricultural University also could not find that the diseases were caused by the use of endosulfan. The NIOH was directed by the Indian Council of Medical Research to institute a probe following the wide media coverage on the issue. The pesticide industry found flaws in the analysis of the blood plasma of the alleged victims by the Coimbatore-based Salim Ali Centre for Ornithology and Natural History, SACON. Though the pesticide industry wanted the SACON to set right the flaws, it refused to review its analytical report.

The first national disability census conducted by the Census Commissioner of India in 2001 had found that the southern districts of Kerala were more hit by various diseases and disabilities than the northern districts. Despite the propaganda by NGOs and activists, diseases were found to be less in Kasargod district than in other districts of Kerala. The census report refuted the theory that people fell ill in large numbers because of the aerial spray of the pesticide in Kasargod.

Following the public outcry and the strident campaign in the media, the state government appointed a committee headed by Dr A. Achuthan, an environmental activist. The Achuthan committee examined the report of the CSE. The committee while agreeing with the known toxicity of endosulfan could not pinpoint whether the diseases in Enmakaje gram panchayat were actually caused by the aerial spraying of endosulfan. The committee noted that 'there are reports of health problems from the gram panchayats adjacent to the Plantation Corporation. But there is no evidence to attribute these directly to endosulfan pollution; there is no evidence to completely deny it either'.

However, anti-endosulfan activists coined the slogan based on the Achuthan committee report that 'absence of proof is not proof of absence' by which they meant that though the committee could not get any proof, it did not mean that there was no proof.

The National Human Rights Commission, NHRC, directed the Indian Council of Medical Research, ICMR, to study the issue following its suo motu cognizance of a report in *India*

Today magazine in 2001. The ICMR, in turn, directed the National Institute of Occupational Health, HIOH, to study the problems of the villagers. The NIOH blamed the aerial spraying of endosulfan for the diseases in the exposed area. However, the US-based Environ International, a scientific institution, rubbished the NIOH report in a lengthy scientific article published in 2012.

Meanwhile, the National Human Rights Commission, NHRC, which registered a suo motu case based on a report in the *India Today* magazine later weeded out the case since it found the matter sub judice as a case was then pending in the Kerala High Court. However, the NHRC again registered another suo motu case based on a report in the *Hindustan Times* in 2010. The reports, both in India Today and in the *Hindustan Times* which were suo motu taken cognisance by the National Human Rights Commission appeared highly biased and controversial since the reports supported the anti-pesticide lobby without taking the views of the pesticide manufacturers, the plantation corporation and the Union Government. But the *Hindustan Times* report said that the aerial spray of endosulfan was still being continued which was a travesty of truth. The fact was that the aerial spray was stopped around 2000 following agitation by the local people.

The NHRC ordered the state government to pay compensation of ₹ 5 lakh each to the next of kin of the deceased and the same amount to the physically and mentally retarded victims. However, the NHRC solely depended on the impugned study by the NIOH without considering all other previous studies which found no link between the diseases and the pesticide spray.

The NHRC Chairman Justice K.G. Balakrishnan said in the report that there were more than 6,000 endosulfan victims in the sprayed area. The NHRC seemed to be in a hurry to fix the blame on endosulfan. The NHRC chairman who compared it with the Bhopal gas tragedy visited only a few houses of the victims in the sprayed area before submitting his report to the government.

But the Kerala government paid ₹ 1.5 lakh each to the next of kin of those who reportedly died due to the pesticide spray as well as to the bed-ridden to comply with the NIOH direction to pay ₹ 5 lakh each to the victims.

The Endosulfan Nodal Cell prepared a list of 4,182 patients and sanctioned them a monthly pension ranging from ₹ 1,000 to 2,000. But the Plantation Corporation Protection Council moved the High Court pleading that nobody had died of endosulfan spray and no diseases were caused by the pesticide use. The PCK Protection Council alleged that those who died due to excessive drinking of alcohol and use of tobacco were included in the endosulfan 'death list' following political pressure. It also contended that the list of endosulfan patients was bogus and fabricated by officials at the connivance of political leaders. The endosulfan victims' list which the PCK protection council received through the Right to Information Act carried no details of diseases of the victims and in many cases no date of death was mentioned in the list. The government also failed to reply to the scores of letters sent by the Plantation Corporation Protection Council about the bogus victims of endosulfan and also about the misappropriation of government funds by the NGOs.

Finally, the government was compelled to review the endosulfan list following which the list of 4,182 victims which was drawn up following the medical camps was whittled down to just 1,632. The number was far below the state and national average of mentally and physically retarded persons including cancer patients. This exposed the blatant untruth that endosulfan spray had caused large number of diseases and mass deaths as had happened in the wake of the Bhopal gas tragedy.

The State government instituted a team of doctors from the community medicine department of the Kozhikode Medical College in 2011 to study the issue. The KMC committee had found that there were more diseases in the non-sprayed area of Banam than in Muliyar, a sprayed village though there were several flaws in the report. But details showing the list of the diseases were withheld by the Democratic Youth Federation of India, DYFI, in its writ petition to the Supreme Court demanding ban on endosulfan. The DYFI, the youth wing of the Communist Party of India (Marxist), CPM, presented only 16 pages of the 53 page report of the KMC in its affidavit to the court. However, the Supreme Court slapped an ad-interim ban on production and use of endosulfan in the country on May 13, 2011 following the writ petition filed by the DYFI.

The CPM and its youth organisation were used by the European Union in a proxy war against endosulfan. The booklet 'Endosulfan – a Kerala story' published by the state health department was a highly fraudulent publication, but it was used by the DYFI to get endosulfan temporarily banned in the country.

The European Union countries dominated the Conference of Parties, COP, at the Stockholm convention on Persistent Organic Pollutants Review Committee, POPRC meet in May 2011 in Geneva. All political leaders of the state including Chief Minister V. S. Achuthanandan were the star campaigners for the ban on endosulfan. Achuthanandan undertook a fast in front of the Martyr's Column in Kerala's state capital while the Stockholm convention was in progress in Geneva. The fast by a Chief Minister of a state was shown through video conferencing at the venue of the POPRC meet.

Though the letters sent by the PCK Protection Council to the Chief Secretary, the Chief Minister and all other ministers and officials concerned failed to bring any reply, the Government asked the Plantation Corporation of Kerala to pay compensation to the victims. Even though the PCK Protection Council moved the High Court, the PCK was compelled to pay ₹ 27 crore to the government in May 2012 as its initial payment. The amount was utilised to pay a part of the compensation to the alleged victims as ordered by the NHRC.

However, the Endosulfan Peeditha Janakeeya Munnani, EPJM, (the People's Front of Endosulfan Sufferers) continued its agitation demanding more compensation to the so-called victims. In a conciliatory move, the government conceded most of the demands of the EPJM including setting up of a tribunal to settle the claims of the victims.

The Justice C.N. Ramachandran Nair Committee appointed by the government to explore the possibility of forming a tribunal submitted its report to the government in August, 2013. The committee recommended to the government to set up a tribunal with limited powers headed by a district level judge. The committee said that the tribunal would not have any power to demand compensation from the PCK or the pesticide manufacturers. Further, only those living within one kilometer of the PCK estates would be eligible for compensation. But the action committee wanted the government to reject the recommendations of the Justice Ramachandran Nair Committee.

2

MISERIES OF KASARGOD VILLAGERS

Circled by a chain of green hills, the area where endosulfan was sprayed is hauntingly beautiful. In the foothills of the cashew plantations there were several houses located in the valley. Viewed from above, the thick canopy of trees below appeared like thatched roofs atop the houses. The mist-like spray of the pesticide that wafted in the air has little chance of penetrating the leafy tangle below and eventually to fall into the water bodies.

Those not familiar with the topography of the area would think that most of the sick and the diseased could be found in the houses located in the foothills of the plantations where the pesticide was sprayed for 20 long years. Naturally and logically the victims could be found there. But actually the houses of the suspected victims were located some six to ten kilometers away and in some cases 15 to 20 kilometers from the nearest cashew plantation. However, the pesticide was not sprayed extensively in the entire villages as widely reported in the media; but the spray was confined to the top of the hills, some 100 to 150 meters wide, above the cashew plantations.

What turned out to be a crucial phase of the agitation was the visit of opposition leader V. S. Achuthanandan in Swarga, Vaninagar and Padre, the villages reportedly 'worst affected' by the aerial spray of endosulfan. The visit of the opposition leader of the state assembly in 2002 boosted the morale of the anti-endosulfan activists. The media statement of Achuthanandan that it was a great pesticide tragedy unparalleled in the history of the country caught the attention of most of the political leaders. Since Achuthanandan was regarded as a crusader supposedly fighting for the poor, his views on endosulfan spraying and the unusual diseases were taken seriously by the people. Given the charisma of V.S. Achuthanandan, the anti-endosulfan activists first roped in the opposition leader hoping that his intervention on the issue would bring them rich dividends. And their expectations proved right as the dormant anti-endosulfan agitation ultimately became a sort of mass movement triggered and contrived by foreign funds.

Achuthanandan first visited the house of Kumaran Master of Swarga, a retired school teacher who was once a communist activist. The word Swarga in Malayalam means heaven and according to anti-endosulfan activists, there were so many victims in the village of Swarga. A native of Uduma in Kasargod, Kumaran Master had worked in a Kannada school on the Kerala-Karnataka border.

On the fateful day, several journalists were accompanying the motorcade of the opposition leader in the morning. He started his journey from the government guest house where his trip was joined by political leaders and of course by the media corps. Before they reached the area, some activists who were awaiting the opposition leader on the road ran towards the house. Unaware of what was happening, media persons and camera men also ran behind them. They entered the house and inside was Kumaran Master sprawled on a cot with his grotesquely distended belly heaving slightly. It was a pathetic sight; Kumaran Master greeted the opposition leader getting up from his bed with some difficulty. Some of the activists helped him to sit on the cot.

Before the opposition leader reached the house, the local activists told Kumaran Master to repeat what they had wanted him to tell the leader. We were watching the scene through the window, standing quiet on the veranda of the house and we clearly heard what they had told him.

It was the first conspiracy hatched by the local anti-endosulfan activists. The activists wanted Kumaran Master to describe himself as a victim of endosulfan though he was not. But the local activists least expected that media persons would be standing right on the veranda of the house near the window listening to what the activists wanted him to tell the opposition leader.

He opened a conversation with Achuthanandan introducing himself as a former communist activist. Then Achuthanandan changed the subject saying that agriculture minister K.R. Gowri, herself a communist, was responsible for the spraying of endosulfan. Achuthanandan and K.R. Gowri were once comrades-in arms, but became sworn enemies when the latter was expelled from the Communist Party of India (Marxist) in which they worked together for decades.

Achuthanandan apparently wanted to settle the old scores with K.R. Gowri and that was the reason why he became active in the anti-endosulfan movement. K.R. Gowri had once stated in the state legislative assembly that nobody had died of endosulfan spraying.

As directed by the local activists, Kumaran Master told him that he used to conduct manual spraying of endosulfan in the small patch of vegetable garden he owned and thus he became a victim of the pesticide. His disease was then clandestinely described as related to endosulfan spray. The photo of Kumaran Master was published in the colour posters printed by the Malaysia-based Pesticide Action Network Asia and the Pacific, PANAP, in its worldwide campaign against endosulfan. It was part of a conspiracy hatched by anti-endosulfan activists that his picture appeared on the PANAP colour poster.

Any patient who appeared pathetic and horrible in real life would appear in anti-endosulfan picture-post campaign. Evidently, Kumaran Master was not a victim of endosulfan though he suffered from cancer. It was an instance of disinformation spread by PANAP all over the world as part of the worldwide campaign and conspiracy against endosulfan. In the midst of the controversy, no media person turned up in Swarga to verify the fact whether Kumaran Master was a victim of endosulfan spray.

It was the first visit of a political leader to the house of a suspected victim of endosulfan. The visit of Achuthanandan lent political importance and the picture of Kumaran Master with his huge and heaving belly was telecast by the electronic media. The print media later used the picture whenever it published a report on endosulfan. Kumaran Master thus became a pathetic logo of the anti-endosulfan reports.

There were many such patients in both the sprayed and non-sprayed areas. Once I had reported the story of a man with a grotesquely extended belly undergoing treatment at the General Hospital in Kasargod. The doctors attending on him had said that the patient suffered from cirrhosis of liver since he was a heavy alcoholic. In tribal colonies of Kasargod where locally brewed liquor was freely available, one can normally come across such patients. The plight of Kumaran Master who was a cancer patient was widely used in the media and it was the first instance of the activists misleading media persons.

Achuthanandan and his team left for another house of a suspected victim. There a 12-year old boy was both physically and mentally challenged. He suffered from cerebral palsy. This house was located some five kilometers away from the cashew plantation of the PCK. The media persons asked the local people whether the helicopter which sprayed endosulfan had flown over the place. Uttering the word 'no', a local man ventured the answer that the spray might have been drifted in the air to reach the place. We asked the villagers whether there were similar cases in the neighbourhood houses as well, but we were told that there was none. Even though some local people volunteered more information on the diseases to the media persons, they were shooed away by the local activists.

Media persons went from one house to another located far away from each other. They saw that only isolated families living far away from the cashew plantations were struck by diseases and no families staying directly below the plantations were affected by the spraying. But there was no clear answer from the local activists who chose to ignore the question.

Wherever media persons visited they could see only scenes of misery: bed-ridden children lying pathetically on dirty mats and moving feebly their emaciated legs. Life seemed to be ebbing out of their delicate frame. Their parents were taking great pains to look after them and even then the burden of finding money to feed them was thrust upon their shoulders. We talked to the neighbours, especially the old people. They told us that the place had a history of such diseases. Several children had died before they reached ten years of age. The diseases existed in the villages even before the aerial spraying of endosulfan started in the area, they said in a hushed up tone.

The opposition leader also visited Vaninagar school where some children suffering from Down's Syndrome were studying. The Head Master allowed the visitors to see the children and they were brought to his room. These children came from different places and were dull in their studies. The mentally challenged children came from both the sprayed and non-sprayed areas. They stood before the visitors barely trying to smile.

After visiting the children, Achuthanandan called aside Sree Padre who was the local spokesman of the anti-endosulfan agitation indicating that he wanted to talk. They talked in private in a secluded corner of the school for some time. No third person heard the conversation. Only Achuthanandan and Sree Padre knew what transpired between them.

Sree Padre was a vociferous anti-endosulfan activist and a crusader against pesticide industry. As he was keen to make it appear that all diseases were caused by the aerial spraying of endosulfan, it was but natural that he might have told his views to the opposition leader. Achuthanandan was soon 'convinced' after the talk that all the diseases were caused by the spraying of endosulfan as was reflected in his press statement later. Admittedly, this gave a mighty push to the already aggressive campaign against the pesticide.

Achuthanandan was eager to get a fair image of himself in the media and among the people. Media gave him the aura of a crusader against all sorts of evils. The entire media and the people were later carried away by emotion. What had transpired at the talk between Sree Padre and Achuthanandan at the secluded corner of the Vaninagar school on that fateful day decided the fate of the anti-endosulfan agitation. Thereafter, Achuthanandan became a strong votary of the anti-endosulfan agitation. He would issue media statement whenever anyone said that no people had died of endosulfan spray.

Then politicians after politicians visited the sprayed areas with journalists in tow as the media ballooned off the issue in the entire state. The political leaders would hold press briefings after visiting the area and none of them had any doubt regarding the cause of the diseases. A hungry media ever eager to get spicy stories played up the issue; the media reporters were also happy that the reports, laced with their imagination, started appearing on front page of most of the newspapers. Not to be left undone, the national media, many of them of repute, landed on the calm and tranquil area of Vaninagar and Swarga to report on what was described as a colossal human tragedy next only to the Bhopal gas disaster.

I was part of a media team when the then BJP state president C. K. Padmanabhan visited the sprayed area. After visiting some houses and meeting the mentally challenged children at the Vaninagar school, Padmanabhan addressed the media on the ground of the school. But most of the patients he had visited had oral cancer which was the tell-tale evidence of tobacco use.

In his address to the media, Padmanabhan wanted a thorough scientific investigation into the causes that led to various diseases and also wanted an epidemiological study. But his demand for a scientific probe was resented by local anti-endosulfan activists who told him that since the Centre for Science and Environment, CSE, had already conducted a study in the area there was no need of further studies. Anti-endosulfan activist Dr Mohan Kumar who appeared visibly upset then remonstrated with the BJP leader saying that so many political leaders were coming to see the children, but none of them did anything to help the hapless victims.

Media persons visiting the sprayed area would normally ask the question where the pesticide was sprayed. Pointing out to the cashew plantations, located some five to six kilometers away on the slope of a chain of hills, the local people would say that it was sprayed exactly there. They would say that the mist like particles would be carried away in the wind spreading in the entire area. Was there any chance that a child far away from the sprayed area would fall ill considering the fact that the pesticide was sprayed only twice a year and that the particle was very thin?

The quantity of endosulfan used was 1.37 litre per hectare. If endosulfan had really affected the entire area, it would have become a major tragedy with each household having a sick child. The media persons who visited individually and collectively in the area had witnessed that in most cases the victims' houses were located far away from the sprayed areas. Most importantly, except for Kumaran Master, the activists had not taken the media persons to the houses of other suspected victims since it was feared that it would expose the entire cooked up stories.

A few months before the Stockholm Convention on Persistent Organic Pollutants Review Committee, POPRC, in April 2011, the focus of the entire media was riveted on Kasargod. The media was agog with speculation that endosulfan would be banned worldwide at the POPRC meet. Media persons across the country were under pressure to send spot stories. Thus, a number of media persons descended on the tranquil villages of Swarga and Enmakaje. Many of them had the contact address of anti-endosulfan activists. They became the stenographers of the anti-endosulfan activists as they had no time to visit the suspected victims since their houses were scattered in the whole area. So they took the easiest method of writing what the anti-endosulfan activists had wanted them to report.

It was then that Shaju Philip, Kerala reporter of the *Indian Express* called me. He wanted to visit the sprayed areas and see for himself the agonies of the victims and report it for the Sunday edition of the paper. We first decided to visit the Enmakaje gram panchayat which sprang to the media limelight in 2001 following the Endo controversy. Padre, a village in Enmakaje gram panchayat, was described by the media as an endemic area severely hit by the aerial spray of endosulfan.

It was a place where landowners had cruelly exploited the poor. They treated them in an inhuman way; the workers were treated worse than cattle. The workers employed for farming including Dalits and tribes would be served tea in coconut shells and meals in areca nut sheaths. The food was served to them in most unhygienic surroundings. Social organisations had to wage a continuous campaign against the practice before it was abolished. But remnants of social hegemony still persisted in some rural areas dominated by upper castes. Dalits who took meals at restaurants had themselves to dispose of the plantain leaves in which they had taken the meals. In some remote areas even those invited for marriage functions had to discard the leftovers of the food served to them. But educated families detested these practices.

Most of the fertile lands in Enmakaje belonged to the landowners. The whole region was once ruled by tribal chieftains; then came the Jains followed by Brahmins from various places in the country. The poor had only the rocky stretch of land where not even a blade of grass would grow. They lived in the parched land with no drinking water facilities and in horribly unhygienic conditions. About 36 per cent of the villagers in the panchayat used 'suranga' (a horizontal well) water for their daily needs. The surangas were constructed for supplying water for irrigation and not for drinking purpose, but the poor used the suranga water for their daily needs; however, the rich families possessed masonry wells.

The base of the hills would be bored with iron implements forming a tunnel known as 'suranga'. The ground water that flowed through the suranga would be collected in a tank or in open patches of slush. The villagers collected water from the slush by using buckets or from the storage tanks constructed for the purpose. Surangas were located in large numbers in Enmakaje gram panchayat and most of these were unhygienic.

The Dalits would be made to work in the farms of the landowners in return for a pittance and leftovers of food. They stayed in small huts put up outside the farm lands of the landowners. The landowners would pamper them with plenty of tobacco and those addicted would be mentally forced to work for the landowners since they got their daily supply of tobacco. Women and youngsters thus became addicts to tobacco and the habit continued even today. The increasing number of cancer, particularly oral cancer, was the direct result of the habit of tobacco use passed down to the new generation. But nobody cared to probe into the past history of the area to know how the villagers had unusual number of cancer patients among them.

The myth of Jhadadhari, a local deity holds the key to the history of diseases in the area. The surroundings of Jhadadhari shrine were once sacred groves where several varieties of flora and fauna which became extinct long ago in other places still survived. There had been large number of unusual diseases in the whole area, carried on from one generation to the other; and one can read this from the myth.

Local people used to make votive offerings at the shrine

beseeching the deity that the village children be born healthy. The deity of Jhadadhari had the misfortune of being abandoned and revived again after a gap of several years. The villagers believed that the diseases in the villages were due to the curse of the Jhadadhari for abandoning the deity. It was a belief which had its roots in the past; it originated several generations ago when no pesticides were in use and the people pursued the primitive mode of agriculture such as the slash and burn cultivation.

We reached Perla and hired a jeep. Kusappa Poojary, the driver of the jeep was in an enthusiastic mood. He told us that he had taken so many journalists to the houses of the victims. So Poojary knew the entire land like the palm of his hand. First he took us to the house of Jagadish in Swarga whose picture was repeatedly telecast by the media for several times as a victim of endosulfan spray. Poojary, who belonged to a backward caste, told us about several unusual customs in the village. He narrated how the people of backward castes and Dalits were badly treated by the landowners.

We reached the house of Jagadish, a mentally challenged youth. His face which elicited the sympathies of the people had been repeatedly telecast by the visual media. It was a typical picture which would stir one's intimate feelings against the pesticide spray which reportedly ruined his life. But no editor of any newspaper or TV channel took the trouble to verify the truth.

'We could understand that he was mentally challenged only after six months of his birth', said his distraught father. We asked to get his date of birth, but his father said he had no such documents. In order to get an idea about his age we asked his father to give us the record of the medical camp where he had been taken for enrolment in the endosulfan list. His father showed us an old piece of paper in which his age was mentioned as 45, and he was a 15-yearold boy when the aerial spray of endosulfan started in the Perla division of the Plantation Corporation. His father told us that there has been no improvement in his case ever since he became a mentally challenged child after six months of his birth.

Jagadish belonged to a family of areca nut farmers. Villagers in Enmakaje mainly depended on areca nut farming for their livelihood. The farmers suffered when there was fall in the price of raw areca nuts. We saw raw areca nuts spread for drying in the sun on the cow dung smeared courtyard of the house.

Coming back from the house, we discussed our experience. How can a child who became mentally challenged after six months of his birth be a victim of endosulfan when the aerial spray of the pesticide had not even begun? We remembered that his pathetic face on the television elicited so much anger and sympathy among the people. While we were returning we saw a television crew from Mangalore going to his house. They would be showing him as a victim of endosulfan and the viewers of the television would be seething with anger against endosulfan spray. We felt that if only the media had tried to reach at the truth, it could have got more clarity on the issue. But it was too much to expect from a blind media which was totally bent upon to describe the whole issue as a pesticide tragedy.

We then visited the house of Girija, a forty-yearold mentally challenged woman. She was wearing a frock when we visited her and appeared younger than her real age. Like Jagadish, Girija, too, was born some years before the aerial spray of endosulfan began in the area. Since she suffered from the disease by birth, she could not be a victim of endosulfan spray.

It was also the house of a farmer located on higher grounds circled by plantations below. The cultivation was enriched by water from gravity pipes from the hills. Water was available in plenty from the surrounding hills which originated in small springs and eventually flowed down as a rivulet. The people residing nearby collected the water from storage tanks. These were perennial springs and there was no scarcity of water in the neighbourhood.

Girija belonged to the Billava caste. The main occupation of the Billavas was toddy tapping, but they were also employed in other fields. The Billavas were next above the Dalits in the caste hierarchy. They belonged to the Other Backward Class (OBC) and were known by various surnames such as Poojary and Suvarna. In Mangalore, there were several rich Billava families, but in Kasargod they were mostly poor.

In the two houses we visited, endosulfan spray was not the cause of the disease since the victims were born many years before the aerial spray of the pesticide started in the area and yet both of them were enrolled in the endosulfan victims' list.

Who certified that they were victims of endosulfan at the medical camps? Didn't expert doctors from the medical colleges see that they suffered from congenital diseases before the spraying started? But the doctors examined the victims and they had no need to check their date of birth and verify it with the date of spray.

But there was pressure on doctors from political parties to certify that each and every disease in the sprayed area was caused by endosulfan. Besides, the picture of Girija like that of Jagadish was repeatedly flashed on the television screen whenever a story on endosulfan appeared on it. If a newspaper or television channel got pathetic pictures of the victims, they would continuously use them as file pictures without verifying the truth. Since nobody was bothered to verify the truth, the credibility of the news and pictures would not be questioned.

We went to another house. The house of each patient was separated by a long distance. If anyone thought that the houses of the diseased persons were all located in the same neighbourhood, they would be quite wrong.

We got into the jeep. The road was not strait; there were bends at right angles. Kusappa Poojari negotiated each bend with the ease and skill of an acrobat. Eventually we reached the house of another patient. This time we hoped that the diseased person would be a real victim of endosulfan spray.

Another patient, this time a girl of 26 years, stood before us. It was in Vaninagar and her father told us that she can recognise sounds, but could not utter a sentence coherently. Lakshmi was a lovely girl. Her father told us about the aerial spray which occurred some kilometers away. This girl too may not be a victim of endosulfan since the cashew plantation where the pesticide was sprayed was located far away. If she was the real victim of endosulfan we would have seen some more victims in the neighbourhood. We wanted to get the family history of the unfortunate girl. Was anyone in the family hit by the same sort of illness?

Lakshmi's father told us that her elder sister was healthy and was married off. But her cousin sister was also a mentally challenged girl. Lakshmi's father said her cousin sister was staying in Karnataka, a non-spayed area. His answer solved the puzzle. It may be a case of family history. We felt that each case was unique and needed to be studied in detail by collecting details about the family history also.

She belonged to a family of Bunts who were regarded as upper castes. They were known by their surnames of Shetty and Rai. The Bunts were an upwardly mobile and prosperous community and there were many celebrities and film actors among them in Mumbai and Bangalore.

No expert team had probed the family history of the patients. We felt that a study team has to spend a lot of time in the house of a patient to gather various data; the morbidity status of the surrounding villages; the family history, the hygienic condition of the place, the general health of the family, the income of the family members and how much amount the family spends on food and medicine. In fact, a multi-disciplinary study team has to gather a lot of information on a particular patient. Without any family data it would be unscientific to pin the blame solely on pesticide spray for all the miseries in the village.

We visited Swarga, a sprayed village on the way. Twenty-fiveyear old Narayana was a mentally retarded youth. The house was located several feet below the road. We reached the house by negotiating a narrow path which eventually led to the house. While coming back from the house we met his father since Kusappa Poojari knew him personally having taken some media persons to the house before. His father told us that after six months of his birth he developed fever on a night. At dawn he took the child to a doctor. He said his son never regained from his sickness, began as fever on that fateful night.

Narayana belonged to a family of Marathi Naiks. There were so many Marathi Naiks in the endosulfan victims' list prepared by the district administration. There were a sizable number of them in the endosulfan 'death list' also.

The Marathi Naiks were the soldiers of the British army in Maharashtra. They were persecuted by the British following the First War of Independence in 1857 and the Maratha rebellion. After the suppression of the mutiny, the community of soldiers were scattered throughout the West Coast. Some of them migrated to the south. There were so many gradations of people among them—menials, cooks, barbers and soldiers—all belonging to the caste hierarchy. There were Dalits and upper castes among them.

They were commonly known as Marathi Naiks. The word 'Naik' in military parlance denoted the lowest rank in the army. The Gowdas among them possessed firearms and they were the upper caste among the Marathi Naiks. They were delinked from the scheduled tribes' list by the Union Government following an anthropological study conducted by the Kozhikode based KIRTADS, an institution established for conducting research and studies on tribal affairs. However, they were once again included in the list of scheduled tribes after a prolonged agitation supported by most of the political parties.

The migration of Marathi Naiks reached the further end of South Kanara district in Hosdurg Taluk which is now part of Kerala. The Marathi Naiks were isolated in the wilds after they were hounded by the British. They suffered from social inequalities. Anthropologists had studied the migration as well as the cultural and social isolation of the Marathi Naiks which made them vulnerable to various diseases. They joined the cultural and social milieu of Enmakaje after some years following the suppression of the mutiny. They migrated to Enmakaje after leading an isolated life for several years.

In most of the houses where we visited the cases were mostly of Down's Syndrome and one of its causes was the marriage between blood relatives. Early marriage of girls which was a customary practice in the villages also contributed to the birth of babies with congenital abnormalities. It also contributed to the risk of cervical cancer in teen aged mothers and other gynaecological problems.

We then called it a day after visiting some more houses of the patients and returned to Kasargod town. Located to the northernmost tip of the state, Kasargod was a much neglected district of Kerala. Because of its proximity to Karnataka, Kasargod is noted for its cultural and linguistic diversity. People of the district mostly depended on the neighbouring city of Mangalore for healthcare and educational needs. A place with vast stretches of rocky and barren lands, Kasargod once belonged to Karnataka.

However, after the reorganisation of states on linguistic lines in 1957, Kasargod became a part of Kerala. Those opposing the merger of Kasargod with Kerala started the anti-merger agitation. Though various Kannada organisations still demanded the amalgamation of Kasargod area north of Chandragiri river with Karnataka, the pro-liberation movement was now in a dormant state. It was only recently that institutions of higher learning, tourism centres and government undertakings started coming up in Kasargod district.

3

ABHORRENT SOCIAL CUSTOMS AND STRANGE DISEASES

Shaju Philip and I continued our journey to the pesticide sprayed areas the next day also and we first visited Muliyar, a sprayed area in the morning. There we met two brothers—Balakrishnan and Manikantan—with skin diseases whose pictures had appeared widely in the media. Their body bore marks like the scale of a snake and the skin appeared all wrinkled. The boys belonged to a family of pottery makers known as Moolya. The picture of the two boys was published by the Pesticide Action Network Asia Pacific (PANAP) in a colour poster which was circulated internationally. The PANAP poster had also carried the picture of Kumaran Master of Swarga. The boys were the favourites of the visual media which had repeatedly telecast their pictures. Their names had also figured in the endosulfan patients' list. Except for the skin problem, the boys did not seem to have been hit by any other diseases.

Manikantan and Balakrishnan were born with the skin disease. Their house was located one kilometer away from the Kottoor division of the Plantation Corporation of Kerala.

Skin diseases were very common among the people both in the sprayed and non-sprayed areas. In a temple near Kumbla, devotees would take the dip in the temple tank during the annual festival to cure themselves of skin diseases. People from different parts, including Karnataka, would wash themselves in the temple pond, a natural lake, every year during the annual festival.

A strange social custom which had its connection with the cure of skin diseases existed in the area. People, mostly Dalits and lower castes would roll over the leftovers of food partaken by Brahmins. The belief was that if they rolled on the leftovers, it would help cure their skin diseases. So the people rolled themselves on the plantain leaves after Brahmins had taken their meals apparently to cure their skin diseases. So, according to the belief, rolling over the plantain leaves of the leftovers would offer both the cure and prevention of skin diseases. Obviously, taking dip in the temple pond and rolling over the leftovers suggested that people suffered from skin diseases in early times also.

The system known as 'Mathe–Mathe Snana (taking bath in leftovers) once prevailed in some temples in Kasargod. However, the ritual was abolished following protests by the people. But the system still prevailed in nearby Karnataka where Dalit organisations used to stage protests at its venue every year. People from Kasargod used to visit this temple in Karnataka every year to cure their skin diseases by rolling on the leftovers. However, the Karnataka government now intended to prohibit this practice by enacting a law. The anti-endosulfan agitators had propagated that the large number of skin diseases in the area started with the aerial spraying of the pesticide.

Another most abhorrent social custom also prevailed in the area. Landowners would invite the Dalits and other lower castes in their villages ostensibly to celebrate the occasion when a married woman in the household became pregnant. The food consisting rice and curry would be placed in a large vessel near the landowners' house. The food would be mixed with pieces of nails and strands of hair of the pregnant woman. Unsuspecting and hungry people of the lower castes would eat the meals by scooping out the rice and curry from the vessels with a wooden ladle.

The belief was that if the Dalits ate the meals mixed with the pieces of nails and strands of hair of the pregnant woman, it would ward off the evil eye said to have been cast on her; it was also believed that it would facilitate an easy delivery for the woman. According to the activists of the Dalit welfare movement, the system still prevailed in some areas in Kasargod. The organisation has, therefore, warned the Dalits against taking such meals at the invitation of the landowners and upper castes.

However, the various committees constituted by the Central and State governments to study the alleged ill-effects of endosulfan spray failed to analyse the socio-cultural factors that may have played its part in creating various types of diseases. According to the parameters of medical anthropology, people who were treated and exploited cruelly in a society would suffer from various diseases.

After leaving the house of Balakrishnan and Manikantan we travelled to the office of the Plantation Corporation in Muliyar. We talked to the manager of the estate. He said the PCK workers who had sprayed endosulfan without taking any safety precaution—not even wearing gloves - were still healthy and they did not have any disease even though they were exposed to the pesticide spray. We talked to the workers, especially women and they said they did not feel giddiness while preparing endosulfan compound for aerial spray.

We were told that endosulfan had fallen all over the head and shoulders of Gangadharan Nair, a PCK worker while loading its compound in helicopter tank. Since he was working as supervisor of the PCK estate in Chokkomoola we went there to meet him.

Gangadharan Nair said endosulfan had fallen all over his body and he was literally drenched in the pesticide. Immediately he took bath in a nearby pond. He said what the anti-endosulfan activists were saying all along was baseless and untrue. They had once threatened the PCK workers and asked them not to cooperate with the aerial spraying of the pesticide.

We went to a house located in front of the PCK office in Chokkomoola. A middle-aged man in the house said he had been working in Karnataka during the years when the pesticide was aerially sprayed and so he was not aware of what had happened then. However, the women in the household volunteered the information that they had all seen the helicopter spraying endosulfan. The open well in the house was not covered during the spray, they said. A bad smell would linger in the air for sometime after the spray and the surroundings would be enveloped in a mist-like vapour, but nobody in the house developed any disease because of the aerial spray, they said.

We then walked down the hill slope through a boulder-strewn road. Except for jeeps, no other vehicles can pass through the road. We visited some houses of former PCK workers located in the valley of the once cashew-clad hills. The women in each household repeated the same thing as the women workers of the Muliyar estate had told us. There were no diseases among them; the diseases were mostly seen among those residing in far away places from the PCK plantations, they said. But such diseases had no connection with any pesticide use, they said.

While returning, we stopped in some places in Muliyar town and asked the villagers about the diseases. They said there were several types of ordinary diseases in the area as seen everywhere, but could not say whether it was all caused by the aerial spray of endosulfan. They said that the children of some rich parents were included in the endosulfan list and their families were getting free ration. The children were mentally challenged, but their parents were rich and could afford expert medical treatment for their wards. They lived in comfortable houses and owned costly cars. Yet they availed the benefit of free ration. They told us that a man, a native of Muliyar, was a heavy alcoholic and he died of alcohol abuse. But his name was included in the endosulfan 'death list' and his family received ₹ one lakh from the government as compensation! His son was an anti-endosulfan activist.

Swarga and Vaninagar villages in Enmakaje gram panchayat, located on a sprawling hillock would turn cold during winter and rainy season. So the natives took to the drinking of potent arrack to escape from the cold climate. So the drinking of illicit brew began to tell upon their health. Many became alcoholics and suffered from cirrhosis of liver. Since it was cold in the top, the use of tobacco was also high, especially among women. The youngsters chewed packed tobacco laced with narcotic substance. The chewing of tobacco and drinking of spurious liquor exacted its toll, but all deaths have now been attributed to endosulfan spray.

On another occasion, I visited the sprayed area along with Rupa Jha, a senior editor with the Delhi BBC. The BBC crew visited the sprayed area on July 22 and 23, 2011 after the Supreme Court slapped a country wide ad-interim ban on endosulfan in May, 2011.

We started our journey from Kasargod town on an evening and we first proceeded to Kuntar near Adhoor. Rupa Jha who had already contacted some anti-endosulfan activists was apparently keen to visit Kuntar where she was told that there were some patients. Day light was fading when we reached the house which was located on a knoll. We climbed the terraced higher grounds and reached a small house overlooking the valley.

It was a Tulu speaking family; but a contact person whom we had picked up on the way translated in Malayalam what the patients, all of them being relatives had said. I translated what I gathered from Malayalam. But the BBC crew spoke no Malayalam, Tulu or Kannada. As there was scarcely any day light left to take the pictures of the family, the sound bite of the patients in Tulu was taken. Rupa Jha said it could be used for the BBC Hindi radio programme after dubbing the talk of the Tulu patients into Hindi.

On a cursory glance of the victims, I soon gathered that the diseases were caused not because of aerial spray of endosulfan because the PCK plantation was located far away.

There was very little chance of the pesticide spray, scudding across the hills, falling in the area and causing the diseases. The illness, it seemed, was mainly caused by poverty, malnutrition and squalor.

The next morning we went to the Buds School in Perla where a number of children, most of them below ten years of age were brought by their parents in the morning. The care taking of the children by special teachers of the school would continue till the afternoon when they would be taken back home in the vehicles hired for the purpose.

As we reached the Buds School early, we could see the children being taken out and carried bodily by their parents from the vehicles. The children belonged to both the sprayed and non-sprayed areas; it was a pathetic sight and the BBC crew took the pictures of the children being taken to the school, one after the other. Some of the mothers hailed from Karnataka but were married in the sprayed areas. They had their delivery in the non-sprayed areas in Karnataka. The children at the Buds School mostly suffered from Down's Syndrome; they were lying on the floor with mothers hovering around them. They shared their problems among themselves of bringing up the children. The BBC crew took the pictures of the children and their terrible plight. All the use of endosulfan including the aerial spray was stopped in the area ten years before and yet deformed children were still being born, both in the sprayed and non-sprayed areas.

We then proceeded to Karadka where there was a ten-year old boy hit by hydrocephalus. The picture of the child was used in the booklet 'Endosulfan-the Kerala story' published by the state health department.

Abhilash's father was an areca nut farmer. He refused permission to take the pictures of the child and also to cooperate with us. He said so many journalists, including television crew had come to report about the boy, but his son was not so far included in the endosulfan list and, therefore, not getting any benefit. 'My son is not an exhibition piece', he said.

But at last he agreed to cooperate when Rupa Jha said she would ask the Endosulfan Nodal Cell officials to include the child in the list. The mother of Abhilash belonged to Karnataka, but was married in Karadka. Since the family could communicate only in Malayalam and Kannada, I translated what they had said. Abhilash's mother said the doctor attending on the child had said that he was hit by hydrocephalus.

I visited the sprayed area along with a photographer on another occasion. First we went to a house on the Madhur Road in Kasargod town to see a sick child who was included in the endosulfan list. The parents of the child belonged to Kanhangad, a non-sprayed area. The mother and child were staying in the house along with her father. Appu, the ten year old boy was bed-ridden and he was suffering from cerebral palsy.

In Nullipady in Kasargod town, a non-sprayed area, there were two patients, both related to each other and staying in the same house. Both of them were in the endosulfan list. Two-year old Thushar was able to walk, but was speech impaired. Thirty-four year old Dinesh was mentally challenged. The parents of the two suspected victims were getting a total amount of ₹ 4,000 per month. Thranath Acharya, a carpenter and father of Thushar said he was not going for any work since he was attending to his son and the other mentally challenged youth in the same house.

There were three children, all staying in the same house in Mangalpady and closely related to each other; they were suffering from hydrocephalus. Mangalpady was a non-sprayed area lying on the coastal belt. Surgery on the head of the eight-year old Farzeena, daughter of Abubacker was conducted in a Mangalore hospital. The family incurred ₹ 2 lakh for the surgery. The names of the three children were included in the endosulfan list.

One year-old Iflal and his brother Inhal suffered from the same problem. 'Their heads are growing and we are worried', said his mother. This exposed the widely held belief and contention of the anti-endosulfan activists that it was the pesticide spray which caused hydrocephalus as they were living far away from the sprayed area.

There were so many cases of hydrocephalus in the district both in the sprayed and non-sprayed areas. According to doctors, hydrocephalus was an old disease. One of the important findings of the various committees was that the incidence of hydrocephalus was the direct result of the pesticide spray. But there were people who believed that incidents of hydrocephalus in the area were due to some other factors which the health department should bring out, instead of blaming the pesticide spray. They said that heaping continuous blame on the pesticide spray for causing hydrocephalus would not bring out the truth and help eradicate the disease.

We went to Muliyar, a sprayed village, and met Chandu Nair. Sixty-year old Chandu Nair was born with a genetic disease. He was speech impaired. But he was married and have two healthy grown up children. His name was in the endosulfan list. Ramakrishnan of Jinnadkam in Muliyar, a physically disabled man was in the endosulfan list. He was getting the pension for the disabled besides the monthly pension for endosulfan victims. He became disabled after he fell into a well. He was running a small shop and his family stayed at the back of the shop. But he did not tell that he became crippled after falling into a well.

On another occasion, I visited Enmakaje along with Shelvin Sebastian, principal correspondent with the New Indian Express in Kochi. Since Shelvin Sebastian was a regular contributor to the Sunday Express, he wanted a special story for the Sunday issue of the paper.

Since he was my colleague, he called me to help him and we hired a jeep and were soon off to Enmakaje. Jeep driver Ravindra Shetty told us he lived near the plantation of the

PCK in Perla. He had seen the helicopter aerially spraying endosulfan when he was young. He said despite the aerial spray there were no diseases in his area. All the people were healthy, he said.

We went to a house in Perla where we met a youth crawling on his knees on the veranda of the house. The youth was aged about 45 and he was being taken care by his aged mother who attended to his needs. There was an abandoned tricycle in the house compound. The youth's mother told us the tricycle was donated by a local organisation to facilitate his movement. The press photographer with us took the picture of the youth crawling on his knees. His name was included in the list of endosulfan victims.

Shelvin Sebastian was keen to meet Dr Mohan Kumar, an anti-endosulfan activist and he went to his clinic in Ethadka. But I stayed back since Dr Mohan Kumar was not happy about the media reports I had filed on the endosulfan issue. Shelvin came back after holding a detailed conversation with Dr Mohan Kumar. He told me that according to Dr Mohan Kumar, the youth we had visited sometime before and who crawled on his knees was not a victim of endosulfan. Dr Mohan Kumar told him that the youth became disabled after falling from a coconut tree some years before.

In most of the houses we could see children suffering from Down's Syndrome and their houses were separated by some distance. We could see everywhere the unmistakable hallmark of poverty and squalor. We stopped near a cashew plantation where red and yellow cashew apples were hanging from the tree. Ravindra Shetty plucked a few fruits and cleaned them with the water he had brought for drinking. He then started eating the fruits. 'These are pure fruits', he said, 'because no pesticide was ever sprayed on the cashew trees here for the last several years'.

We went to a nursery school where we were told that a child hit by epilepsy was studying. The mother of the child was also working as teacher in the same nursery school. But she told us that her daughter was not a victim of endosulfan since there had been no pesticide spray in the area where she was living with her child. In some houses we could see that parents had more than one disabled child. In some houses there were four or five deformed children, a few of them being bed-ridden.

The incidence of tuberculosis was widespread in the sprayed area. The erstwhile Madras government had constructed a TB sanatorium in Pariyaram in nearby Kannur district. The areas of Kasargod once belonged to Kannur district before the formation of Kasargod district. TB was prevalent mostly among the poor and there were so many patients hit by TB in the endosulfan list as well as in the death list.

There was high incidence of TB among the Koragas who eked out their living by weaving baskets using forest creepers. The Koragas were an ancient community living in Enmakaje and in the adjacent areas of Karnataka. The Koragas reportedly migrated to South India from another continent thousands of years ago. According to anthropologists, long stay of a community in an area would even out the physical differences in course of time and so the Koragas also came to resemble any other ancient tribes in the Indian sub-continent. Yet some of the Koragas had strong resemblance with their African cousins. The Koragas were on the brink of extinction and now because of government intervention their number was on the increase.

Tuberculosis was an ancient disease. But for anti-endosulfan activists, TB was caused by the use of pesticide spraying. According to anthropological studies, Columbus and his fellow European explorers were accused of killing the natives of America with germs and weapons.

The early sailors were accused of bringing with the bugs of illness unknown in America including small pox, measles, influenza, malaria and tuberculosis. But a study conducted by the anthropologists of the university of Chicago in 1990 unearthed genetic material from mummified remains of human beings. The study said that the natives of America had so much TB in earlier times also. But the mystery was solved following the study that the early migrants to America from Asia who crossed the Bering Sea bridge and migrated to the new continent took the disease to the new world. Those migrants thousands of years before Columbus landed in America carried the TB to the new continent, it was revealed in the anthropological study.

The allegation of the activists was that aerial spray of endosulfan created all sorts of diseases for thousands of persons in eleven gram panchayats of the district. The Enmakaje gram panchayat was a virtual ethnological museum with various tribes having distinct ethnicity living in the area for several generations. The tribes were living there much before the advent of others. They were mostly the migrants from distant continents.

Kasargod was generally regarded as a confluence of different culture and languages. Seven languages were spoken in Kasargod. Muslims in Uppla and Manjeswaram who migrated from north India spoke Urdu or Hindi. The Kannadigas spoke Kannada or Tulu; in the border areas of Kasargod Muslims conversed in Beary dialect, a mixture of Kannada and Malayalam; the Marathi Naiks spoke Marathi, Kannada and Malayalam.

Because of the migration of different ethnic groups, Kasargod villages became a confluence of various diseases also. Several ethnic groups in Kasargod villages migrated from far distant places. The Arabs and Turks who reached the coast of Malabar for trade married the local women. There was a mixture of Arab blood in the population of Kasargod. Their culture and food habits constituted the mixture of several ethnic groups.

Each ethnic group had their traditional diseases which pursued them through generations. Though the tribes had their traditional diseases which originated from their distinctive ethnicity, several diseases in the area seemed to have been brought by migrants from far distant places.

For instance, some years ago there was an outbreak of sickle cell anemia among the Paniyas in Wayanad which was widely prevalent among the people of Africa. It was only then that the medical fraternity realised that the Paniyas had genetic connections with the African people. Most of the tribal population including the Paniyas in Kerala and Tamil Nadu suffered from sickle cell anemia. There were reports that the tribal families in Attappady in Kerala also suffered from the disease.

Diseases may also occur due to food habits. There were complaints of cancer in a village in North Malabar. The reason was that the villagers were in the habit of eating river crabs which were available in plenty in the river estuary clogged with all sorts of industrial waste from the nearby motor workshops. The eating of crabs by some of the villagers who found its meat a delicacy developed cancer after some years. The river crabs grew up by consuming industrial waste and other pollutants.

According to media reports, the number of patients suffering from kidney diseases was on the increase in Malappuram district of Kerala. Alarmed, the District Panchayat in Malappuram formed the Kidney Patients' Welfare Society in 2007. The KPWS received as many as 2,106 applications for conducting dialysis during the past six years after its formation. As many as 297 patients had undergone treatment in the district following kidney transplantation till 2013. According to media reports, Kerala found itself in the grip of diabetes which has been on the increase in the state.

The anti-endosulfan activists generally ignored or mocked at the suggestion that there were acute diseases in non-sprayed areas also. There was unusual number of mentally retarded children in Mogral Puthur grama panchayat, located near the seaside where no pesticide was ever used since it was not a farming village. The residents mostly lived with the money sent by their relatives from the Arabian Gulf countries. In this village, there were 193 mentally challenged persons, a figure higher than that of all the mentally challenged persons in Swarga, Vaninagar and Padre villages put together.

I visited Mogral Puthur accompanied by a social worker. I could see the same scenario which I had seen in the endosulfan sprayed villages. The diseases were also the same—hydrocephalus, Down's Syndrome, mental and physical retardation. Like the villages in Enmakaje, the victims' parents were all poor struggling hard to look after their sick and infirm children. There were two or three mentally challenged children in a family.

Jithin Raj and his sister Sisira of Kottavalappu were both mentally challenged children. Their parents were unable to go for work since their presence was required for looking after them. Diseased and sick children died young in the villages. A ten-year old boy stricken with polio died in Pookkara village while a girl in the neighbourhood succumbed to her illness when she was eight. In some areas there were deformed children in each household. There were as many as 36 mentally retarded children in the surrounding areas of Erial, a small town.

The staff of the Kerala State Institute for Mentally Challenged had conducted a house-to-house survey of the mentally challenged for two days in the area. The staff who conducted the survey was of the opinion that they have not seen such a large concentration of mentally retarded children anywhere in the state. It was a cluster of multiple diseases that one can see in Mogral Puthur.

According to the study conducted in Mogral Puthur, the density of the population was the main cause of the diseases. Then there was also the problem of lack of spacing of children. Many of the mothers in the area had given birth to children whose age difference was hardly one year. Early marriages and lack of medical awareness on the part of the expectant mothers also contributed to the illness. Marriages between closely related people were yet another cause for the diseases.

The villages located to the north and eastern areas of the district adjoining Karnataka were also disturbingly prone to various diseases. What one normally heard were horrible stories of strange diseases stalking the entire area. The coastal areas of the district especially from Kasargod to Manjeswaram were endemic to various diseases. The Kerala State Handicapped Development Corporation had conducted camps in three places on the coastal belt in 2005. Surprisingly, a total of over one thousand mentally challenged and bed-ridden patients were brought to the camps. This has proved that something was troubling the villagers which caused a large number of diseases. Diseases as found in the sprayed areas were prevailing in Paivalige, a village on the Kerala–Karnataka border, though it was a non-sprayed village.

A one-day survey conducted by a team of volunteers in Neeleswaram block panchayat in Kasargod district, a non-sprayed area, baffled the organisers. Volunteers in seven batches visited 8,000 houses of the block panchayat. Though they found large number of patients suffering from cancer, asthma, mental retardation and physical disabilities, the organisers refused to publish the results fearing that the villagers would be isolated and the people would become outcastes in their own land.

Diseases were everywhere in Kasargod district, mostly among the poor. The culture and way of living of the people in the area—whether pesticide was sprayed there or not—were one and the same. A girl belonging to Uppla died as she developed a malignant tumour at the back of her head. It grew in size and became as big as her head. The girl who was normal developed the tumour when she was studying in primary classes. The leg of another girl began to swell and it had to be amputated, but the girl died shortly. Both girls belonged to non-pesticide sprayed areas.

Significantly, the rich and the landowning class were not hit by the spraying of the pesticide. All the commotion was created by the landowning class. Perhaps, they found a way out to escape from the blame of the young generation in the village who would point an accusing finger against landowners who most cruelly exploited the poor. But they found an easy way out to escape from the blame—endosulfan was the cause of all the diseases!

4

AN EXPERIMENT WITH UNTRUTH

On February 21, 2001, the New Delhi based Centre for Science and Environment convened a media conference in Delhi to announce that its own laboratory test had found 'alarming high levels of endosulfan in samples of water, milk, fruits, vegetables and blood collected by it in the village of Padre in Kasargod'.

Announcing this to media persons, CSE director Sunita Narain said this alarming high levels of endosulfan was responsible for causing a variety of health ailments including cancer among the people of Padre. The CSE concluded the media conference with a strong demand to ban endosulfan throughout the country.

It was the CSE's first experiment with untruth through cunning fabrication of the data it collected from the village of Padre. The whole incident smacked of scientific cover-up. It turned out to be a big success as the media believed everything what the CSE had projected. The media conference was flashed across the nation. The rest was history with environmental activists demanding ban on endosulfan as the issue became emotional in Kasargod. Those who questioned the CSE's findings were accused as agents of the pesticide industry. It showed that the NGOs and the environmental activists would go to any extreme to create sensational stories in the media.

The CSE study was named 'analysis of samples from Padre village in Kasargod district of Kerala for endosulfan residues'. The investigators who conducted the study in February 2001 were Dr Padma S. Vankar, Dr Rashmi Mishra and Dr Sapna Johnson, all scientists. Technical assistance on collection and storage of samples was given by M.K. Prasad, coordinator of the Environmental Centre of the Kerala Sastra Sahithya Parishad and V.R. Raghunandanan, Associate Professor and veterinary toxicologist with the International Rural Technology Centre, Palakkad. However, Sripathy Kajampady, a doctor in Perla helped in collecting the samples.

Under the caption "impact of endosulfan on health – scientific evidence" the CSE report said 'Exposure to endosulfan may result from, for example : breathing air where it has been sprayed ; drinking water contaminated with it; eating contaminated food; touching contaminated soil; smoking cigarettes made from tobacco contaminated with endosulfan residues ; or working in an industry where endosulfan is used. Proper protective clothing (safety goggles, gloves, long sleeves, long pants, respirator) is needed to prevent poisoning when handling endosulfan'.

The CSE and the Kerala-based NGO Thanal formed an unholy alliance among themselves in the beginning of 2001 with the support of the European Union. Thanal which supported the CSE was helped by the UK-based Pesticide Action Network (PAN) funded by the European Union in its campaign against endosulfan in Padre. The CSE collected the technical details on endosulfan from the website of the Pesticide Action Network which was included in its study report.

It was the result of the study conducted by the CSE which was announced at the media conference in Delhi. The CSE admitted in its website that the sponsor of the study and supporter of the programme was the Delegation of the European Commission in India, New Delhi. The institutional support was given by the Swedish International Agency, SIDA, New Delhi. Most important, the pollution monitoring laboratory of the CSE was funded by the European Union and the Delegation of the European Commission in India to analyse the pesticide residues in the village of Padre.

What was the interest of the European Commission and the SIDA to conduct the endosulfan residue study in the village of Padre in Kasargod? The national media never investigated the involvement of the SIDA and the European Union in the study. The media in Kerala which prided itself that it was the pioneers of investigative journalism did not take any efforts to investigate. But the answers given by the Union Government under the Right to Information Act exposed the whole link between foreign funds and the CSE.

The Ministry of Home Affairs had replied under the RTI Act that the CSE had received a total of ₹ 53.21 crore from 1999 to 2006. The CSE had received a foreign contribution of ₹ 3.9 crore in 2001 during the study of the endosulfan residues in the village of Padre. (The Ministry of Home Affairs informed this to a RTI activist vide letter No.\21022\582009-FCRA-1 dated, February 2 , 2009 in reply to his query under the Right to Information Act. The answer was given by S.K. Shahi, Deputy Secretary to the Government of India of the Ministry of Home Affairs).

But the Delegation of the European Commission in Delhi had to admit later to the Endosulfan Manufacturers and Formulators Welfare Association through a letter that it had given funds to the CSE to catalyse the formation of pressure groups.

What was the content of the study? In the introduction itself, the CSE report said that the Plantation Corporation of Kerala, PCK, had become a silent killer in North Kerala. 'The aerial spray of endosulfan, a deadly 'organochlorine pesticide', and other toxic chemicals in their plantations had seriously damaged the health of the children, women and men', the study revealed. But the CSE report failed to conduct a study on 'other toxic chemicals' reportedly sprayed by the PCK.

In the report of the Pesticide Residue Monitoring Study, the CSE introduced itself as a Non-Governmental Organisation based in Delhi. 'Its main aim was to undertake scientific studies to generate public awareness about food contaminated by pesticides and heavy metals'.

According to the introduction in the report, the CSE said that 'It provided scientific services at affordable prices at communities that cannot obtain scientific evidence against polluters. This can be crucial at times in a court of law when a community may be fighting against a polluter in its area. Given the state of scientific research in India-most of it is restricted to national defense and food security; this is an effort to use science to achieve ecological security. The laboratory will also provide paid services to become financially self-sufficient'. Most importantly, the CSE said that 'the funds to set up the laboratory have come from the European Union.'

According to the CSE, the pesticide used by the Plantation Corporation of Kerala, PCK, was endosulfan. 'It has already been banned in most of the developing and developed countries. The international negotiation by the United Nations Environmental Programme, UNEP, to ban such persistent organic pollutants has already shortlisted 12 chemicals and endosulfan is expected to be the 13th in the list'.

A good opportunity was, therefore, presented to the CSE to hasten the end of endosulfan as residents of the pesticide sprayed villages in Kasargod, according to the CSE, 'complained of ailments such as headache, dizziness, skin lesions, sudden abortions, neurological disorders, epilepsy, cerebral palsy and cancer'. As endosulfan was listed as the 13th pesticide to be banned for being a persistent organic pollutant, the CSE did not waste the opportunity to conduct a pesticide monitoring study in the village of Padre in Kasargod. As stated earlier, it has to be stressed that the study was supported by the Delegation of the European Commission in India and the institutional support was given by the Swedish International Agency, SIDA.

The CSE said in its report that 'younger generation was losing its immunity and occurrence of fever and other diseases was very high. The cattle and dogs die within one week after spraying. Stream fishes and the whole water body and the soil are contaminated with chemicals'.

The CSE then offered to conduct laboratory tests on samples collected from the village of Padre free of cost in its newly established laboratory. The CSE had said that its intention was to 'provide paid services to become financially self sufficient'. However, it decided to conduct laboratory test of samples free of cost in Padre. This showed its peculiar interest in conducting the test in the village. If everything was to be taken together—first, the institutional support given by SIDA, second, the support from the European Union which also funded a new laboratory for the CSE, and most important that endosulfan was listed as the 13th pollutant to be banned during the time—it gave a clear insight into the real motive of the CSE and the European Union in conducting the pesticide residue test in Padre.

The CSE report itself was a string of untruths which made a mockery of the basic principles of science. It collected samples from human milk, vegetables, butter, bovine milk and water. The study team also collected blood samples from the residents of Padre.

The analysis of the report was mind boggling. Some of the villagers carried an average of 108 to 196 ppm (parts per million) of endosulfan in their blood. The report said that Dr Mohan Kumar, an anti-endosulfan activist from the very beginning of the agitation carried 115.19 ppm of endosulfan in his blood! It was nothing but a blatant violation of the basics of science.

Also, endosulfan residues ranging from 6.65 ppm to 9.19 ppm was found in filtered water samples. This was 2,000 per cent to 3,000 per cent higher than its maximum water solubility of 0.32 ppm. It was similar to saying that the CSE can extract nine kilogram of salt from one litre of sea water!.

According to the principles of science, no human being can ever carry 115.19 ppm of endosulfan residues, which was 13,000 per cent higher than the lethal level in one's blood and can still be alive. Dr Mohan Kumar still remained healthy even after ten years of the CSE analysis of his blood samples. According to the critics of the CSE study, even suicide victims who took endosulfan to take their own lives had less than 10 ppm of endosulfan in their blood. The CSE report was subsequently published worldwide by the Pesticide Action Network, PAN. It was also circulated at the venue of the international conventions on pesticides in Rotterdam and Stockholm.

The ignorance about ppb and ppm among ordinary people came in handy for environmental activists and NGOs to create and plant fear among the people. The ppb stands for Parts Per Billion and the ppm stands for Parts Per Million and 1,000 million makes one billion. The general public would be easily frightened when media projected the pesticide residues because they had been told frequently that all pesticides were killers. There was no doubt that pesticides were killers. However, pesticides were not designed to kill human beings, but only insects and rodents that caused threat to farming activities.

Apart from Dr Mohan Kumar, the CSE had tested the blood samples of some more people to detect the endosulfan residues and the results were again mind boggling. Kittana Shetty, 21, staying near the Kodenkeri stream had 109.5 ppm of endosulfan residue in his blood! But the maximum permissible limit of endosulfan in blood was shown as 'not available' in the report. But the endosulfan residue in the blood sample of Muthakka Shetty, mother of Kittana Shetty, was even more mind boggling; it was as high as 196.47 ppm !

Lalitha, 35, living near the Kodenkeri stream had 176.47 ppm of endosulfan residue in her blood. Her both parents died of neurological problems and her sister died of cancer. Vishnu Prasah Kulkarni, 16, suffering from epilepsy had 108 ppb of endosulfan in his blood. In all these cases the maximum permissible limit of endosulfan in blood was shown as 'not available'.

A total of 28.24 ppm of endosulfan residue was detected in a fish sample collected from a tank in Kajampady in Padre near the cashew plantation. But the lethal dose of endosulfan was shown as 0.7 ppm. Similarly, a live frog had 10.35 ppm of endosulfan in its tiny body, but the maximum permissible limit was shown as 0.7 ppm. The milk collected from a cow in Kumbadaje contained 57.2 ppm of endosulfan!

All the samples were collected in February, 2001 and the last aerial spray was conducted in the village on December 26, 2000. But a scientific team of the Kerala Agricultural University could find endosulfan residue of only 2 ppm and that too in an open hill near the cashew plantation during the same period.

The CSE had also targeted the soft drink industry. On August 26, 2006, the CSE released a sensational report to the media claiming that its analysis had shown pesticide residues in all 57 soft drink samples collected from Indian market. The pesticide residues, according to CSE, ranged from 2.65 ppb. There was much public outcry when CSE alleged that there were pesticide residues in soft drinks. There were accusations against the government that it was doing nothing to prevent poisons being bottled and sold as soft drinks.

After releasing the report, the Union Ministry of Health constituted a six-member expert committee to scientifically examine the claims made by CSE since it was highly perturbed by the findings. The committee in its report released in September 2006 stated that the 'results and conclusions reached by the CSE in its report cannot be accepted on its face value. The expert committee said in its report that sample methodology used by the CSE did not have a scientific and statistically valid base.

These were but a few examples of the unscientific analytical results released by the CSE. The investigators, a few of them belonging to the prestigious scientific institutions in the country, deliberately falsified the results with dubious motives.

But surprisingly, the country did not have any specific law to prevent scientific fraud though most of the developed countries have passed such laws for punishments for laboratory frauds. Therefore, environmental laboratory crimes needed to be considered on par with environmental crimes and should form an integral part of the Environmental (Protection Act), 1986. Its aim should be to detect, investigate, punish and prevent laboratory frauds in the country.

The United States Environment Protection Agency has established a laboratory fraud directorate to specially investigate all such frauds. The Chinese Ministry of Science and Technology enacted a set of rules to tackle misconduct of scientists working in government funded institutes and science programmes. Punishment ranged from suspension to life time disqualification.

Anti-endosulfan activists of Kasargod were supported by Pesticide Action Network, PAN, the Environment Justice Foundation, EJF, and I-PEN (International POP Elimination Network). The purpose of the NGOs was to effectively use the media to generate negative publicity against endosulfan. The journalists who exposed the untruths were mocked and denigrated in the internet. The new media came in handy for them to implement their hidden agenda.

The systematic campaign to ban endosulfan, a generic pesticide started in 2001. However, the conspiracy at the Persistent Organic Pollutants Review Committee, POPRC, meet in Geneva began in 2007. The pesticide residue monitoring study conducted by the CSE was aimed towards this objective. Statistics from the European Commission showed that between 2002 and 2008 the funding of the Environmental Non-Governmental Organisation, ENGO, increased from €3.9 million to €8.5 million. The ENGOs also included the Pesticide Action Network, PAN, which had helped the Thanal in Kerala to fuel the anti-endosulfan agitation in Kasargod. Funded by the European Commission, the ENGOs became proxy to the EU and carried on campaigns against generic pesticides. Available information showed that endosulfan was ten times cheaper than the patented pesticides of the European Union countries. The EU pesticide manufacturers wanted to market their costly pesticides in India, but it was bound to cripple the already burdened farmers of the country.

With an estimated sale of 35 million litres, endosulfan was among the top 10 generic insecticides in the world. But European Union was the largest manufacturer and exporter of pesticides in the world. Therefore, it wanted the elimination of endosulfan from the world market by substituting it with its patented, high priced and highly profitable pesticides.

The EU, thus, financed environmental activists in the country to generate scientifically erroneous reports. Thanal was the most active NGO engaged in the anti-endosulfan campaign in Kerala. It has been receiving foreign funds to work against endosulfan in the state. The patented pesticide lobby in the European Union manipulated and took control of the Persistent Organic Pollutants Review Committee convention to campaign against endosulfan with the sole objective of eliminating it from the international market.

India and China, the major users of endosulfan protested against the unlawful procedures at the POPRC convention. But the protests were of no avail as the European Union used its clout to silence the delegates of India and China at the convention. It was exposed at the convention that Sweden was taking the initiative to eliminate endosulfan from the global market. It was the Swedish International Agency, SIDA, which rendered institutional support to the environmental impact study of the CSE in the village of Padre way back in 2001.

Sree Padre, an anti-endosulfan activist acted as a conduit between the CSE and journalists across the state to plant its press releases. A press release of the CSE was sent through e-mail to Sree Padre on June 28, 2002. It was captioned 'An industry of death wins". The press release said:

'A hard hitting expose by the CSE showed how the pesticide industry connived with Government officials and scientists in Kerala to successfully lift the ban on a deadly pesticide. At stake here is the integrity of the state Government's decision-making for generations far into the future. It not only spells irreparable harm for the residents of Kerala, but also makes a mockery of the public health concerns. A recent confidential report by the National Institute of Occupational Health, NIOH, Ahmedabad, has unequivocally blamed endosulfan, an organchlorine pesticide as the reason for the unusually high cases of diseases and deformity in Kerala's Kasargod district. Endosulfan is either banned or restricted in many countries.'

The e-mail was sent in 2002 and at the time the conspiracy of the NIOH scientists was little known. The NIOH report was later criticised by Dr O.P. Dubey committee and Dr C.D. Mayee committee. The US environmental organisation called Environ International exposed the NIOH report in March 2012.

The CSE press release said 'when Down To Earth' first broke the story in February 2001, both the Union and the State Government imposed a ban on spraying of the deadly pesticide in Kerala. But shockingly, the Kerala Government lifted the ban on March 22, 2002 based on two industry-sponsored studies—the one by the Frederick Institute of Plant Protection and Toxicology, FIPPAT, Kancheepuram, Tamil Nadu, and another by the Kerala Agriculture University'.

'Surprisingly, both these reports did not find any trace of endosulfan residues even though these samples were collected within a few months of the last aerial spraying by the Plantation Corporation of Kerala since the mid-1970's on its cashew plantations. However, after the NIOH study which was conducted 10 months later following the spraying, conclusive evidence of endosulfan residues in water and blood samples were collected from Kasargod', the CSE release said.

According to CSE, 'the 4,100 crore pesticide industry was working overtime on a no-holds-barred campaign to promote endosulfan sales and ensure their own survival'. It said India was the largest producer of endosulfan in the world. 'The murky games of the industry include disinformation campaigns, involving misleading advertisements, and manufactured scientific data by sponsoring 'scientific' studies and influencing Government scientists and officials. For the time being, the strategy seems to have worked. The silent screams of Kasargod's residents have fallen on deaf ears', said the CSE communication.

The CSE reached the peak of its disinformation campaign when it said 'the State Government officials are taking recourse to this dangerous slide away in the fact that legally they cannot continue the ban. But Section 27 of the Insecticides Act, 1968, under which pesticides are regulated clearly states that the State Government can either extend the ban or issue fresh order. It is apparent that the A.K. Antony Government has preferred complicity with the pesticide industry to public health commitments.'

Clearly establishing the link between Thanal and the CSE way back in 2002, the e-mail said 'This damning NIOH report was kept a secret because it clearly implicates the pesticide industry, said Jayakumar C. of Thanal, a Non-Governmental Organisation fighting for the victims. The Down-To-Earth's latest cover story on endosulfan conspiracy on July 15 issue gives a blow by blow account of the pesticide industry's deadly intent to profit over public health'.

The CSE communication again established the earlier link between Sree Padre and other activists when it gave the names of three activists fighting against the industry in Kerala. They were Sree Padre, Kasargod, Jayakumar C. and Sridhar R. of Thanal, and Dr Sripathy Kajampady of Kasargod. They were not mere anti-endosulfan activists, but were those fighting the pesticide industry. Significantly, they started the fight against the pesticide even when no study had proved that endosulfan was responsible for the so-called strange diseases they had attributed to the pesticide spray.

It was the CSE which started the whole campaign against endosulfan with the huge funds from the European Union countries with intend to destroy Indian agriculture. But unfortunately, there was none to speak for Indian agriculture and the need to feed its huge and burgeoning population. It again showed that the intention of Thanal and the CSE was to destroy Indian agriculture with funds from the European Union, EU. Surprisingly, the Indian Government could not think that it was a thoroughly anti-national act indulged in by the CSE and Thanal, a Kerala-based NGO.

The Colorado based Global Greengrant Funds had given $ 9,500 to Thanal which conducted anti-endosulfan activities in Kasargod from 2001. This included 1,150 dollars received by Dr. Mohammed Asheel, Assistant Endosulfan Nodal Officer in Kasargod for his trip abroad to take part in the Stockholm convention of the Persistent Organic Pollutants Review Committee, POPRC meet. The website of the Global Greengrant Funds had published the details of the funds given to Thanal and Dr. Mohammed Asheel.

In a letter sent to Prime Minister Manmohan Singh on June 21, 2010, the Endosulfan Manufacturers and Formulators Welfare Association demanded an expert committee inquiry into the monitoring study of pesticide residues conducted by the CSE in Kasargod with financial support from the European Union.

The Association informed the Prime Minister that the information obtained under the Right to Information Act suggested that the CSE had received ₹ 53.21 crore (about 10 million Euros), most of this from the member states of the European Union.

'Using the funds the CSE conducted a pesticide residues monitory study. The report had found alarming levels of endosulfan residues in water and blood samples taken from a pesticide sprayed village in Kasargod district claiming that it was causing a host of health problems'.

Most importantly, the Association informed the Prime Minister that European Union covertly circulated CSE report worldwide using the NGOs who were financially supported by EU such as the Pesticide Action Network, PAN, as well as in global forums such as the United Nations Environmental Programme, UNEP, causing considerable panic and regulatory restrictions against endosulfan worldwide.

'But to the general public, the highly visible campaign in Kasargod in Kerala may appear to be driven by local NGOs. But in reality, the campaign was funded and facilitated by European Union countries mainly because of strong economical and commercial reasons. The campaign was driven to exterminate endosulfan, a widely used pesticide from the world', the letter said.

However, the delegation of the European Union in Delhi admitted to the Endosulfan Manufacturers and Formulators Welfare Association that it had given funds to CSE. In reply to the association on May 20, 2010, the EU said the funds were provided to catalyse the formation of pressure groups and that it cannot be held responsible for the results of the study, their correctness or the usage of the results.

The association informed the Prime Minister that 'there were streaks of unmistakable imperialism in its response. The EU showed zero accountability to the scientifically flawed report for which it had funded'. The Association pointed out that the provisions of the Foreign Contributions Regulations Act, 2006, did not allow foreign contribution in India if it was likely to affect prejudicially the scientific and economic interest of the country. The act also expressly stated that the foreign contribution should not lead to incitement of an offence.

'The scientifically flawed report generated by the EU through CSE and made public worldwide does prejudicially affect the scientific and economic interests of India. It is well known that generating a scientific report by means of fabricated data is an offence', the letter said.

The Association then made a strong plea that the EU must scientifically demonstrate that it was possible to find 9.19 ppm of endosulfan residues in filtered water samples as per the methods adopted by CSE in its study which it had sponsored. This should be demonstrated in a government institute or government accredited private laboratory in the presence of experts. 'If the EU and the CSE could accept the challenge and fail to prove it, the impugned study must be withdrawn', said the association.

Another remarkable suggestion of the association to the Prime Minister was that an exclusive law must be introduced in the country to permit publication of foreign funded scientific study involving environment or health of the people only after it has been peer reviewed by government appointed experts. This would send a strong signal to those who take the soft route of environment and health to achieve hidden economic agenda. Though the Association wanted the Prime Minister to order an expert inquiry into the issue to bring out the truth, the probe never materialised. Nor was the CSE prepared to demonstrate its 'findings' before any expert committee.

On July 21, 2012 Kerala Chief Minister Oommen Chandy shared dais with Sunita Narain of the CSE in Kasargod. They met during the so-called National Workshop on Rehabilitation of Endosulfan Victims. Addressing the workshop Sunita Narain reiterated what she had stated earlier—'what has happened in Kasargod was similar to the Bhopal gas disaster'.

5

FRAUDULENT STUDIES BY SCIENTIFIC INSTITUTIONS

The Science, Technology and Environment Department, STED, which later became the Kerala State Council for Science, Technology and Environment, KSCSTE, a government undertaking, had taken a stand supporting the anti-endosulfan agitation from the very beginning. It was sympathetic to the agitation and was under the influence of the NGOs which spearheaded the agitation in Kasargod.

The bias of the STED was evident as early as 2001 when the government constituted a committee of scientists including those in the STED to study whether any environmental health hazards occurred due to the aerial spray of endosulfan.

A government order issued on May 15, 2001 said 'it is noticed that certain unusual diseases are spreading among the inhabitants of Padre village of Enmakaje gram panchayat in Kasargod district due to the aerial spraying of pesticides using helicopter by the Plantation Corporation Kerala Ltd'.

The government order itself was biased since it had 'noticed' the spread of certain unusual diseases in the village of Padre. This was an instance of the government itself caving in before the false propaganda carried on by some NGOs regarding the so-called strange diseases.

A committee was constituted by the government with Dr Kamalakshan Kokkal, principle scientist, STED, as convener. Dr Kamalakshan Kokkal, a native of Kasargod was a sympathiser of the anti-endosulfan agitation. The committee comprised V. Gopinathan, head of the department of Geology, Kasargod Government College, T.C. Madhava Panicker, president of the Kasargod Peoples' Forum and Dr C. Thampan, scientist of the Central Plantation Crops Research Institute, CPCRI, in Kasargod. However, T.C. Madhava Panicker and V. Gopinathan supported the anti-endosulfan campaign from the beginning. Two other committee members were Dr K.C. Ajith Prasad and P. Sreekantan Nair, both scientific officers of the STED.

The terms of reference of the committee was to enquire and report on any environmental problems prevailing in the area and also to examine the complaints on suspected spreading of unusual diseases among the inhabitants. The committee has to suggest suitable remedial measures to overcome environmental crisis, if any.

As stated earlier, the order was issued on May 15, 2001. But towards the end of 2012 everything ended up as the proverbial storm in a tea cup as the so-called strange diseases became ordinary diseases such as mental and physical retardation, cerebral palsy, cancer, head ache, joint pain, tooth ache, jaundice, eye problems, ear ache and other silly ailments.

Looking back, one could see that how erroneous and biased was the order of the Kerala government issued in 2001 when it said that 'certain unusual diseases are spreading among the people due to the aerial spraying of endosulfan'. It was found in 2012 that the diseases were not unusual in nature since almost all the disease were common that could be found everywhere. This showed that the state government, too, was carried away by the propaganda of Thanal and the Centre for Science and Environment.

According to the executive summary of the 'scientific report' of the STED, the problem was confined not only in Enmakaje gram panchayat but also in its hinterlands. The STED admitted in the executive summary that it depended on secondary data available, factual representations submitted by aggrieved persons, people's representatives, media, NGOs, Pollution Control Board and the district administration. But most of these were biased. The NGO was Thanal from whom the team collected evidence. Besides, the media was highly biased since it was in the forefront of reporting the 'Endo tragedy' which it had termed as another Bhopal gas disaster. The Pollution Control Board had also been highly biased in its report which led to the ban on endosulfan in the state.

The STED report said 'as the area is away from urban and semi-urban areas, the environmental problem related to any industries or wastes are of remote possibility. The only anthropogenic activity that needs special mention in the area is the aerial spraying of endosulfan practiced by the Plantation Corporation of Kerala, PCK.'

During the spray time, said the STED report, people suffered from suffocation and many of the inhabitants had breathing problems, irritation in eyes, headache, cough, skin diseases and body weakness following the aerial spraying. But the workers of the Plantation Corporation who were directly exposed to the pesticide by carrying out the work of mixing and loading endosulfan in helicopter should also have felt giddiness and other symptoms than the local people; but they did not suffer from any such symptoms, and were still found healthy. The committee collected the oral version of the local people among whom the NGOs had conducted a relentless and ruthless campaign before it started its proceedings.

It was also evident, according to the report, that unusual 'abortion rate among women and animals, birth of handicapped children among the inhabitants were similar to the effects that endosulfan may cause'. The committee depended on the available secondary data or the oral version from the people. The Thanal and other NGOs had been making strident campaign in the sprayed villages that the diseases were indeed caused by the aerial spray of endosulfan. It had conducted a series of campaigns among the people way back in 2000. The data on congenial problems, irritation in the eyes, head ache, suicidal tendency were all put into the head of the unsuspecting villagers as part of the propaganda by the NGOs.

The scientific committee should not have depended on secondary data. It could have collected the primary data at sources from hospitals, veterinary clinics, from the birth and death registers in local body offices. The committee could have collected material evidence from poly clinics on dizziness, irritation of eye and the rate of abortion.

It was the height of bias to allege that 'many of the health problems found among the inhabitants are similar to the effects that endosulfan may cause'. Since there was no history of diseases breaking out following the aerial spray of endosulfan in any other places of the country or for that matter anywhere else in the world, there had been no follow-up studies on endosulfan's affect on human beings. Without any previous data how could the scientific committee of the STED reach the conclusion that the diseases were similar to the effect of endosulfan? All studies on endosulfan were nothing but 'rat studies'.

Interestingly, the scientific committee came to the conclusion based on secondary data that 'prima facie aerial spraying of endosulfan was to be the causative factor of unusual diseases among the people of the area. But it was not clear how the 'scientific committee' arrived at the conclusion to blame endosulfan spray for unusual disease in the area.

The STED scientific committee which recommended the ban on the aerial spray of endosulfan, however, made a somersault and remarked that 'the role of endosulfan as the exact cause factor is presently neither denied nor proved beyond doubt in this area'.

A few years later, the STED was reconstituted as the Kerala State Council for Science, Technology and Environment, KSCSTE, and it conducted a detailed study on endosulfan residues in the sprayed area. But the pesticide industry sent a request to the public information officer of the KSCSTE to provide details of the soil samples it had collected from the exposed area for the study. It wanted to analyse the soil samples on its own. However, the Public Information Officer rejected the plea of the pesticide industry even though the request was made under the Right to Information Act.

The public information officer replied to the pesticide industry that the information requested by it was not available in the office. The information sought under the RTI Act included details of confirmatory test, details of residue analysis and information regarding the chromatograms. The pesticide industry in its appeal to the appellate authority said that the reply was perfunctory and violated the provisions of the Right to Information Act.

The pesticide industry said the very purpose of the RTI Act was to enable a citizen to have access to information under the control of the public authority. According to the RTI Act, the information meant any material stored in any form, including the data stored in electronic equipment. The state Government had given ₹ 10 lakh to the KSCSTE to conduct the study.

The residue analysis of endosulfan was conducted by the Centre for Water Resources Development and Management, CWRDM, one of the seven research and development centres of the KSCSTE. Therefore, public information officer of the KSCSTE should have collected the information from the CWRDM, said the pesticide industry.

But the truth eventually came out much to the embarrassment of the KSCSTE and the CWRDM. On May 15, 2013, CWRDM's principal investigator and head of the water quality division told journalists that the residues of endosulfan were still present in the soil samples collected from different panchayats from Kasargod district. The fourth and latest phase of the continuing study undertaken by the CWRDM pointed out to the greater persistence of endosulfan in soil and sediment samples than in water samples, according to media reports.

Though the pesticide industry had asked for details of the soil samples conducted by the KSCSTE under the Right to Information Act, the reply was that the information was not available. But the fact was that the CWRDM functioning under the KSCSTE and which conducted the soil tests had details of the test sought by the pesticide industry. This showed that both the scientists of the KSCSTE and the CWRDM had something to hide and they were helping the powerful NGOs which received foreign funds in the anti-endosulfan agitation.

The pesticide industry also criticised the collection and identification of samples which was done with the help of NGOs, panchayat employees and health officials. The industry alleged that it was not a standard practice since the help of soil experts was not sought by the KSCSTE. The pesticide industry also questioned the KSCSTE for not putting the required information on its website as required under the RTI Act.

The KSCSTE then informed the media that it would conduct another soil test in the sprayed area. It was clear from the decision of the KSCSTE to conduct another soil test that there were serious lapses in its earlier test.

The result of the soil testing conducted by the KSCSTE in the beginning was seized by Thanal. It released the report to selected media persons who reported that the entire soil in the sprayed area was contaminated with endosulfan residues. But the fact was that the soil was contaminated only at the helicopter take off points in the PCK plantations. It was but natural that such spots would be spoilt with endosulfan residues. But this was magnified in the media to suggest that the entire PCK plantation land was contaminated with poison.

But the scientists changed the stand when the question of acquiring land for the Central University of Kerala in Peria, a sprayed area, came up for discussion in the media. The KSCSTE which was entrusted by the Central University to prepare a pesticide - free clearance report said that the whole area was bereft of any pesticide residues. The Central University wanted the clearance report since Peria was located to construct buildings for the Central University to house its headquarters and the main campus.

The report of the KSCSTE also carried an analysis of the environmental impact of pesticide spray. The report was prepared by Dr K.S. Vijayan, former Chairman of the Kerala Biodiversity Board. The report was appended to the KSCSTE report. He said in the report that the sprayed area was once rich in floral and faunal diversity, but it lost its rich diversity following the spraying of endosulfan.

He reported that a large number of wild animals including the Nilgiri languor, tiger, jackal and wild boar completely disappeared from the sprayed area. Even though Dr Vijayan had reported that wild boars had disappeared from the area, the farmers in the village submitted a complaint to the District Collector that their crops were periodically destroyed by herds of wild boars from across the Karnataka border. But forest officials contradicted the report of Dr Vijayan. They said that Nilgiri Langurs were never spotted in the area. They said tigers had disappeared from the area long ago though one or two of the felines occasionally strayed into the land adjacent to the sprayed area from the Western Ghats region.

Environmental NGOs used scientists to create unfounded fears and anxieties in the minds of the gullible public with the aid of false and fabricated data, alleged the pesticide industry. There was a hidden agenda behind all this. It was to attack the pesticide industry by conducting fraudulent scientific studies and propagate it through the internet. Efforts of these scientists benefited the foreign countries. As a result, fruits and vegetables from India could not find a ready market in Europe because of the propaganda made by a group of NGOs supported by con scientists, according to the pesticide industry.

The best example to corroborate this charge of pesticide manufacturers was the experiments conducted by the scientists of the Indian Institute of Technology, Kanpur.

When the Delhi-based Society for Scientific Values wrote to the IIT Kanpur about the scientific misconduct of a prominent scientist, the IIT director did not respond to the letter. An application under the Right to Information Act sent to the IIT authorities also failed to produce any response. When a reminder was sent, a terse one line reply from the Public Information Officer of the IIT said no complaints of research and scientific misconduct against the scientist was received. At last the IIT management was compelled to give substantial information after the Central Information Commissioner pulled up the institute for its lack of meaningful response. The CIC directed the administration to supply complete and correct information about the disinformation campaign and fraudulent research conducted by the scientist.

A senior research scientist from the IIT Kanpur appeared as an expert in the TV show 'Satyamev Jayate'. In the TV show titled 'poison in our plate' the senior research scientist liberally resorted to scare mongering about pesticides citing certain findings from an earlier IIT Kanpur research study on pesticide residues in breast milk from Bhopal in Madhya Pradesh.

The study had asserted that there were alarming residues in breast milk samples ranging from 400 to 800 per cent higher than its acceptable daily intake, ADI. The Centre for Environment and Agro Chemicals, CENTAGRO, a platform of farmers, agricultural scientists and members of the pesticide industry collected information on the study under the Right to Information Act from the IIT Kanpur. The CENTAGRO alleged that it was an instance of falsification and fabrication.

The CENTAGRO sent a letter to the secretary of higher education, Ministry of Human Resources and Development seeking action against the scientist. It stated in the letter that the method used in the study 'organochlorine and organo-phospherous pesticide residues in breast milk in Bhopal' was wrong in analysing endosulfan residues. In residue analysis, the alfa endosulfan, beta endosulfan and endosulfan sulphate should have been analysed separately'.

But the published study did not follow this essential procedure and in the process the study erred seriously. The study showed serious limitations, omissions and errors. Besides, the study was fundamentally flawed and looked dubious. The scientist had made the declaration that the study was carried out at the IIT Kanpur which provided analytical facilities. Strangely, the IIT said that there was no record available to show that the study was conducted at the IIT Kanpur.

Questioning the study, the CENTAGRO wondered whether it was an example of dry-labbing which meant publishing a research study without conducting any laboratory tests. It said in the letter that the whole study sensationally discussed in the T V show 'Sathyamev Jayate' looked shady both scientifically and legally'.

According to the CENTAGRO, the scientific misconduct at IIT Kanpur was not confined to one particular department. In 2010, an international journal 'Bio-technological Advances' retracted two research papers published by the scientists of the IIT Kanpur working at the institute's department of biological sciences and bio engineering. The papers were retracted since they were found to have been plagiarised from various sources including the Wikipedia.

The CENTAGRO said in the letter to the Union Minister that an institute directly under the President of India should set and maintain high standards of scientific integrity. Finally, it emerged that both the KSCSTE and the CWRDM were another IIT Kanpur spreading disinformation.

6

THIS WAS WHAT HAPPENDED AT THE POPRC CONVENTIONS

European Union, the largest producer and exporter of pesticides in the world has 600 companies employing about 27,000 workers manufacturing pesticides worth 9.9 billion Euro, the largest in the world. Therefore, Europe has a significant share of 60 per cent in world's pesticide export. (*Source:* Data from Eurostat/FAO.)

The European Union had used its clout in the Rotterdam convention and Stockholm convention to eliminate pesticides widely used outside the European Union countries which were not manufactured in the EU. The European Union also targeted the pesticides which commanded good export volume. If generic pesticides were to be eliminated, the EU could manufacture its substitute pesticides which would be highly priced and patented by the European Union. This would yield high profits for the EU-based pesticide manufacturers. Multilateral Environmental Agreements, MEAs, involving chemicals in Rotterdam convention and Stockholm convention were effectively used as trade restrictive tools either to curb or eliminate pesticides that posed threat to EU's global trade in pesticides. It was a trade war in the modern times.

Since the US was not a party to these conventions, the EU's writ ran exclusively and remained almost unchallenged. The EU was, therefore, aware of its supremacy in scientific publications and data generation and used them to aggressively scuttle any dissenting voices during deliberations of Multinational Environmental Agreements. Besides, the EU facilitated proxy attacks and aggressive campaigns through environmental activists within and outside these conventions. For instance, the aggressive campaign conducted by the Delhi-based Centre for Science and Environment and the Kerala-based NGO Thanal.

The campaign against endosulfan started in 2001 when the Delegation of the European Commission in India and the European Union funded a laboratory to the Delhi-based CSE to conduct the residue analysis of endosulfan in the village of Padre in Kasargod district.

The Persistent Organic Pollutants Review Committee, POPRC, held every alternative year is known as the Stockholm convention. It is being held as part of the United Nations' Environment Programme, UNEP. The third meeting of the POPRC was held from November 19-23, 2007 in Geneva; the fourth meeting was also held in Geneva from May 4 = 8 in 2009. The fifth POPRC meet was held from April 25 to 29 in Geneva in 2011.

However, the conspiracy against endosulfan began in 2007 when the European Commission, EC, on behalf of the European Union submitted a detailed proposal at the secretariat of the Stockholm Convention proposing to list endosulfan under the convention for its elimination for being a persistent organic pollutant. After one month, it published a document on September 26, 2007 which stated 'that the secretariat was satisfied that the EU's proposal met the requirement of Annex D'. The EU's proposal was then listed for examination by the Persistent Organic Pollutants Review Committee-3 (POPRC-3).

According to the Annex D criteria, there were some conditions to be fulfilled if a pesticide qualified to be listed as a persistent organic pollutant. However, the POPRC-3 did not examine the proposal, but simply noted in its final report that 'vital information required for consideration of endosulfan had not been made available to it.' The POPRC then asked the notifying party (European Union) and others including observers to supply the missing 'vital information' before it began to examine the EU's proposal at its next meeting-POPRC-4-to be held in Geneva from May 4 – 8, 2009.

India's view was that the procedure adopted was not in accordance with the rules of the convention. Article 8 of the convention required incomplete proposals to be set aside by the POPRC. It did not allow the notifying party or others to amend the proposal after initial verification by the secretariat.

Simply put, the secretariat was first satisfied that the EU's proposal met the annex D criteria and naturally the EU's proposal was listed for examination by POPRC-3. But the POPRC-3 should have set aside the proposal then and there as per rules. But it asked the notifying party (European Union) including observers to supply the missing 'vital information'. A proposal which missed the vital information was incomplete and as such it should have been set aside by the POPRC-3, according to India.

But what happened in the case was the violation of the rules of Article 8 of the convention. Article 8 does not allow the notifying party to amend the proposal after initial verification by the secretariat. Thus, postponing of the examination of the EU proposal from POPRC-3 to POPRC-4 and allowing the EU to amend its proposal during the interim period was against the provisions of the convention. India, therefore, wanted the convention to reverse the decision since it lacked legitimacy.

Another grievance of India was that the Chair of the POPRC- 4 chose to take decisions by majority votes instead of consensus on two occasions. First, it was to admit amended version of unexamined EU proposal and secondly to uphold the amended EU proposal that it met Annex D criteria to classify endosulfan as a persistent organic pollutant. This was done despite objections from committee members. The convention and rules of procedures did not permit substantive decisions to be taken by a majority, but it has to be taken by consensus. According to India, these decisions, therefore, lacked legitimacy.

Indian member at the convention, therefore, submitted a dissenting note requesting that the report may be appended to the convention report. But the secretariat of the POPRC convention did not append the note of dissent and India argued that this was against the principles of transparency of the convention.

As an unmistakable instance of conspiracy against endosulfan, the Draft Risk Profile, DRP, for chemicals was prepared by the European Commission. It was, however, prepared under a contract with a private firm called Green Planet Research, headquartered in Madrid in Spain. But according to rules, the Draft Risk Profile has to be prepared by the POPRC itself, but astonishingly it was entrusted to a private firm in which a former official of the POPRC secretariat reportedly held a supervisory position.

The Stockholm convention did not have any provision to allow the notifying party- the European Union- the privilege of preparing the Draft Risk Profile of a chemical pesticide. The Indian officials expressed strong concern and resentment at the questionable practice. Since the Draft Risk Profile of endosulfan was prepared by the Green Planet Research, it amounted to a clear conspiracy, said the Indian officials.

Another conspiracy against endosulfan was that the convention unilaterally ignored the numerous validated data from the tropical countries that clearly showed that endosulfan did not merit the Annex D criteria as a Persistent Organic Pollutant for elimination. The Indian Chemical Council, the Crop Life International and China had submitted several scientific data at the convention showing that endosulfan was not a persistent organic pollutant in tropical countries including India.

India argued at the convention that about 95 per cent of endosulfan was used in tropical countries such as India and China where concentration of pests was the highest. Unlike in cooler climates, endosulfan did not bio-accumulate in tropical countries and it would dissipate in soil there. The studies conducted in cold countries and in laboratories there did not reflect the field conditions in tropical countries, according to the scientific data submitted by the Indian Chemical Council, the Crop Life Insurance and China at the POPRC meet.

India suggested at the conference that in view of the additional information and data furnished at the conference regarding the condition prevailing in tropical countries, the convention should review the entire issue in accordance with the rules and spirit of the convention. India's argument at the convention was that the decision at the Stockholm convention should be made in strict accordance with the text of the convention as approved by the rules of procedures.

India raised four issues in its position paper regarding the lack of transparency and bypassing the rules and procedures of the convention at the behest of some European Union countries. The main issue concerning India was the genuine doubt as to how the POPRC-3 noticed 'missing vital information' in the proposal of the European Union without even examining it. India urged the secretariat that it could check the voice recording of POPRC-3 proceedings to explain as to how the missing information was noticed without examining the EU proposal.

India argued that the normal procedure in the case was that the secretariat first received proposals and verified whether it contained the information to qualify for the Annex D criterion against a persistent organic pollutant. Once the secretariat was satisfied in this regard it can send the proposal to the POPRC to ascertain whether it fulfilled the Annex D criteria. In the case of endosulfan, the PORPC was granted power to seek supplementary or additional information in violation of the procedures.

The Article 8 of Stockholm convention wanted the POPRC to be flexible and transparent as it could not usurp the functions of the secretariat. Further, Article 8 did not permit the POPRC to seek additional vital information.

The second issue raised by India and China related to the voting option in this regard given by the Chair of the POPRC-4 conference. China and India submitted a conference room paper challenging the Chair for giving the voting option. The convention rules did not allow the POPRC to decide by vote to accept the amended proposal whose original version was found to be lacking the vital information. India and China argued that the original incomplete proposal of the EU should have been set aside at POPRC-3 itself without giving it another lease of life from POPRC-3 to POPRC-4.

However, at the end of the examination of the EU proposal, the opinion of the POPRC-4 was divided whether listing of endosulfan met the Annex D criteria or not. The Chair of the convention once again ruled to take a decision by majority voting by quoting Article 19 of the convention. But Indian and Chinese members said at the meet that according to Article 19 'the committee shall make every effort to adopt its recommendations by consensus'. If all efforts at consensus have been exhausted, such recommendation should as a last resort be adopted by a two-thirds majority vote of the members.

The Rule 45 of Rules of Procedures expressly stated that decision on matters of substance should be taken only by consensus. It meant that while procedural matters may be decided by a vote, all substantive decision in the convention must be taken by consensus. India argued that whether a proposal met the Annex D criteria or not was a substantive decision and it could not be taken by voting. In other words, a substantive decision could be arrived at only through a consensus as per Rule 45 of the procedure. Taking decisions on substantive matters by vote was clearly inconsistent with the conventions' text. India, therefore, argued in its position paper that the voting decision by the Chair of POPRC-4 on the EU proposal on listing endosulfan as a persistent organic pollutant was invalid.

India raised the issue of ignoring the dissenting note submitted by Dr G.K. Pandey, member from India at the POPRC-4 convention. The convention did not make public the dissenting note submitted by Dr Pandey. Since dissenting notes formed an integral and perhaps inevitable part of pluralistic discussions in multilateral forums, it needed to be made public in the interest of transparency and good governance.

Dr G.K. Pandey's dissenting note at the POPRC-4 said that India and China had submitted a conference room paper on the first day of the convention explaining why the EU proposal on endosulfan was procedurally unacceptable for consideration. India also submitted another conference room paper bringing out deficiencies and inadequacies in the EC's proposal on endosulfan explaining why and how it failed to meet the Annex D criteria. India urged that the paper be annexed to the final report of POPRC-4.

During the deliberations India objected to the unfair practice of allowing the European Union countries to submit a pre-drafted review of its own proposal to guide the discussions on a pre-conceived path.

India pointed out that such a practice was both unfair and unlawful in a multilateral convention as it went against the principle of fairness and justice. It was rather strange to permit the notifying party to submit a self-review of its own proposal and subsequent self-claim that it passed Annex D review for acceptance by POPRC. The Stockholm convention cannot allow this, India argued.

During the deliberations India repeatedly pointed out that the data presented in EU proposal failed to consider the data generated from other countries such as tropical region countries including India. Therefore, India argued that Annex D evaluation was not done in a fair and transparent manner as mandated in Article 8 of the convention taking account all information. India also repeatedly pointed out that Annex D criteria were not at all met by the EU proposal.

India, therefore, protested at the Chair's decision to go for voting on substantive nature in contravention of what was provided in the convention and rules of procedures – more specifically Rule 45 of rules of procedures. Indian representative read out relevant provisions and its right interpretation and explained that the 'decisions' were different from 'recommendations' under the convention.

Most importantly, India objected to the final adoption of the proposal to declare endosulfan as a persistent organic pollutant, POP, submitted by Sweden, a member of the EU- the notifying party-as though it was prepared by POPRC members. Remember, it was the Swedish International Agency, SIDA, which gave institutional support to the Centre for Science and Environment, Delhi, to conduct the pesticide monitoring study in Padre village in Kasargod. It all substantiated the European Union conspiracy against endosulfan with the active involvement of Sweden.

In short, India reiterated that the decision taken on European Commissions' proposal regarding endosulfan suffered from series of procedural, technical, legal and ethical improprieties. India, therefore, strongly protested against this and requested the fourth Conference of Parties, COP, to comprehensively examine the above before deciding to accept or reject the recommendation of POPRC-4 in this regard.

Another issue raised by India was that the European Union which was the notifying party at the POPRC-3 and 4 conventions was allowed some privileges violating the rules and procedures. Firstly, it was allowed to postpone and amend its initial proposal between POPRC-3 and 4 conventions. It was allowed the privilege of pre-draft evaluation and supply it to POPRC-4. Again, it was allowed to prepare the draft risk profile of endosulfan for and on behalf of the POPRC-4.

India expressed protest over the violation of rules. It said that text of the convention and the rules of procedures would allow none of these privileges to the EU which was the notifying party. Ideally, the notifying party should not have unilaterally pushed its proposal through various levels of decision making by the POPRC.

In view of the procedural lapses India suggested that the decisions made by the POPRC-3 and 4 on EU proposal on endosulfan be disapproved and set aside. India was firmly of the opinion that decisions of Stockholm convention should be made in strict accordance with the text of the convention and approved rules and procedures. COP-4 might also suggest ways as to how to prevent and correct such breaches in future, it said. Since Stockholm convention was an important Multilateral Environment Agreement, MEA, India was committed to ensure that its implementation did not, by design or fault, deviate from the text of the convention.

However, the fifth Persistent Organic Pollutant Review Committee meet held in Geneva from April 25 to 29, 2011 was firm in its decision to find an alternative to endosulfan. It was during this meet that Kerala Chief Minister and communist leader V.S. Achuthanandan staged a fast at the Martyrs' column at the state capital on April 25 demanding ban on endosulfan. When China, a communist country, with whom the CPM still maintained fraternal relations was protesting against the POPRC decision on endosulfan along with India, Achuthanandan joined the European Union camp against endosulfan. But the CPM never explained the anti-EU stand taken by China at the POPRC meet.

The decision, however, was taken amidst protests by India and China against the proposal to find an alternative to endosulfan. The conference took a series of decisions to replace endosulfan with an alternative pesticide. The meeting decided to undertake a work programme to support the development and deployment of alternatives. The countries attending the meet as well as the observers were requested to submit to the secretariat of the POPRC the information on chemical and non-chemical alternatives to endosulfan. The meeting suggested the countries to take into account the technical feasibility, cost-effectiveness, efficacy and risk factors. The meeting also suggested to take into account its availability and accessibility.

The Secretariat was requested to gather and compile information and make them available to the countries and observers attending the meet. The summarised information in this regard was to be given to facilitate the work on the Persistent Organic Pollutants Review Committee to its seventh meeting.

The seventh meeting of the POPRC was requested to assess the alternative to endosulfan in accordance with the general guidance on finding alternatives and substitutes on the basis of information provided by parties and observers. However, priority has to be given to information on alternatives for crops using high volumes of endosulfan. The POPRC was also asked to prepare reports for the Conference of Parties, COP, at its sixth meeting on the assessment of alternatives to endosulfan.

However, when the fifth POPRC meet was in progress in Geneva in April, 2011, an e-mail from Australia surprised all delegates. The e-mail was sent by Prof Ivan Kennedy of the Faculty of Agriculture and Environmental Chemistry at the University of Sydney. The e-mail opposed the move to declare endosulfan as a persistent organic pollutant, claiming that the basis on which the ban was being proposed was invalid.

According to Prof. Kennedy, 'chemicals are assets' and he was primarily against any ban on chemicals. 'There were elements which fostered hatred and blamed chemicals for some other causes. I am opposed to the decisions taken on grounds of paranoia. They should be taken in a scientific manner and the law should be good', he said.

'We need stewardship from manufacturers and marketers for the safe use of endosulfan. The risks should be assessed and the chemicals use monitored', he said in the e-mail message.

He said Australia had used 10,000 tonnes of endosulfan in three lakh hectares, especially in New South Wales and Queensland. The chemical was sprayed 10-12 times a year intensively. The use of the chemicals was monitored and no problems were found, he said.

Compared to DDT, which can persist in the environment for decades, Dr. Kennedy explained that endosulfan's short life meant, in most conditions, that it was reduced to negligible conditions in a few months or even days on plants.

He said although it was not used in many fresh food crops in Australia, but when it was used there was a withholding period which meant that by the time foods reached the market, minute traces of endosulfan above maximum residue levels (MRLs) were virtually non-existent.

'The POPRC had relied on cherry-picking the data, and testing in unrepresentative laboratory to classify endosulfan as a persistent organic pollutant. The review at the meet had shown that POPRC had failed to establish that endosulfan met the criteria as a POP. Taking such an extreme precautionary measure towards important tools for agriculture, as advocated by the green movement, placed the global food security of billions of people at risk', he said. Instead of global ban on endosulfan, Prof. Kennedy recommended a phase out period for the chemical at least for 10 years.

Professor Kennedy acknowledged that in large doses endosulfan was a toxic substance. 'Toxic chemicals necessary for efficient agriculture production will always be with us, but these should all be in constant review. There is evidence accepted by medical authorities that endosulfan has been handled safely in Australia', he said.

According to the status report on endosulfan filed by the Union Government in the Supreme Court, as many as 3,333.21 metric tonnes of endosulfan were used in 24 states out of 35 during 2009-10.

The largest user was Haryana with 644 metric tonnes followed by Bihar (500 tonnes), Maharashtra (450 tonnes), Uttar Pradesh (385 tonnes), Rajasthan (177 tonnes),Tamil Nadu (170 tonnes) and Punjab (110 tonnes). However, Arunachal Pradesh, Meghalaya and Mizoram used one metric tone each. States and Union Territories such as Jammu and Kashmir, Kerala, Manipur, Nagaland, Sikkim, West Bengal, Chandigarh, Andaman and Nicobar, Dadra and Nagar Haveli, Daman and Diu and Lakshadweep used zero quantity of endosulfan. While Kerala banned the use of endosulfan, its neighbouring state of Karnataka used 350 tonnes of endosulfan.

According to the documents filed in the Supreme Court, endosulfan was exported to as many as 29 countries during 2009-2010 while anti-endosulfan agitation was going on unabated in Kerala. The countries included US, UK, Australia, China, Spain, Belgium, Venezuela, South Africa, UAE, Maldives, etc. The contention of the anti-endosulfan activists was that endosulfan was banned in the US, UK and Australia, but the documents exposed the claim.

The Union Government filed the status report in the Supreme Court in connection with the writ petition filed by the DYFI. The status report on endosulfan filed by the government assumed significance since it reflected the official version of a country as opposed to the views of NGOs fighting the pesticide.

According to the status report, 'endosulfan is an organochlorine compound. It is a broad spectrum insecticide and controls many important chewing and sucking pests in various crops. Three formulations of endosulfan are registered under the Insecticides Act, 1968, for controlling insect pests in various crops such as rice, wheat, sugarcane, cotton, jute, maize, cocoa, groundnut and mustard'. From the above it was evident that the Union Government viewed endosulfan as a useful pesticide.

The status report said that the annual worldwide production of endosulfan was reported to be about 18,000—20,000 metric tonnes, MT. The most important reason why the European Union countries were interested in easing out endosulfan from India was that it was the largest producer of endosulfan with annual production of about 9,900 metric tonnes. The biggest endosulfan manufacturer in the country was Hindustan Insecticides Ltd., a public sector company with an annual production of 5,500 metric tonnes followed by Coramandal Fertilizers Ltd, with 2400 MT and the Excel Crop Care Ltd with 2008 metric tonnes.

According to the status report ' endosulfan was developed in the early 50s. It is produced in China, Israel, Brazil and the Republic of Korea. Endosulfan is used in varying amounts in Argentina, Australia, Brazil, Canada, China, India, the USA and some other countries.'

Regarding the controversy over endosulfan in Kerala, the status report said that 'following adverse health effects reported from Kasargod district, (mild mental retardation, learning disabilities, cerebral palsy, cancers and skin diseases) several committees were appointed by the state government from 2000 onwards to review the effect of endosulfan on human health and environment. The origin of the problem was aerial spraying of endosulfan in cashew plantations by the Plantation Corporation of Kerala, PCK, reportedly since 1981.'

The status report said that 'a survey by District Medical Officer, Kasargod in Padre village during December 2002 found slight increase in occurrence of disease pattern observed in the sprayed area when compared to the non-sprayed area. It also concluded that disease pattern was the same in both areas. Hence it was suggested that a detailed clinical study was needed to prove the cause of the disease'.

Regarding the current status of endosulfan in Kerala, the state where the controversy first arose, the report said that the use of endosulfan has been banned in Kerala vide directions of the High Court in 2001. The Union Ministry of Agriculture vide its notification on October 31, 2006, has also kept the use of endosulfan in Kerala 'on hold' pending finalisation of an epidemiological study by the Kerala government. The Kerala State Pollution Control Board in its order on 19, November 2010 has also banned the use of endosulfan in any form in Kerala until it was proved safe.

According to the status report, endosulfan was reviewed by the committees appointed by the Union Government. Endosulfan was reviewed by the Union Government through Dr S.N. Banerjee committee in 1991, Dr R.B. Singh committee in 1999, Dr Dubey committee in 2003 and Dr C.G. Mayee committee in 2004. All the committees recommended the continuation of the use of endosulfan in the country.

According to the status report, a meeting was held in the ministry of agriculture on November 23, 2010 to review the issues related to endosulfan. The committee noted that the endosulfan-related health effects had not been reported in other states where it was used extensively. It, however, noted that in order to establish endosulfan-related health effects and to take a national view on endosulfan, a detailed and comprehensive study has to be done covering other parts of the country. The Director General of the ICMR was requested to initiate a comprehensive study covering Haryana, Bihar, Maharashtra, Uttar Pradesh and Karnataka–the states which were the largest users of endosulfan.

The status report relating to the Stockholm convention was interesting as it clearly exposed the bias of the POPRC convention against endosulfan. Under the heading 'Our position is the following' the Union Government made its stand clear towards the POPRC conventions.

'At the national level there have been some studies indicating the adverse health impacts of endosulfan. These studies, however, are confined to Kasargod district of Kerala. Significantly, the status paper said 'no adverse environmental or health effects related to endosulfan have been reported from any states other than Kerala, even though it was used in much large quantities in other states'.

According to the provisions of the Stockholm convention, it was not sufficient for a chemical to have the characteristics of a persistent organic pollutant, POP, for its listing, but it should also have significant adverse health and environmental effects. This has not been conclusively established, said the status report.

'Our position was that the European Union proposals concerning endosulfan considered by POPRC-3 and 4 suffered from several flaws and we submitted a conference room paper, CRP, at the fourth meeting of the Conference of Parties, COP, to the Stockholm convention'. India's concern has not been addressed by COP-4. Besides, POPRC resorted to voting on substantive issues as against the established practices and precedents.

Quoting the guideline document provided by POPRC, India lashed out at the practice of declaring certain pesticides as persistent organic pollutants and adopting more harmful pesticides than the one which was sought to be phased out.

India quoted the guideline document which said that 'the objective of promoting the use of alternatives under the convention is to protect human health and the environment. Simply replacing persistent organic pollutants with other hazardous chemicals should therefore be avoided and safer alternatives should be pursued'.

The guideline document said, 'what is termed as a safer alternative is an alternative that either reduces potential for harm to human health or the environment or that has not been shown to meet the Annex D screening criteria for listing a chemical under the convention as a persistent organic pollutant'.

But the POPRC meet flouted the very guidelines it had issued, said the status report. For, in respect of many of the alternatives suggested in POPRC meetings, incomplete information has been provided. Further, many of the so-called alternatives to endosulfan exhibited POP characteristics, some of them in higher degree on certain parameters than endosulfan'.

The status report elaborated on the advantages of endosulfan use over other registered alternative insecticides in the country. For instance, it said 'that malathion which was considered as alternative insecticide to endosulfan cannot control the destructive phase of insect pests of crops such as cotton, paddy, pulse and oil seeds as endosulfan does. On the other hand, the use of narrow spectral pesticides would lead to multiple application of pesticides and increase the pesticide burden and costs', said the status report.

7
AN AGGRESSIVE AGITATION

Anti-endosulfan agitation began on a low key and slowly gathered momentum around 2003-04. In the beginning there had been no vociferous campaign and agitation against endosulfan which was witnessed in the beginning of 2011 in Kasargod in the run up to the Stockholm convention. The agitation passed through many ups and downs. It flared up some times when ignited by NGOs and political leaders, but then remained dormant for a prolonged period, forgotten by all when other local issues dominated Kasargod. The issue would come alive after sometime with the NGOs reviving the agitation fuelled by foreign funds. Environmental activists Medha Patkar, Sugatha Kumari and CSE Director Sunita Narayin had all addressed the rallies on a number of occasions. So also were senior journalists B.R.P. Bhaskar and T.J.S. George besides writers and intellectuals from Kerala and outside.

Apart from veteran CPM leader V.S. Achuthanandan, Congress leader V.M. Sudheeran and CPI leader Binoy Viswom were the star campaigners of the anti-endosulfan agitation. CPI leader Annie Raja also visited the sprayed area saying that the anti-endosulfan agitation would be taken up at the national level. While some of the intellectuals knew that the agitation was triggered by foreign funds, others were quite ignorant of it. They came on their own to support an issue which attracted country wide attention. They also played an active role in the agitation since they were sincere to the core concerning the fight for environmental rights.

Dr Mohan Kumar and Sree Padre were some of the early campaigners against endosulfan. After basking in the media limelight in the beginning, their interest on the endosulfan issue tapered off and their place was taken up by those who craved for publicity. The new green activists were nowhere in the limelight when Sree Padre and Mohan Kumar were making the initial campaigns with the active support of Thanal and the CSE. Evidently, the NGOs fueling the agitation were looking for more efficient, talented and fierce organisers who could unleash an aggressive agitation to achieve their goal. The NGOs then roped in former Naxalite leaders having better organising capacity than others and who had a network of support groups across the state.

When the anti-endosulfan agitation was taken over by former Naxalite leaders those who kicked off the campaign in Padre village soon withdrew themselves from the scene. But Mohan Kumar attended some of the functions organised by the second rung leaders of the anti-endosulfan agitation, but Sree Padre was not much active in the movement and remained aloof from the protesters. He, however, supported the movement from outside.

Dr. Mohan Kumar had once remarked that people would not believe that there were so many victims of endosulfan in the sprayed area when more than 4,000 persons were enlisted as endosulfan victims. He was indirectly mentioning about the enrolment of patients with silly diseases and those having no diseases at all in the endosulfan list following political pressure. He was of the opinion that the seriousness of the issue was lost when political parties took up the issue as a mass movement.

Thanal, a Kerala-based NGO started its activities in the endosulfan sprayed villages from the very beginning. It first convened the meetings of villagers with the help of the local campaigners. The NGOs started campaign with the anti-endosulfan literature downloaded from the internet. The villagers were told at several meetings that endosulfan had wreaked havoc in most of the countries of the world and those countries had now banned endosulfan because of its deleterious effect on human health.

The villagers were made to believe that the use of endosulfan was at the root cause of all the diseases in the area. Meetings of honey-bee farmers were also convened by the NGOs. The honey-bee farmers were complaining of the mass disappearance of bees following the aerial spray. This was made use of by the activists and the sentiments of the farmers were exploited by the activists and the NGOs. The mass disappearance of honey-bees was reportedly due to a disease which affected the bees at the time all over the region. Interestingly, the anti-endosulfan campaign in Kasargod and the alleged diseases and sufferings of the people were disseminated across the world through internet and the social media. Therefore, it was a two pronged campaign—one directed on the suspected diseases in Kasargod and the other on the international turf about the deleterious effect of endosulfan all over the world by focusing on Kasargod incident. The campaign in Kasargod, thus, attracted worldwide attention through the omnipresent media network.

However, except for holding media conferences in metropolitan cities, the pesticide industry shied away from the scene. Even in the midst of campaigns and agitation against endosulfan, the pesticide was not banned in the country. So the pesticide industry carried on its business unmindful of the widespread campaign and noises that the activists were making as if it was of no concern to the manufacturers. The industry, thus, failed to make an aggressive intervention on the issue countering the widespread campaign of anti-pesticide activists. Most important, it failed to understand the ramifications of the international campaign. It had to later regret its lack of awareness on the issue saying that there had been no adequate response from the industry even though it became the favourite whipping boy of the environmental NGOs.

The vociferous campaign indulged in by the NGOs gradually produced its result. The study conducted by the Centre for Science and Environment, CSE, and the orchestrated campaign by NGOs led by Thanal coupled with the media campaign created a situation in the state in which the court was compelled to ban endosulfan first in Kasargod and then in the entire state.

The Munsiff Court of Kasargod first issued a stay order in February 2001 following a petition filed by a woman who worked in the state agriculture department. The court stayed the use of endosulfan in the cashew estates of the Plantation Corporation of Kerala. Subsequently, the Kerala State Pollution Control Board banned the use of endosulfan in the state in 2004. All the ban orders were issued in the wake of the countrywide campaign conducted by the CSE.

The campaign in the state was run by Thanal with the support of the UK-based Pesticide Action Network, PAN. The Union Government was also carried away by the frenzy of the campaign which resulted in its ban in Kerala. The Union Ministry of Agriculture issued a gazette notification on October 25, 2005 inviting objections and suggestions from all persons likely to be affected within 45 days.

However, in consideration of the suggestions from stake holders, the Union Government issued the order on October 31, 2006 prohibiting the use of endosulfan in Kerala by invoking the Insecticides Act, 1968. The order said that the use of endosulfan in Kerala 'shall be kept on hold till such time that the results of the epidemiological study to pin point the factors responsible for the health problems in the village of Padre become available and a decision is taken by the Central Government'.

But the ban order came into effect only in Kerala while the farmers in the neighbouring states of Karnataka and Tamil Nadu were still using endosulfan and were transporting vegetables to Kerala grown by using the pesticide.

As a result of the strident campaign, the Kerala government had earlier banned the aerial spray of endosulfan on February 18, 2002. The government issued the directions invoking the provisions of the Insecticide Act, 1968. The government stated in its order that aerial spraying of endosulfan would continue to be prohibited in all crops in the state. The Perla division of the PCK covering Padre and Muliyar villages would observe a pesticide holiday for a period of five years.

The government made it clear that the PCK would undertake only ground-based spraying of pesticides in its cashew plantations after following due safeguards for prevention of contamination of water bodies in accordance with the packages of practices recommended by the Kerala Agricultural University.

The government directed that all spraying operations of PCK in its cashew plantations would be carried out under the direct technical supervision of a joint Kerala Agricultural University–PCK expert group. This group would provide technical guidance regarding plant protection operations in PCK cashew estates.

The government also directed the Agriculture University to set up a small cashew research unit in Perla utilising the infrastructure of the PCK. The government then lifted the ban on the use of endosulfan for all crops and plantations in Kerala in the light of the directives. But even then the aerial spraying of endosulfan was not allowed by the government.

But the anti-endosulfan activists moved the High Court provoked by the government order lifting the ban and sought a permanent and total ban on the use of endosulfan throughout the State. The High Court observed in its judgment that both sides had presented an array of technical literature and records. It said that the court's function was not to decide on an issue which was essentially a matter for technical experts to decide.

The court then pronounced the order on August 12, 2002 temporarily banning endosulfan. The order said 'pending further decision by the expert committee appointed by the Central Government, the use of endosulfan or any of its trade names would not be permitted to be used within the state until further orders'.

The court then observed: 'we make it clear that we have not passed the above interim order by holding that endosulfan is inherently dangerous, but purely as a precautionary and defensive measure as in our view balance of convenience lies in granting interim prohibitory order during the period when the matter is pending consideration before the Central Government'. The court then declined the request of the counsel of the Pesticide Manufacturers and Formulators Association to stay the order to move the Supreme Court.

But the screw was tightening on endosulfan all the while and the European Union conspiracy was reaching its logical conclusion with continued media support. The NGOs supporting the agitation used the LDF government and the DYFI, the youth organisation of the CPM as tools to implement their hidden agenda. Surprisingly, it was the CPM which professed a clear cut and unambiguous anti-imperialist stand which was first roped in by the agitators.

The pesticide industry was given a rude shock by the Supreme Court judgment on May 13, 2011 imposing ad-interim ban on the pesticide. Since there was nothing wrong on the part of the pesticide industry as it was carrying on its normal business activities recognised under the law, the industry had never expected as severe a setback which resulted in the temporary ban on endosulfan for eight weeks. It was only then the pesticide industry realised the full potential of the European lobby and the anti-endosulfan agitators in Kerala and Delhi. The industry was too late to take up any tangible action.

The anti-endosulfan agitation had the backing of the CPM-led district panchayat in the very beginning. The District panchayat, the apex body of the three-tier gram panchayat in India, implemented the 'Thanal' housing project for bed-ridden patients in the sprayed area. Though a part of the fund was taken by the district panchayat in the housing project, it was Thanal, an NGO, which gained from the deal since the name of the project was named 'Thanal housing scheme'. It took advantage of the name of the housing project and this exposed the close connection between Thanal and the district panchayat.

Apart from the district panchayat, P. Karunakaran, MP who represented the Lok Sabha from the Kasargod constituency and was the Deputy Leader of the CPM in the House rendered all help to the anti-endosulfan agitation fuelled by the funds of imperialist countries of the European Union.

According to Karunakaran, he has been raising the endosulfan issue in the Lok Sabha from 2004. The people of Kasargod had experienced the severity of a man-made tragedy such as the endosulfan disaster. The activities of V.S. Achuthanandan first as the opposition leader and then as Chief Minister of the State had served to focus the issue before the conscience of the nation, he said.

P. Karunakaran MP raised the issue in the Lok Sabha on July 7, 2004. He called the attention of the House on the 'suspected unusual diseases and unnatural deaths in the endosulfan sprayed area'. He told the Lok Sabha that the aerial spray of endosulfan constituted a threat to the life of the people as well as to the flora and fauna and, as a result, many persons from the area were still suffering from heart and lungs related diseases. When members of the Lok Sabha from Kerala had earlier raised the issue, the government had said that a team of scientists of the Indian Council of Agriculture Research had presented a report to the government after visiting the exposed villages. He told the Lok Sabha that it was an unscientific report which was prepared by the team without taking the views of the people in the affected area.

P. Karunakaran MP again took up the issue in the Lok Sabha on August 23, 2005. He apprised the Lok Sabha that a serious situation had developed in the sprayed area because of the aerial spraying of endosulfan for the past 20 years. He said the environmental and health problems were on the increase. He told the Lok Sabha that 'thousands of people had been bed-ridden following the aerial spray'. The Kerala government had appointed Dr Achuthan commission and Dr Sivaraman, the then health director, to study the issue. The latter had reached the conclusion that the aerial spraying of endosulfan was at the root of the problem, Karunakaran told the Lok Sabha.

He claimed that he brought before the attention of the Lok Sabha the 'plight of hundreds of children crawling on their knees; of the blind people and of patients hit by asthma and cancer'. Addressing the Lok Sabha he pleaded for help to the victims and their immediate rehabilitation. The parliament member said that with his intervention on the issue, the NABARAD, the apex bank for rural development, had sanctioned ₹ 137 crore in the exposed area to improve the infrastructure facilities in the region.

P. Karunakaran MP also demanded the total ban of all pesticides in the country. Even though he was the Deputy Leader of the CPM in the Lok Sabha, the CPM leadership did not respond to his statement on the need for a total ban on all pesticides in the country. The aggressive campaign by P. Karunakaran against endosulfan underlined the fact that he might have been misled by the NGOs fighting endosulfan with the funds of the European Union countries.

All political parties, especially the CPM, found an opportunity to activate their workers and organise agitations demanding ban on endosulfan. Then most of the political parties started conducting campaigns for the total ban of the pesticide. But it was not until 2005 that the district administration was jolted into action to conduct medical camps and give help to the suspected patients following a mass campaign by the NGOs supported by most of the political parties. A Study Congress was organised by the district panchayat which was ruled by the CPM and other Left parties.

Thanal befriended the media to help it in its persistent campaign against endosulfan. Since the media got juicy stories on the issue, it made use of the opportunity to boost its circulation and readership among the people. The persistent media campaign attracted the people who also started believing that the spraying of endosulfan was the root cause of the diseases and demanded that the pesticide be banned.

The activists used the opportunity provided by the campaign to make money. They formed organisations to channelize foreign funds, ostensibly to help the so-called victims but to spend the money for their own use. As many as 20 organisations sprang up in the area lobbying with the media to help them. The fake studies conducted by these organisations, many of them religious outfits, concluded that the diseases were indeed caused by the aerial spray of endosulfan. This was intended to raise funds from foreign religious organisations. The NGOs also exerted influence on the heads of educational institutions with the result that students were forced to campaign against endosulfan on the streets. The students took out rallies in the town holding placards calling for the total ban on endosulfan. Teachers also joined the rallies.

Even the district administration was carried away by the propaganda. It made an appeal to the world community to contribute liberally for the victims. Its website said 'endosulfan tragedy in Kasargod (India) has given us a jolt after the Bhopal tragedy and the struggle has gained momentum. This is not a struggle to eliminate a few pesticides, but a struggle for peace and harmony and the struggle for the continuity of life on the Earth.' The website also appealed to the global community to help the victims. An account was later opened with the State Bank of Travancore, Kasargod branch, to receive foreign funds.

There were some funny incidents during the anti-endosulfan campaign. The NGOs campaigning against the pesticide invited writers and novelists to see for themselves the 'pitiable condition' of the endosulfan victims. Their accommodation, food and journey to the sprayed area were arranged by the NGOs. But they arranged 'something more'. A group of writers and novelists landed in Kasargod and the next day they proceeded to meet the victims. After visiting the victims, they seemed to have been thoroughly overwhelmed by 'grief'. As soon as they reached the Government Guest House where their overnight stay was arranged, they tucked into the sumptuous meals. The writers had to address the media after finishing their visit, but many of them could barely stand up since they were all wobbling. Their incoherent mutterings and unintelligible talks constituted their address to the media. This showed that they treated the whole issue in a frivolous way.

The anti-endosulfan activists also exploited the situation to the hilt to get foreign funds. Several organisations came up later, all pleading for help to the victims and appealing to the international community. At first there was only one organisation—the anti-endosulfan action committee— which comprised all activists fighting against the pesticides. But differences of views soon cropped up among them when money became the sole motivating force for the agitators. Some of them were against singling out endosulfan alone for elimination and they soon felt that all pesticides were poison and the campaign should focus on the need to promote organic farming and bio-pesticides to obviate the use of all chemical pesticides. Poet Sugathakumari, an environmental activist of Kerala who came to Kasargod for anti-endosulfan campaign expressed the view that the agitation against endosulfan should be a symbolic fight to eliminate all pesticides. According to her, 'all pesticides are poison and people feel panic to take food since all the food was contaminated with pesticide residues'. Her speech in Kasargod created a pesto-phobia among the people.

But others were of the view that the fight should continue only against endosulfan which, according to them, was primarily responsible for the miseries of Kasargod villagers. Then another organisation called 'Endosulfan Peeditha Janakeeya Munnani', EPJM, (People's Front for the Sufferers of Endosulfan) was formed and this organisation happened to be a protégé of an NGO. As the earlier activists of the anti-endosulfan action committee joined en mass in the new organisation, the former action committee became defunct.

The EPJM was led by Ambalathara Kunhikrishnan who had better organising capacity than other leaders and he was also well known among various social groups in the area. His call for action brought activists from various parts of the state to take part in the agitation. However, despite Sugathakumari's plea to take up the fight against all pesticides, no agitation was conducted in Kasargod against the pesticides which were either banned or restricted in other countries, but which were still being used in India. So instead of fighting against all pesticides the campaign was confined mainly against endosulfan.

Pesticides banned in other countries were still being used in the country. But anti-endosulfan activists never targeted other harmful pesticides. According to a statement filed by the Union Government in the Supreme Court, as many as 67 pesticides which were banned in other countries were still being used in the country. The DDT which was categorised as a persistent organic pollutant was permitted for restricted use in India. The pesticide review committee headed by S.N. Banerjee and R.B. Singh permitted the restricted use of DDT along with other pesticides banned in some countries of the world.

Endosulfan Victims' Support Aid Group, Envisag, was formed by a group of activists to channelise funds from abroad, especially from Gulf countries to help the so-called victims. Mothers who gave birth to children suffering from hydrocephalus were brought to the venue of the agitation to publically exhibit them before television cameras. Soon, the agitation by the Envisag attracted media attention since several mothers having deformed children participated in the campaign. Reporters of newspapers having Gulf edition were pressurized to send the reports for publication in the Gulf edition to channelize funds from abroad.

The Envisag again organised a fast in the town with deformed children most of whom hit by hydrocephalus. They came from Nenjamparamba in Karadka gram panchayat where there were a number of children hit by hydrocephalus. The anti-endosulfan agitators fabricated a story that the PCK workers had buried endosulfan in the village. But the plantation corporation strongly denied the allegation of the activists. The PCK had no need to bury the excess endosulfan since the corporation had the facilities to take back and store the excess endosulfan. The PCK had stored excess endosulfan in its premises when the pesticide was banned in the state by the Kerala High Court in August 2002.

The anti-endosulfan activists were playing tricks to hoodwink the officials of the Endosulfan Nodal Cell. They had raised a hue and cry that several families living around Nenjanparamba—where the excess endosulfan was allegedly dumped by the PCK workers—were suffering from various diseases. As can only be expected, a pliant media played up the issue. The district authorities enlisted the help of the Centre for Water Resources Development and Management, CWRDM, in Kozhikode to test the soil and water content of the hillock around Nenjamparamba.

The CWRDM scientists who collected seven samples of soil from the area said none of the samples contained endosulfan residues. This exposed the blatant lie of the anti-endosulfan activists that the surroundings of Nenjamparamba were highly polluted and that children were still being born with deformities.

The activists blamed the PCK alleging that its retired workers failed to cooperate with the probe. The anti-endosulfan activists had collected evidence from the local people, but none of them could point out the exact spot where the excess endosulfan was reportedly dumped by the PCK workers. According to the activists, the excess quantity of endosulfan was dumped in 2003 when the anti-endosulfan agitation was at its peak. But no activist could pin point the exact spot where endosulfan was buried along with its barrels. The version of the anti-endosulfan activists was that the contents from the dilapidated barrels flowed through a horizontal well, known as suranga and it got mixed up with the underground water to cause diseases in the whole area.

At the end of 2011 another organisation was also formed. It was christened Non-Imperialist Funded Endosulfan Action Committee, NIFEAC. The contention of the new outfit was that all the organisations working in the field had been receiving funds from imperialist countries to carry on the anti-endosulfan agitation. The new organisation crossed horns with the EPJM alleging that it has been receiving massive foreign funds through Thanal. The NIFEAC also conducted some campaigns on its own, but the flow of funds to the outfit from local sources was soon blocked by other organisations in the field. There has been severe infighting among various organisations which were tearing at each other's throat.

Many religious organisations also entered the fray. The prominent among them was Solidarity, an organisation flouted by the Jamaat-e-Islami. Its activists visited the sprayed villages doling out help to the families of disabled and bed-ridden children. It periodically arranged food such as rice and vegetables and built up a rapport with the families. The Solidarity brought disabled children on trains to parade them before Parliament House in Delhi. It was not concerned about the plight of the disabled children who had to endure much suffering on the way to Delhi.

The activists selected a tree in the town calling it *'oppumaram'* (signature tree). Canvas was draped around the tree and the activists coming from various places affixed their signatures or wrote slogans on the canvas. Most of the organisations made use of the opportunity to bask in the media publicity. Some of the artists painted pictures on 'endosulfan disaster' on canvas while some others arranged music programmes. Political leaders who were sidelined in their parties also became active in the anti-endosulfan movement. They wanted to raise their sagging political image by offering themselves as crusaders of the anti-pesticide campaign. Some political leaders took to environmental activism to keep themselves afloat in the media limelight.

As the anti-endosulfan campaign reached its feverish pitch in 2011, some religious mutts in the state also committed help to the victims. The heads of the mutts told media persons that they would construct houses for the victims modeling on the houses they had constructed for tsunami victims. It later proved to be their initial response since nothing materialised and no houses were built for the victims. It was an example of the media campaign influencing the people and institutions in every walk of life. Some film personalities also pledged help on a large scale, but it too never materialised.

Youth activists undertook fast in front of Central Government offices demanding ban on endosulfan in the run-up to the POPRC convention in Geneva. The venue where they undertook the fast was embellished with the pictures of national leaders and freedom fighters. The friends of the fasting youths collected money from the public. They also collected funds from shop owners and business persons.

In the beginning, both the CPM and the CPI were against the anti-endosulfan agitation. The CPM was afraid that if the agitation gained momentum, it would lead to the closure of the plantation corporation where substantial number of workers belonging to the CITU, the trade union wing of the CPM were working. The CPM activists had beaten up the activists of a local club on December 22, 1999 when they took out a silent protest march to the office of the Plantation

Corporation in Muliyar demanding compensation to the victims. The CPM-DYFI activists even vandalised the office of the local club when the activists were holding a protest meeting against the aerial spray of endosulfan.

The CPI was against the agitation since the portfolio of agriculture was managed by a succession of CPI ministers. But when the NGOs kicked up the agitation, the CPI and the CPM had to fall in line because every political party supported it. The CPM and its youth wing made a somersault and it also organised a state–wide *hartal* (**shut down**) a few weeks before the Stockholm convention demanding total ban on endosulfan throughout the country.

The opportunism of the CPM was exposed on the issue of endosulfan. The DYFI had organised a series of agitations against the State government accepting the loan of the Asian Development Bank, ADB, alleging that the economic interest of the state would be affected if the loan was to be accepted by the government. The DYFI had even blocked the officials of the ADB who came to negotiate with the government on the loan. But the CPM-ruled grama panchayat in Pallikkara in Kasargod implemented an agriculture programme funded by the ADB which was implemented by the Central Plantation Crops Research Institute, Kasargod.

The CPM's anti-imperialist stand was made clear when it withdrew its support to the first UPA Government at the Centre on the issue of India signing a civilian nuclear pact with the US. Such a party unabashedly supported the anti-endosulfan agitation in Kasargod funded by the European Union.

8

KERALA CHIEF MINISTER'S FAST HELPS THE EUROPEAN UNION

CPM leader V.S. Achuthanandan who was the Chief Minister of Kerala when the Stockholm convention was held in Geneva went on a fast at the Martyr's Column in the State capital on April 25, 2011 demanding ban on endosulfan. Achuthanandan as the opposition leader had visited the pesticide sprayed villages of Swarga and Vaninagar in 2002 which gave the nascent anti-endosulfan agitation in the village of Padre a mighty push. The fast was stage managed by Thanal since it used him as a tool to further the economic interest of the European Union. The video footage of the fast was shown at the venue of the POPRC convention in Geneva. Achuthanandan read out a message sent by Dr Mohammed Asheel, Endosulfan Nodal Officer of Kasargod from the venue of the meet in Geneva.

The officials and members of the European Union at the Stockholm convention who were exerting pressure on India and China to ban endosulfan were much delighted at the video footage of V. S. Achuthanandan, a hardcore communist, holding the fast demanding ban on endosulfan. Everything was pre-arranged by Thanal as Dr Mohammed Asheel attended the Stockholm convention with the money provided by the Global Greengrants, a US-based funding agency. Astonishingly, neither Achuthanandan nor the Communist Party of India (Marxist), CPM, were aware that the European Union was co-opting them as tools to serve its global economic interest.

Interestingly, on the same day when Achuthanandan was undertaking the one day fast, the DYFI—the youth organisation of the CPM— filed a writ petition in the Supreme Court demanding ban on endosulfan. The DYFI counsel stressed the nature of urgency of the case in its writ petition to the Supreme Court stating that Stockholm convention was scheduled to be held from April 25, 2011. The Supreme Court later slapped an ad interim ban on endosulfan on May 13, 2011 on the strength of the writ petition. Thus the DYFI and the CPM served the economic interest of the European Union countries. Besides, P. Karunakaran MP, deputy leader of the CPM in the Lok Sabha had vociferously demanded ban on endosulfan during a discussion in Parliament on the issue.

Flouting government norms, the Kerala government sponsored the trip of Dr Mohammed Asheel to Geneva to attend the Stockholm convention camouflaging him as an independent observer. This clearly exposed the interest of the Marxist led LDF government in Kerala in the on-going move for a global ban on endosulfan.

Though it was mandatory that the State government should take the prior consent of the Union Government to send its employees to attend an overseas conference or on any such assignments, the State government did not take any consent from the Central Government. The State Government sent Dr Mohammed Asheel as a representative of Thanal, a non-governmental organisation. But the government issued an order on April 23 that travelling allowances and other expenses of Dr Asheel would be met from the National Rural Health Mission. It was a clear violation of rules as the funds of the NRHM were misutilised with the consent of the State government.

Dr Mohammed Asheel had told media persons that he attended the convention as a representative of Thanal. This showed that the State government had not obtained the permission of the Union Government for deputing an official of the State government to attend an international conference on behalf of an NGO.

Surprisingly, apart from flouting the norms of the Union Government the State government issued the order to meet his expenses from the funds of the National Rural Health Mission. But according to the finance division of the NHRM, the State government should not make any changes in its allocations or re-appropriation among different components without the approval of the Union Ministry of Health and Family Welfare.

Not only Achuthanandan, but other district and state level leaders of the CPM also joined the chorus in Kerala for banning endosulfan. All the feeder organisations such as the student and youth wing of the CPM were pressed into service to unleash a vigorous anti-endosulfan campaign. Not to be left alone, the CPI also joined the anti-endosulfan agitators. The party organised separate programmes such as marches to the collectorate. The meeting of every trade union and service organisations passed the resolution demanding the ban.

The Bharatiya Janata Party had also joined the fray. It had conducted a separate campaign demanding ban on endosulfan. It was not so much interested in the agitation as it was already hijacked by the Left parties such as the CPM and the CPI. The BJP had organised an agitation which was rather funny. Its cadres jumped into the sea in Kasabha beach in Kasargod. The police prevented them from jumping into the sea. Yet they broke the police cordon much to the surprise of the police. But they came ashore after surf bathing in the sea for quite sometime, even as the police watched the whole show because all the youths selected to jump into the sea were experienced fishermen.

The BJP leaders of Kasargod seemed to be ignorant that Rajendra Singh Rana MP, former state vice-president of the BJP in Gujarat had inaugurated a massive rally of endosulfan workers in Gujarat demanding withdrawal of the NIOH report in 2010. In a letter to Prime Minister Manmohan Singh on November 16, 2010, M. Rajendra Singh Rana said the scientists of the NIOH had fabricated its report and that it was all fraudulent. He said the effects of endosulfan on human beings as claimed by the NIOH were totally baseless and fabricated by the NIOH scientists. He, therefore, appealed to the Prime Minister to take steps to withdraw the NIOH report to prevent damages to the image of the country abroad.

But Congress had in the very beginning taken a hazy stand. It had not taken a forthright stand on the issue. But the party maintained a discreet silence when the anti-endosulfan agitation was going on. It kept quiet when the then Union Minister of State for Agriculture K.V. Thomas said at a function held at the CPCRI in Kasargod on October 10, 2010 that nobody had died of endosulfan spray. He was then verbally attacked by all political parties except the Congress. The statement later generated a controversy and helped revive the agitation which was then in a dormant state.

What the Congress lacked was made up by Oommen Chandy when he became the Chief Minister in May 2011. He continued the tradition of the previous LDF government. He said the UDF government was committed to the cause of helping the endosulfan victims. At a function held in Kasargod to distribute the remaining amount of ₹ 50,000 to the dependents of those reportedly died due to the aerial spray of endosulfan, Oommen Chandy said that he had discussed the issue with the Union Government which would soon formulate a package to help the endosulfan victims. He made a very prominent statement then which was welcomed by all anti-endosulfan activists. He said Prime Minister Manmohan Singh would visit the sprayed area. The activists were thrilled at the statement of Chief Minister Oommen Chandy. It was also unofficially announced that the Union Government would announce a huge package to help the victims.

A national workshop was organised in Kasargod by the District panchayat and the National Programme for the Rehabilitation of Persons with Disabilities, NPRDP, on July 21 and 22, 2012. Though it was intended as a consultative workshop 'on comprehensive rehabilitation of endosulfan victims and rejuvenation of Ecosystem' in the district, it was really meant as part of the on-going campaign against endosulfan. It was Thanal which pulled the strings from behind the curtain. The fund for arranging the workshop came from the district panchayat and the NPRPD. It was sheer waste of money as nothing tangible emerged out of the workshop. A project for ₹ 6.28 crore was drawn up at the workshop for the rehabilitation of the victims.

The rehabilitation project was really intended to help an environmental NGO since it was part of its Community Based Rehabilitation, CBR, mission. The rehabilitation would be done with government funds, but the NGO mostly reaped the benefits.

In a farcical act, the old stock of endosulfan remaining at the various estates of the Plantation Corporation of Kerala was 'detoxified' by a team of officials of the pollution control board, state agriculture department and the district administration. It was codenamed 'Operation Blue Spring'. The old stock of endosulfan in dilapidated barrels was transferred to new drums in June 2012 calling it 'detoxification'. The officials wore 'space suits' while transferring the pesticide. The transferring of endosulfan to new barrels with much media publicity was part of the aggressive campaign to make it appear that endosulfan was as dangerous as nuclear weapons. It was without taking any precaution that the workers of the PCK had sprayed endosulfan in its estates. Since they were experienced, the workers of the PCK could have easily transferred the excess endosulfan to new barrels without wearing the 'space suits'. The farce of filling the endosulfan in new barrels also entailed hefty expenses by the government.

The NGOs working in the field were regularly paid money and as many as ten persons of an organisation in the field were on the regular pay roll of an NGO. There was not much public support to the agitation at the end of 2012 since so many people knew that the whole agitation was a fraud.

The culture of organising mass movements was unknown in Kasargod, a place which used to witness smuggling of contraband goods from Gulf countries in the early 70s. A tag of 'communalism' has always been attached to the place because of recurring religious strife resulting in communal clashes in the area. However, the place witnessed mass movements on two issues demanding tracing of missing girls, in two separate incidents.

A 13-year-old girl and a native of Coorg was reported missing from a house in Goa where she was working as a domestic servant. The head of the family belonged to Kasargod. The agitation to trace the girl became a mass movement with all Muslim organisations and political parties joining together in support of the cause. The action committee also undertook continuous fast in the town. The agitation demanding tracing of the girl who had also worked as a domestic help in Kasargod, threw up a new crop of leadership. The agitation was called off with the arrest of the owner of the house and his wife when the remains of the girl were recovered from a graveyard in Goa.

Soon after another mass movement followed demanding the tracing of another girl. After months of agitation and continuous fast, the girl was eventually traced in an orphanage. These agitations demanding tracing of the missing girls saw mass movements in Kasargod. The anti-endosulfan agitation was also taken up by the same leadership which learnt that Kasargod was also a fertile land suitable for organising mass agitations in which a cross-section of people irrespective of religion and politics participated with much enthusiasm.

There was a lull in the aggressive campaign of the activists in the beginning of 2013. The first phase of the agitation which culminated in relay fast in front of the collectorate spanning three months was however withdrawn following assurance by the government. But the government once again failed to live up to the expectations of the action committee which triggered the second phase of the agitation.

The anti-endosulfan activists lit a symbolic flame in the premises of the collectorate in the first week of January 2013 preparatory for the impending agitation. It was organised by the Endosulfan Peeditha Janakeeya Munnani, EPJM, the only organisation remaining active in the field of agitation. It, however, started an indefinite fast from February 18 on its second leg of the fast demanding setting up of a tribunal to give adequate compensation to the victims. The EPJM also demanded that the payment of monthly pension should continue and it should not be stopped within five years. The fast near the bus stand was inaugurated by senior journalist B.R.P. Bhaskar. The agitation was revived at the instigation of some NGOs.

Meanwhile, the District Collector issued a press statement denying the allegation of the action committee which stated that the government was not listening to the demand of the agitators. The District Collector said the government was implementing the recommendations of the National Human Rights Commission. It had already paid ₹ 1.5 lakh each to the bed-ridden and the physically disabled. An amount of ₹ 1.5 lakh each was also deposited in the account of the next of kin of 400 deceased victims, he said.

On the eighth day of the fast, mothers of the so-called endosulfan victims blocked the National Highway holding placards. The front leaders alleged that though the fast was started some days before, no officials visited the agitators even though the health conditions of those undertaking the fast deteriorated.

However, two activists of the EPJM who were undertaking the fast were arrested and removed to hospital by the police. The district authorities later reached the venue of the fast and held discussions with the agitators. But the action committee said that it was not satisfied with the reply given by the district authorities.

Unlike the past agitation demanding compensation which lasted for 90 days, there was not much mass participation in the agitation this time. The crowd was captive as they were ferried in vehicles. Most people who participated in the agitation came from outside. However, local political parties made a bee line to the venue of the fast since the party leaders wanted to enjoy the media limelight. Though it was announced that the National Highway would be blocked by 'endosulfan mothers', those who participated mostly were women volunteers. Some of them were even spinsters and on the regular pay roll of an NGO which controlled the agitation.

After the arrest and hospitalisation of the two activists on indefinite fast, another anti-endosulfan activist started the fast. This time the fast was undertaken by Dr D. Surendranath, a green activist.

Chief Minister Oommen Chandy sent District Collector Mohammed Shaheer and N.A. Nellikkunnu, local MLA to hold discussion with the agitators. They told the agitators that the government would form a committee to study the issue of waiving the arrears of bank loans availed by the families of the victims. The committee would examine whether the loans were taken for the sole purpose of treatment for the victims. The representatives of the government also appealed to the agitators to withdraw the fast.

But the agitators remained firm in their stand that unless they received a written assurance from the government, the agitation would not be withdrawn by the action committee. The committee wanted a written assurance from the government that the monthly pension of the victims would not be discontinued after five years.

Senior Congress leader V. M. Sudheeran visited the fasting volunteers. He wanted fresh medical camps to be organised to ensure that relief and rehabilitation measures reached the genuine victims. Since the spraying of the pesticide was conducted by the government owned Plantation Corporation of Kerala, it was the duty of the administration to provide medical treatment and compensation to the victims. He said the Union Government, the Plantation Corporation and the pesticide manufacturers could not abdicate their responsibility on the issue.

As the media gave unstinted support to the agitation, more people started visiting the venue of the fast from across the state. School children from other districts came to the venue pledging solidarity with the agitators. The organisers of the agitation put to use their best mobilising capacity to bring more and more people to the venue. But there was not much participation of the villagers from the pesticide sprayed areas.

The venue of the fast became a platform of uniting all extremist elements. They included Hindu and Muslim extremist outfits. It also turned out to be a forum for uniting former Naxalite leaders. After Naxalism was put down by the government in the late 60s leading to the killing of Naxalite leader Varghese in Wayanad on February 18, 1970, the Naxalites found themselves at the receiving end of police action leading to the disintegration of the movement in Kerala. Significantly, the second phase of the fast began on February 18, 2013, the 43rd death anniversary of the Naxalite leader Varghese. But the Naxalites regrouped themselves by forming environmental or human rights organisations under various innocuous names. A former Naxalite organisation appeared in the form of protector of environment triggering agitation against tourism projects in Bekal in Kasargod. The same group started agitation against the proposed nuclear power plant in Peringom in Kannur district in the early 90s. However, it seized the leadership of the endosulfan agitation to mobilise the people in collusion with some NGOs.

The action committee which has been conducting an indefinite fast for 36 days called off the agitation following discussion held with Chief Minister Oommen Chandy as well as with other ministers, officials and political leaders at the state capital on March 25, 2013. The fast undertaken by Mohan Kumar, a social activist of Payyannur attracted the media attention since he refused to end his fast even though the district administration appealed to terminate the fast. Mohan Kumar began the fast after Dr D. Surendranath was arrested and admitted to the hospital.

According to the terms of the settlement, the government would appoint a committee to examine the question of setting up a tribunal as demanded by the action committee to provide compensation to the so-called victims. The committee would include Law Secretary as convener, Advocate General and Director General of Prosecution as its members. The committee wouid examine the liability of the pesticide companies to the victims and the scope for setting up a tribunal.

It was agreed that a three-member committee would study the demand of the action committee for waiving the bank loans taken by the families of the victims. The Chief Minister said that the list of endosulfan victims eligible to receive assistance would be expanded on the basis of fresh medical camps that the government would organise.

He said the geographical boundaries of 11 gram panchayats where endosulfan was sprayed would not be a limitation for identifying fresh victims. Persons who had lived in the exposed panchayat and later shifted their residences to other non-sprayed areas as well as those exposed to the pesticide drift outside the sprayed panchayats on the district border would also be considered.

The Chief Minister announced that as many as 366 cancer patients and those identified as bed-ridden, mentally challenged and disabled at the medical camps held in August and December 2011 would also be included in the list. The total number of 1,632 patients would go up to 2,295 and they would be eligible for compensation as recommended by the National Human Rights Commission.

The Chief Minister said the remaining 3,205 identified 'victims' would continue to receive benefits announced by the state government. Altogether, 5,500 persons would be getting assistance. He said 12 more hospitals would be added to the list of hospitals in which the victims can get free medical care.

With the winding up of the indefinite fast by the Endosulfan Peeditha Janakeeya Munnani, EPJM, newspapers devoted its pages to their usual campaign that people outside the district were also hit by endosulfan spray. The media published news of distraught mothers outside the district who came to the district endosulfan nodal office carrying their children hit by hydrocephalus and other diseases. The media, by its relentless propaganda, had created an impression that diseased persons, even from outside the district, were the victims of endosulfan spray.

Thus, the Endosulfan Nodal Cell granted relief to the alleged victims born outside the sprayed area. It was intriguing that children were still being born even after 13 years following the cessation of the aerial spray and that too outside the sprayed villages. Now it was clear that if children were being born after 13 years of the winding up of the aerial spray in places located far away from the sprayed area, there was some other reason for the birth of deformed children. But instead of holding a medical probe to find out the cause of the diseases, the government attributed each and every birth of deformed children to the aerial spray of endosulfan conducted several years before.

On July 9, 2013, the media published a report under the caption 'relief for young endosulfan victim' which said that Badsha, a young victim was given ₹ 1.5 lakh as part of the first instalment of ₹ 5 lakh announced by the State Government for the seriously affected patients. The amount was handed over to the family by National Rural Health Mission Programme manager Dr Mohammed Asheel. Badsha was born in Chengala, a non-sprayed area. The amount was given mainly because the media projected Badsha as a victim of endosulfan as part of the on-going campaign. The government had already agreed to the demand of the anti-endosulfan action committee that the patients in non-sprayed areas near the sprayed villages would also be given help even though the place belonged to another district.

Ayishath Rubeena, a three month old girl born in Manjampara, a non-sprayed area died in a Mangalore hospital on July 9, 2013. Ayishath Rubeena was born with a congenital disease. The Endosulfan Nodal Cell agreed for her treatment and the girl was first admitted to the General Hospital in Kasargod and then shifted to a private hospital in Mangalore where she died.

According to media report, Ayishath Rubeena was the fourth child of Ahammed and Beefathima of Manjampara, located a long distance from Karadka estate of the plantation corporation where aerial spray of endosulfan was stopped in January 2000. The couple has only two surviving children now. The eldest son Mohammed Mukthar had undergone six surgeries before he was six and he was now able to walk. The second child Mariam Mubeena was born without any disease. The third child Mujeeb was born with the same disease as suffered by Ayishath Rubeena. The child lived only for two years. Before his death, Mujeeb had undergone two surgeries. From this one can get a fairly good account of the family history of diseases of the children born to Ahammed and Beefathima. In this case, three children of a couple were born with congenital diseases and out of them only two children survived. But strangely, the aerial spray of endosulfan, conducted many years before, was blamed for the congenital diseases of the children.

Thus, a one-and-half-year old boy, described as an endosulfan victim by the media got help from the Endosulfan Nodal Cell for treatment. According to media report, Manish, the one-and-half year-old boy, was born in Golikkatte in Badiadka with a growth on his neck. The unfortunate child would not have received any government help if he was not described as a victim of endosulfan.

Nobody wanted to know whether the child was born after 13 years since the cessation of the aerial spray of endosulfan. The child's house was located a long distance away from the cashew plantation of the PCK. Anti-endosulfan activists had conducted the campaign arguing that the endosulfan residues would remain in the soil for decades after the spray.

The officials of the Endosulfan Nodal Cell were, therefore, very careful to avoid any adverse criticism against them. So they scanned every newspaper for the report on sick children crying for help. The regional newspapers were in the forefront of publishing such reports. Even otherwise, newspaper readers generally contributed money or pledged help to distraught families in the state where children were born with congenital diseases even though the sick children were not the victims of any pesticide spray.

Moved by the media reports, the local branch of the Canara Bank decided to give ₹ 50 lakh for the benefit of the alleged victims as part of the bank's Corporate Social Responsibility, CSR, programme. Addressing a media conference, the Canara Bank officials said three houses would be constructed for the victims with the money apart from earmarking sufficient amount for the educational needs of the affected children. But the Canara Bank offered the money for the so-called endosulfan victims unmindful of the fact that the fake victims were the creation of the media.

One of the demands of the action committee which had conducted a 36-day long fast was to constitute a tribunal to pay compensation to the victims. Though the government had consistently opposed the demand in the beginning that setting up of a tribunal was not feasible, the government at last agreed to the demand of the action committee following its indefinite fast. As a preliminary step in this regard the government appointed Justice C.N. Ramachandran Nair as the chairman of the committee which was expected to report to the government on the feasibility of forming such a tribunal.

But all hell was let loose when Justice Ramachandran Nair made certain remarks to the media when he visited Kasargod to hold a sitting to elicit the views of the public and the action committee on the issue of setting up the tribunal. The anti-endosulfan action committee represented by the Endosulfan Peeditha Janakeeya Munnani, EPJM, protested against the remarks by Justice Ramachandran Nair who said that Plantation Corporation of Kerala and the pesticide manufacturers could not be blamed for the alleged diseases. He had also said that what was needed was not a tribunal, but a project to rehabilitate the victims. He warned that a tribunal would take a long time to settle the individual claims and the endosulfan manufacturers and other stake holders would challenge the setting up of the tribunal entailing prolonged litigation.

The action committee said Justice Ramachandran Nair visited Kasargod with a preconceived notion to scuttle the formation of the tribunal. The action committee therefore wanted the government to change the profile of the committee by inducting new members.

The committee collected evidence from the people in an open session held at the collectorate conference hall on July 20, 2013. Members of the public as well as anti-endosulfan activists demanded setting up of a tribunal with adequate power. The commission also received written submissions given by the public on the issue.

However, the committee submitted its report to the government on August 6, 2013 recommending the formation of a tribunal with limited powers for identification of victims and adjudication of compensation claims. According to the recommendations of the committee, the proposed tribunal would not be competent to entertain any compensation claims from the Plantation Corporation of Kerala which sprayed endosulfan in its plantations for 20 years. The tribunal would also not be competent either to claim compensation from endosulfan manufacturers. Its role would be limited to settling disputes over eligibility for compensation or other assistance as ordered by the government.

The committee proposed to the government that a serving judicial officer of the rank of the district judge be appointed as tribunal to settle disputes through summary proceedings. It also recommended the constitution of an 'Endosulfan Relief Fund' with state funds and through contributions and collections from the Union government, the plantation corporation and others for assistance to the endosulfan victims.

Another recommendation of the committee was to constitute a team of specialist doctors from medical colleges to certify eligibility and categorisation of claimants for grant of relief by the tribunal. The committee also recommended that the state government should set up an agency at the district level to implement the orders of the tribunal. The tribunal and the agency should be established through state legislation.

The committee suggested that the government should not go for litigation against the plantation corporation and it should take over the liability to compensate the victims through the constitution of the relief fund. The committee recommended that the eligibility for assistance should be normally limited to people living within a maximum of one kilometer away from the plantations of the PCK.

As can only be expected, the Endosulfan Peeditha Janakeeya Munnani, EPJM, rejected the recommendations of the Justice Ramachandran Nair committee and wanted the government to set up a tribunal with adequate power to claim compensation from the plantation corporation and the pesticide manufacturers.

Meanwhile, agriculture minister K.P. Mohanan who chaired a meeting of the district level endosulfan victims rehabilitation cell on September 28, 2013 at the Collectorate Hall in Kasargod pledged help to the non-categorised 'endosulfan victims' also. The minister said the non-categorised victims did not belong to the four major groups identified by the National Human Rights Commission for relief and rehabilitation. The minister said a panel of doctors headed by Dr K.P. Aravindan of the Alappuzha medical college had been given the task of categorising the victims for the purpose.

K.P. Mohanan informed the cell meeting that as many as 2,076 victims had been given the first instalment of the NHRC recommended compensation. This included totally bed-ridden patients and those with serious mental and physical disabilities besides those afflicted with 'undiagnosed diseases'.

Amidst resentment at the cell meeting over the report prepared by Justice Ramachandran Nair committee on the issue of setting up the proposed tribunal to decide on the compensation, the minister said steps would be taken to remove shortcomings in the report submitted to the government by the committee.

However, the Endosulfan Peeditha Janakeeya Munnani, EPJM, revived the agitation with an indefinite satyagraha before the official residence of Chief Minister Oommen Chandy in Thiruvananthapuram on January 26, 2014. The EPJM activists who included a number of mothers carrying deformed children shouted slogans in front of the official residence of the Chief Minister in support of their demands. They also brewed gruel in a large vessel on the roadside as part of a symbolic agitation to feed the diseased children and their mothers.

The agitation was apparently revived at the instigation of Thanal, a Thiruvananthapuram-based NGO which has been supporting and financing the anti-endosulfan agitation right from 1999. Rehabilitation of the so-called victims of endosulfan was a community based project of Thanal which received funds from the US-based Global Greengrants.

The government held talks with the EPJM leaders on January 28 in a bid to end the agitation. The agitators had brought a number of diseased children to the venue of the dharna, both from the sprayed and non-sprayed villages in Kasargod. Majority of the children were aged below ten. But the organisers of the agitation found it hard to explain as to how deformed children were still being born even though the use of endosulfan was discontinued in the whole area in Kasargod several years before.

The government once again assured the agitators that all their demands would be considered. True, the government repeated the same assurances given to the action committee following the talks held with the Chief Minister on March 25, 2013 after calling off its 36-day long indefinite fast in Kasargod.

It assured the action committee that all 'eligible victims' in Kasargod district would be given help by the government. According to the terms of the settlement, the government would shelve the report of the justice Ramachandran Nair commission which the action committee had wanted the government to reject. The government assured the action committee that the second instalment of the compensation as ordered by the National Human Rights Commission would be given by March 31, 2014. Besides, medical camps would be held every month in the pesticide sprayed areas.

However, in the face of the repeated threat of agitation by the EPJM, the government decided to enhance the monthly dole for the 'endosulfan victims' by ₹ 200. Accordingly, those receiving a monthly amount of ₹ 2,000 would get ₹ 2,200.

The decision in this regard was taken at a meeting convened by Chief Minister Oommen Chandy on July 1, 2014. The meeting also decided to acquire 25 acres of land of the plantation corporation in Muliyar to 'rehabilitate the victims.'

The land mafia behind the anti-endosulfan agitation had exerted pressure on the government to acquire the PCK land ostensibly for the rehabilitation of the patients. The Plantation Corporation Protection Council had expressed concern over the acquisition of its land since the workers of the PCK would be thrown out of jobs. According to the PCK Protection Council, the land mafia which had long set its eye on the fertile land of the PCK would usurp the land diverting it for some other purpose.

9

DISINFORMATION CAMPAIGN AND FACTS

Dr Romeo F. Quijano, a professor of toxicology at the College of Medicine of the Philippine University visited the exposed area in Kasargod in 2002 and prepared a report within two days. Quijano was sent by a Non-Governmental Organisation receiving foreign money. His report was projected as 'Quijano's report on ill-effects of endosulfan' and was widely reported in the media both in the country and abroad. The Philippinese professor visited the sprayed area only for a few days, but during the limited time he could not have made such a detailed study and spoken about the incidence of stunted growth and miscarriages.

The Pesticide Action Network Asia and Pacific, PANAP, based in Penang in Malaysia was in the forefront of the international campaign against endosulfan. It published a colour poster for international dissemination with the slogan 'Ban endosulfan worldwide !' The colour poster carried the picture of Shruthi, a girl born with four fingers each on both hands which were shaped like antelope horns by birth. It was a freak disease, but anti-endosulfan activists branded her as an endosulfan victim even though she was born in a non-sprayed village. Shruthi would be shown before media persons and political leaders visiting the sprayed area.

The colour poster showed her prominently among other patients. The poster was a collage of patients suffering from ordinary diseases—skin diseases, cancer, mental retardation, Down's Syndrome and hydrocephalus. But none of them were endosulfan victims and their pictures were used in the world wide campaign against endosulfan.

Another wrong propaganda was that endosulfan was banned in 81 countries of the world. But the truth was that the pesticide was either phased out or its registration was not renewed because the pesticide manufacturers failed to provide certain data to the registering authority. All agrochemicals by very nature were toxic and intended to kill insects and fungi and hence they were subjected to rigorous risk evaluation process based on various studies and the data generated.

The toxicology studies related to finding the carcinogenic and mutagenic potential of the pesticides and only after such rigorous risk evaluation process that an agro-chemical would get registered with the recommended dosages and crops for which they would be used. The agro-chemicals also came up for periodical review and additional data or studies in this regard were demanded by the registering authorities or regulatory authorities from their registrants for its continued use. The registrant in the respective country has to submit additional data and studies for continuing the use of a particular pesticide.

Quite often the agrochemicals were withdrawn from use or phased out if the registrants were not willing to invest on generating further data on them for commercial reasons. In fact this was the reason for withdrawal of registration of endosulfan in 2005 in 25 countries and for phasing out of endosulfan in the US and Canada by 2016-17.

This coupled with the propaganda in the internet and the social media network mainly by the Delhi-based CSE in its pesticide monitoring study in the village of Padre in Kasargod, several manufacturers the world over were deterred from generating further data for its continued use. Thus, the false data on endosulfan residue studies had played its part in the phasing out of endosulfan.

The authorisation for endosulfan was withdrawn in Europe in December 2005 as the deadline for submitting relevant data expired in May 2002 and a further deadline in May 2003 for submitting long-term studies also expired. European Union countries were the leading producer and seller of endosulfan in the world for 52 years from 1954 to 2006.

The registrant companies did not submit the data before the deadline. The reason was that the money expended on generating data would be enormous than the profit gained through the marketing of endosulfan as other pesticides, too, were entering the market on a large scale. Since other patented pesticides were available in European markets, the consumers tried to get more effective pesticides according to the climatic conditions of Europe. Besides, there was no need to use endosulfan to kill the pests in European countries which were different from the pests found in tropical countries.

Italy, a member of the European Union re-allowed the use of endosulfan in 2008 for a specified period to control a particular pest which destroyed hazelnut cultivation since the pest could not be controlled by other pesticides.

In the US, the local registrant and the regulatory authorities agreed on a phase out period that will retain use of endosulfan till December 2016. The agreement in this regard was reached with the Environmental Pollution Agency, EPA, of the US. In the agreement, the local registrant said that the endosulfan market in the US was shrinking and the cost of developing and submitting additional data was high. The registrant, therefore, voluntarily negotiated an agreement with the EPA that provided growers with an adequate time frame to find an alternative to endosulfan. In Canada, the local registrant and the registration authorities agreed to a phase out period till December, 2016.

Therefore, withdrawal of registration or phasing out of a pesticide after long use for want of further studies was different from banning a pesticide due to serious health problems. In no other country was endosulfan withdrawn, phased out or banned because of health reasons. Though on a phase out period, endosulfan was being allowed for use on a variety of crops including vegetables in such countries. It was used for veterinary purpose for control of parasites in cattle in the US.

Significantly, the Food and Agricultural Organisation, FAO, had issued a guideline in 1985 in which it had suggested that the standards for acceptance of a pesticide in one country would not necessarily be applied in another country. According to the FAO, an industrial food exporting country with a temperate climate with abundance of fertile land available and having advanced agriculture technology would be different from other countries with a different climate and economy for the use of pesticides. The use of a pesticide should be allowed only if the benefits outweigh the risks, said the FAO.

'The need for pesticides in each country differed widely depending on the crops grown and pests present. Not all crops were grown in all countries. Similarly, not all pests were present in all countries', according to the FAO. It had stated that in a country with a highly developed system of agriculture and adequate resources, the threat of harm to a rare bird species may be a sufficient reason to avoid the use of a particular compound. 'But in situations where vector-borne human diseases, starvation and malnutrition were regularly encountered, the analysis of risks-benefit would result in a different decision'.

Besides, the principle 11 of the Rio declaration on Environment and Development finalised by the United Nations Environment Programme, UNEP, during the Earth Summit in 1992 had clearly stated that environmental standards and legislation could be different in different countries. Thus, environmental standards, management objectives and priorities should reflect the environment and development context to which they apply. Standards applied by some countries may be inappropriate and of unwarranted economic and social cost to other countries, in particular to developing countries. International environmental bodies did not recommend adoption of pesticide regulatory decisions or environmental standards from other countries. Instead, such decisions and standards must reflect the local contexts and needs.

Disinformation campaign was unleashed in Enmakaje gram panchayat following the mass disappearance of honey bees in the early 1990s on the pretext that bee cultivation was affected due to the aerial spraying of endosulfan. The Thanal and the anti-endosulfan action committee had convened the meetings of bee cultivators in the course of the agitation in Enmakaje grama panchayat. The farmers reported at the meeting that the bees were not returning to the hives after flying off to gather honey. The reason was that the bee cultivation was affected by a disease among bees in the entire region. But the disappearance of bees was described as the fallout of the endosulfan spray.

The periodic meetings of bee farmers were organised by the Endosulfan Spray Protest Action Committee, ESPAC, in which the members of Thanal also participated. Sree Padre, an anti-endosulfan activist took the initiative to convene the meetings of bee farmers in Swarga in Enmakaje gram panchayat. Since bee farming was a lucrative business in the area and as several families made a living out of apiculture, the bee farmers were an angry and disappointed lot. Their frustration at the loss of regular income through bee keeping was cunningly made use of by the ESPACK against the spraying of endosulfan.

The bees in entire South India were affected by Thai Sac Brood Virus (TSBV) from the early 90s and as a result many bee colonies got destroyed by the virus causing loss to bee cultivators. The honey outlets in Padre village where bee farmers sold the honey at a lucrative price were shut down one after the other following the mass death of bees. Though the ESPACK and anti-endosulfan campaigners knew the truth, they did not inform the reason to the bee farmers.

The ESPACK and anti-endosulfan activists betrayed the bee farmers. If the bee farmers had contacted the scientists who had studied the subject, the travails of the bee farmers could have been avoided by restoring bee cultivation. According to experts in the field, the method to control the bee virus was to 'dequeen' the affected bee colonies for a few days and then 'requeen' it with a healthy queen from another colony. If the bee cultivators had adopted this method, their loss on account of the death of bees could have been avoided and the bee cultivation restored. But far from helping the bee farmers, the ESPACK betrayed them.

Another disinformation campaign was conducted by government officials and a section of doctors. The government officials included those from the IAS cadre who were vociferous in their stand that endosulfan was a highly toxic chemical.

'Endosulfan, a highly toxic organochlorine pesticide was sprayed in the cashew plantation', wrote V.N. Jithendran, former District Collector, Kasargod, in a draft paper to the workshop on endosulfan held in Kasargod in July 2012. Endosulfan was aerially sprayed with the consent of succeeding District Collectors of Kasargod. Surprisingly, the first few paragraphs of what Jithendran had written were also repeated in the paper presented by Dr Mohammed Asheel, Endosulfan Nodal Officer.

The articles were written as discussion documents for a workshop held in Kasargod on July 21 and 22, 2012. Each of the discussion papers lacked clarity and depth and it turned out to be just propaganda materials for the activists. The workshop was organised ostensibly for the 'Comprehensive Rehabilitation of Endosulfan victims and Rejuvenation of the Ecosystem in Kasargod, but in fact it was meant to serve the interest of some NGOs. Though the organisers of the event were the district panchayat and the National Programme for the Rehabilitation of Persons with Disabilities, NPRPD, the real sponsor of the workshop was Thanal. Later the organisers had to admit that more than ₹ 7 lakh was spent to organise a sham programme called the National Workshop-'Concord 2012'. It was another example of the official-NGO-media nexus in Kasargod which in turn was part of the global conspiracy against endosulfan.

Another fallacy in the article presented as a draft report was the one prepared by Balakiran, an IAS officer and sub-collector of Kasargod. He wrote in the draft paper that it was the poor who used the dry firewood from this area for cooking. 'The endosulfan remnants on burning are directly inhaled by the women in the households during cooking', he wrote.

A draft paper presented for the workshop said that 'aerial spray of endosulfan in Kasargod district for about two decades from 1978 has resulted in a disaster affecting the life of human beings and other biological beings. There was astonishing environmental and health related changes in such areas, noted from 1990s onwards. Deformities of limbs of calves had been noticed much earlier. Studies indicate that the main source of toxic material is water, especially for those who take bath in ponds and streams.'

The draft paper said that 'more incidents of congenital anomalies, stunted growth, behavioural abnormalities and other disorders have been observed by physicians working in the area after the aerial spray. Death of various fauna like birds, insects and mammals were also found during this period. Victims or their parents had exposure by watching helicopters which sprayed endosulfan, working in plantations, taking care of the stock of endosulfan, drinking water from surangs (horizontal wells) or living in sprayed areas'.

But when the health authorities re-categorised the list of endosulfan victims in October 2012 for the purpose of paying compensation to the victims as per the order of the National Human Rights Commission, all such diseases were found very rare and far below the state and national average.

Disinformation campaign was carried out through the media that the food items especially fruits and vegetables contained a heavy content of endosulfan residues. This campaign created scare among the people who refused to buy vegetables and fruits in the market. The vegetable and fruit market in Kasargod was hit by heavy losses as the price of locally grown vegetables shot up since the buyers mostly preferred them as endosulfan was banned in the district ten years before. Since locally grown 'organic' vegetables were in short supply, the people were constrained to buy them paying a heavy price.

But the All India Network Project on Pesticide Residues, under the Indian Agriculture Research Institute, New Delhi, allayed the pesto phobia of the people. It provided information that none of the food items in Kerala showed endosulfan residues above the Maximum Residue Limit, MRL.

As many as 2,821 samples of food from Kerala were analysed from October 2006 to March 2007 following widespread outcry in the media that it contained endosulfan residues. But no samples were found with endosulfan residues.

The Joint Meeting of Pesticide Review, JMPR, under the Food and Agricultural Organisation, FAO, of the United Nations held in 1998 had reported that endosulfan was not carcinogenic. Besides, it would not cause irritation to the skin and eye; it would not also cause skin sensitisation.

The Australian Pesticides and Veterinary Medicines Authority, APVMA, under the Australian government said in a report on March 25, 2010 that 'Endosulfan and Carbendazim are two agriculture chemicals that a number of people have claimed are so toxic that it should not be used in Australia. 'The fact that endosulfan is not permitted in some other countries overseas has been used to support this argument', said the APVMA.

The report said 'both chemicals are permitted to be used in Australia because the APVMA is satisfied, on the available scientific evidence that they can be safely used subject to the strict conditions the APVMA imposes. There is no evidence that either chemical is presenting any human health or environmental problem in Australia when used according to these strict conditions.'

However, the propaganda of anti-endosulfan activists was that Australia was one of the countries that banned endosulfan. The Australian government had used endosulfan to contain the acute menace of pests, spraying endosulfan six times a year.

Similarly, a review article on assessment of the developmental, reproductive and neurotoxicity of endosulfan by the department of Pesticide Regulation, California Environmental Protection Agency stated that 'the data shows that endosulfan is not toxic to the development, reproductive, and endocrine systems in the absence of neurotoxin effects which occur at lower doses.'

Further, the review article said that 'the effects observed do not indicate that endosulfan is a direct reproductive or developmental toxicant, nor do they indicate that it is an endocrine disruptor'.

'In none of these studies were there effects on reproductive organs, nor did endosulfan have endocrine disrupting effects in developing animals. It appears the decision is based upon the weight of evidence that endosulfan is not an endocrine disruptor or neurotoxin in fetus, neonates and pups,' the report said.

Besides, the memorandum dated June 9, 2010, of the United States Environmental Protection Agency, Washington DC said that endosulfan is not a dermal sensitizer nor is it mutagenic or carcinogenic' (not likely a human carcinogen)'.

It was widely propagated that aerial spray of endosulfan caused a wide range of diseases in 11 grama panchayats of Kasargod. But according to records, endosulfan was aerially sprayed in several African countries to control flies which caused human sleeping sickness.

At the third meeting of the POPRC held in Geneva from November 19 to 23 in 2007, India, China and Sierra Leone submitted a paper named 'in consideration of a new chemical –endosulfan'. It said that endosulfan was considered by many growers as an excellent and affordable tool in agricultural pest management, especially under the integrated pest management. During more than 40 years of its use, only a few cases of insect resistance have been reported in view of its unique mode of action in insect pests.

According to the paper, 'it is an insecticide of choice for use on cross-pollinated crops in view of its low toxicity to honey bees. Therefore, endosulfan still provides a much needed cost effective crop protection tool in a variety of situations especially in developing countries.' Though it was low toxic to honey bees, the propaganda in Padre village was that endosulfan use had resulted in the mass disappearance of honey bees.

Another finding of the study conducted in India was that 'endosulfan was harmless to wild life. Its toxicity to bees is very low. Toxicity to birds is moderate to high in a laboratory setting, but no poisoning has been reported under field conditions', said the paper presented at the POPRC by India.

Triolochan S. Kathpal, Attar Singh, Jabir S. Dhankar and Gulab Singh of the Centre of Environmental Studies of Haryana Agricultural University had conducted a study on 'fate of endosulfan in cotton soil under sub-tropical conditions of Northern India'. According to the study conducted in 1996, for about the last three decades endosulfan had been widely used for controlling different insect pests of field crops such as paddy, cotton, sorghum, oil seeds, pulses, vegetables and fruit crops under sub-tropical conditions of India.

According to the studies, 'in the cotton growing belt of northern India the compound was recommended for controlling hairy caterpillar, spotted bollworm, semi-looper, etc., on cotton. In recent years, it has been tested for controlling termites in soil as an alternative to aldrin which has been withdrawn from the Indian market since December 1993 due to its high persistence'.

The study by agricultural scientists in Punjab had found that cotton farmers all over the country have been using endosulfan for several years. The farmers used hand pumps to spray endosulfan in cotton fields and yet there were no cases of the farmers affected by endosulfan use.

Endosulfan, an insecticide has been in commercial use for over 50 years. It was recommended and used for control of insect pests and mites on fruits, vegetables, coffee, tea, spices, flowers, forage crops and non food-crops such as cotton and tobacco. It was used in agriculturally important countries such as China, India, USA, Brazil, Australia, Canada, Mexico, Israel, Nigeria and Sudan. These countries accounted for more than 50 per cent of world's area under agriculture.

The World Health Organisation, WHO, had classified various pesticides based on their hazards–extremely hazardous, (Class 1a), highly hazardous (Class 1b), moderately hazardous (Class II) and slightly hazardous. Endosulfan was classified under Class II as a moderately hazardous pesticide. Other pesticides that belonged to Class II category included Copper Sulphate which was commonly applied to control pests in areca nut and coconut trees.

10

SCIENTIFIC STUDIES AND CENSUS DATA DISPEL THE LIES

Almost all the studies on the health and environmental impact [illegible]

[illegible]

with the national average of the disability data [illegible] to the conclusion that the percentage of disability [illegible] population in Kasaragod district was lower than that [illegible] district [illegible] the percentage of the [illegible] other districts.

[illegible] Association [illegible] Vellayani [illegible] the data [illegible] district [illegible] compared the data on the amount of endosulfan [illegible] Kasaragod [illegible] other districts [illegible]

10

SCIENTIFIC STUDIES AND CENSUS DATA DISPEL THE LIES

Almost all the studies on the health and environmental impact of the aerial spraying of endosulfan in the villages of Kasargod for 20 long years were mainly confined to the problems in the exposed area. But no enquiry commission appointed to probe the issue ever made any attempt to compare the percentage of the diseases in the sprayed area with the same type of diseases prevalent in other parts of the state.

Dr K.M. Sreekumar, Associate Professor at the Padannakkad Agriculture College under the Kerala Agriculture University, KAU, examined the statistical data of the disability census conducted by the Census Commissioner of India in 2001. He made a comparative study with the national average of the disability data. But he found to his surprise that the percentage of disability per 1,000 of population in other districts was more than that of in Kasargod district which meant that the percentage of the disability was less in Kasargod than in other districts.

Dr Sreekumar, together with Dr K.D. Prathapan, Associate Professor at the Kerala Agricultural University, Vellayani, presented a paper at the Swadeshi Science Congress held at the Central Plantation Crops Research Institute, CPCRI, in Kasargod on November 7, 2012. They based their study on the data obtained from various medical camps held in the district for the suspected victims of endosulfan. They compared the data on the quantity of endosulfan sprayed in Kasargod with that of other districts, especially in south Kerala.

Their main contention in the scientific paper was that the quantity of endosulfan used in Kasargod district was far below the quantity sprayed in other districts.

However, Dr Sreekumar who presented the paper at the Science Congress was given only very little time to present his views. The Science Congress was apparently dominated by anti-endosulfan activists that led to heated arguments at the venue of the meet.

But the next day, the media published the version of Dr Sreekumar criticizing him that he ridiculed the endosulfan victims in his study. When media persons asked agriculture minister K.P. Mohanan about the scientific paper presented by Dr Sreekumar and Dr Prathapan, the minister was visibly annoyed with the scientists. He told media persons that disciplinary action would be taken against them. The stand of the Kerala Agriculture University, KAU, and the state agriculture department was that no scientists of the KAU and the officials of the department should try to absolve endosulfan from the odium of 'causing so many diseases and thereby giving it a clean chit'.

The paper titled 'where is science on the endosulfan issue?' presented at the Science Congress said that there has been a spate of propaganda that the aerial spray of endosulfan in 11 gram panchayats in the district resulted in a disaster next only to the Bhopal gas tragedy. The propaganda eventually became a truth through relentless campaign carried on by anti-endosulfan activists and the media.

'Therefore, we are making an attempt to examine how much of it was all true in this scientific paper, and for this we are constrained to assume the role of a devil's advocate', they said as introduction to the paper.

They made use of mainly the various information obtained from several sources in the scientific article. First, they collected the classified data from the medical camps held in the exposed area. They also collected the data of the National Programme for the Rehabilitation of the Physically Disabled, NPRPD, and subjected it to the 'Z' test.

According to the presentation at the Science Congress, only just one per cent of the total quantity of endosulfan used in the whole of the country was sprayed in Kerala. The major consumers of endosulfan in the country were Andhra Pradesh (14.3 per cent), Maharashtra (15 per cent), Madhya Pradesh Pradesh (10.1 per cent), West Bengal (9.3 per cent) and Rajasthan (7.5 per cent).

Endosulfan was sprayed by converting 35 % of its compound into a mixture of 0.05% concentrate (500ppm) as per the crop management package recommended by the Kerala Agriculture University. The average use of endosulfan was only 1.37 litre per hectare in the entire PCK estates of the state. Significantly, only limited quantity of endosulfan was sprayed in the cashew plantations of the PCK.

According to the scientific paper, the quantity used for a single crop of paddy in the state was 1.5 litre of endosulfan, as per the crop package of the KAU. It was sprayed twice a year on one hectare for a single crop. It, therefore, required three litres for a double crop of paddy. Similarly, 4.5 litres of the pesticide were used for double crop of paddy as well as for a single crop of vegetable.

According to the scientists, endosulfan fell into the water-logged paddy fields following direct spray on the crop in the rice bowl of Kerala in Alappuzha. Thus, the quantity of pesticide fallen in the paddy fields of Kuttanad in Alappuzha district since 1970 would have been several times more than what was used in the cashew plantations in Kasargod.

It was estimated that an average of seven litres of pesticide were used per year on one hectare of tea plantation in the state. Besides, endosulfan was regularly used three to four times at the rate of 750 ml per hectare on tea plantations every year. Naturally, the effect of endosulfan use should have been higher in tea plantations in south Kerala than in Kasargod district where it was sprayed only twice a year on cashew plantations. It was also estimated that pesticide was used on an average of nine litres per hectare in cardamom plantations in the state. Since the cardamom plantations would be covered under shade, it would take some time for its chemical breakdown under the sun.

Since several streams originating from cardamom plantations constituted the main water sources of the people, those using them should have suffered more health problems than in Kasargod. But the main contention of the anti-endosulfan activists was that it was the aerial spray of the pesticide which caused the diseases.

Rubbishing the contention of anti-endosulfan activists, Dr Sreekumar and Dr Prathapan said the size of molecules of a pesticide from an ordinary sprayer would normally be 336-400 microns thick. If the molecule was bigger in size, there was every chance of it falling into the top soil and even penetrating it. But when it was sprayed aerially, the size of the molecules would be reduced to 145-225 microns thick. Though it would be carried away in the wind, the mist-like spray would reach the top soil only from the leaves of cashew nut trees on which it had fallen. Since cashew trees are deciduous by nature from October to November shedding its green leaves, the soil surrounding the cashew nut trees would be covered by a thick layer of dry leaves.

Since the soil surrounding cashew nut trees was not normally upturned using spades, the pesticide particles would settle on the dry leaves which would be dissipated under the tropical sun from December to January within seven to 15 days. According to studies on the subject, even if small particles of the pesticide lingered on the soil, it would break down and dissipate in the tropical sunlight from February to May.

The commission appointed by the Kerala Agricultural University in its study conducted in 2001 had examined the samples of water, soil and bio-particles in February after 56 days of the pesticide spray. However, it could find endosulfan residues of only two ppm from the open ground in the cashew plantations. Besides, there was very little chance of the pesticide residues, even if it penetrated the soil, being carried away in the water run off to the rivulets below the plantations. Further, the incidence of soil erosion in cashew plantation was very rare and even the summer showers in the month of April and May would not cause soil erosion.

Even if the pesticide residues had been carried away in the powerful monsoon in June and July, it would not reach the rivulets below since it would be washed away in the rains. It meant that the pesticide residues would not enter the human body through drinking water collected from the village water sources. Since there was a tendency for endosulfan to convert itself from alfa and beta endosulfan into endosulfan sulphate, it would stick on to soil particles. In most of the studies, endosulfan residues were found at the bottom sediments of the water bodies and not in the water itself. This happened because the residues would be dissolved at the bottom of the water along with the soil.

Though the Plantation Corporation had supplied plaited coconut leaves to the local people to cover their wells, all surrounding water bodies could not have possibly been covered with coconut leaves. Nevertheless, there had been no complaint of acute toxicity by local people after drinking the water from the wells during the 20 years of aerial spray of the pesticide.

According to studies, the water solubility of endosulfan is 0.32 ppm (parts per million). The endosulfan residues would be degraded into non-toxic particles within 20 days after falling in the water bodies. Even then there was a rare chance of phase reversion of endosulfan in case of aerial spray. If it happened, endosulfan would convert itself either into toxic form or water. If it had happened, there would have been widespread acute toxicity in the exposed area where toxic endosulfan was aerially sprayed. In this case also, there has been no report of the affected people falling sick in the sprayed area. Local people had opposed the aerial spray of endosulfan in Cheemeni and Peria from 1984 itself. If there had been widespread incidence of acute toxicity, they would have started a strong agitation against the spray.

The Plantation Corporation used to erect red flags in its cashew plantations to enable helicopter pilots to see clearly the boundaries separating private cashew estates from PCK land. But, local people used to uproot these flags and plant them in private cashew plantations to get them the benefit of the aerial spray. If there was any report of human toxicity, local people would not have dared to plant the red flags in their lands.

According to the Work Safety Administration of the US, the safety limit of endosulfan spray was put at 0.1 mg per cubic meter of space in an eight hour work schedule. When endosulfan was aerially sprayed twice a year in Kasargod, the concentration of the pesticide in the air was far below the permissible limit in the US.

Endosulfan was aerially sprayed in Ivory Coast to control the tsetse bugs which caused human sleeping sickness, under the supervision of the World Health Organisation for several years from 1970. The WHO itself had studied the health problems in the sprayed area, but there had been no report of adverse health effects there as widely reported in Kasargod.

There was a permissible limit or threshold limit of toxicity for every food article. The Maximum Residue Limit, MRL, in food was determined by the WHO and the various health organisations of the member countries. However, the MRL was fixed neither by the pesticide manufacturers nor agriculture universities. In India, the MRL was decided by the Central Pesticide Board, CPB, headed by the Director General of Health Services.

The MRL of endosulfan in fruits and vegetables is two ppm. Normally, 0.05 per cent (500 ppm) of endosulfan was recommended to be used in fruits and vegetables. According to studies, the maximum residue limit of two ppm would be reached from two to seven days after application. But the

MRL for tea was 24-30 ppm in the US, European countries, Japan and in other agriculture producing countries.

While there was a system to check the MRL value of tea being exported, there was no such system to check the MRL in domestic consumption of tea. The question assumed significance if one considered the fact that consumers were taking at least 24 ppm of endosulfan in their daily intake of tea. This underlined the fact that there was no possibility of endosulfan residues getting in human blood following its aerial spray twice a year in Kasargod. Therefore, there was no possibility of air and water bodies getting polluted by endosulfan residues in Kasargod or its immediate and long term toxicity to human beings or to the flora and fauna.

There were several research papers on how endosulfan reacted in animal bodies. The studies were conducted by injecting poison directly into animals or by feeding them with toxic food. Every experiment has its cause and effect. Administration of medicine in high doses would act as poison. But human body would not function like an animal body in a laboratory setup. For instance, a given dose of paracetamol which was administered to reduce temperature in human body would act as poison in rats. But unlike in rats, human body produced the enzyme which enabled it to dissolve the paracetamol.

Endosulfan was sprayed in specific concentration to destroy pests. But the experiments conducted on human cells or in animals in laboratories could not be depended upon beyond a limit. Therefore, proof of an epidemiological study in the exposed area was important to know whether there was large number of strange and unusual diseases in the sprayed areas.

Dr Achuthan commission which conducted the first official study on the issue in 2002 had suggested a detailed epidemiological study in the villages surrounding the PCK estates. The National Institute of Occupational Health, NIOH, which studied the issue had also suggested a detailed epidemiological study in the surrounding areas. The department of community medicine of the Kozhikode Medical College had conducted an epidemiological study comparing the exposed Muliyar gram panchayat and the non-sprayed Banam in 2010.

But the major drawback of the study was that it did not equally represent both the sprayed and non-sprayed areas. However, the study of the Kozhikode Medical College was presented to the media by deleting some relevant tables which showed that there was not much difference in morbidity rate between the exposed Muliyar and non-sprayed Banam. It was also presented to the Supreme Court in the case filed by the DYFI, the youth wing of the CPM.

The study report of the Kozhikode Medical College said that the blood plasma of 43 persons collected from the sprayed areas were tested at the Salim Ali Centre for Ornithology and Natural History, SACON. It was recorded that endosulfan residues ranging from 2.51 per cent to 170.40 were found in the blood samples. The residues were found following the test conducted by using Gas Chromatography, GC.

But it was only the blood plasma report of four persons which tallied with the record in the print out as per the details obtained under the Right to Information Act. This underlined the fact that the details of the endosulfan residues in most of the cases were recorded wrong.

There were diseases in every society and there was also a national or state average for each disease. The average was arrived on the basis of various studies and the details of which could be obtained from standard medical texts. The Kerala Sastra Sahithya Parishad, a body promoting scientific temper among the people, had calculated state average of various diseases in its studies conducted in 1976 and 2006 and the same data was available in the national census conducted in 2001. But the Kerala health department could not give an answer to the question asked under the RTI Act as to which types of diseases were more prevalent in the sprayed areas of Kasargod.

Dr Sreekumar and Dr Prathapan depended on the data collected from the medical camps conducted in all the sprayed areas in December 2010 and January 2011. The government had pressed into service several vehicles to ferry the patients to endosulfan medical camps besides giving wide publicity to the event through the media. Local volunteers had ferried patients to the camps through house-to-house campaigns. Almost all the patients in the sprayed areas attended the medical camps on the belief that the government would facilitate their continued treatment. These medical camps served to collect most of the data almost on the lines of a door-to-door survey.

As many as 4,226 patients hit by 300 types of diseases were classified as those affected by endosulfan spraying. However, the District Medical Officer, the Director of Health Services and the heads of various medical colleges in the state could not answer the question regarding the factual, clinical and bio-medical criteria used to classify a patient as hit by endosulfan spray. The question was asked under the RTI Act.

The disease of a patient would be categorised as endosulfan related if the doctors at the medical camp answered the question whether they considered the disease as caused by endosulfan. If the answer was 'yes' the patient concerned would be enrolled in the endosulfan list. The list of the diseases was first known as 'endosulfan-related diseases'. Then it was modified as 'peculiar diseases in the endosulfan sprayed area' when the medical authorities could not prove that the diseases were caused by endosulfan spray.

But on examining the list, one could find only ordinary diseases as in every human habitation. Ordinary diseases such as piles, hyper tension, asthma, diabetes, tooth ache, joint pain, cancer, cirrhosis of liver as found in liquor addicts were classified as endosulfan-related diseases by expert doctors of the medial colleges who examined the patients at the medical camps. It was for the first time in medical history that all diseases in a region were classified as caused by a chemical pesticide. But the health department of the state failed to compare the possible diseases of endosulfan spray with the state or national average of diseases even though the crucial data was readily available with the government.

The total population of the 11 sprayed gram panchayats of Kasargod was 2,97,726 as per the 2011 census. If the average live birth was calculated as about 4,000 a year, the prevalence of all types of mentally challenged diseases was 2.5 per 1,000. But the national average of patients with acute mental retardation was four per 1,000. This meant that in any case the number of patients suffering from diseases caused by central nervous system was below the national average. It was widely believed that the diseases such as neuro-behavioural disorders, hydrocephalus, mental retardation and cerebral palsy were associated with the spraying of endosulfan.

There was no data on the annual incidence of various types of cancer in the country. It was possible that the patients hit by various cancers may survive long since it was regarded as long persisting diseases. Therefore, the rate of prevalence of cancer in the country would be more than the number of patients falling victims to cancer every year.

It was known that small quantity of poison would alter the genetic structure. In this case new born babies would have more syndromes which caused genetic disorders. The same would be the state of affairs in all the sprayed gram panchayats. On analysis of the available data, it was evident that the prevalence of various diseases in the sprayed area of Kasargod was almost the same or below the national average.

The endosulfan controversy took its origin from the village of Padre in Enmakaje gram panchayat. If the statistics on the prevalence of various diseases or data on health status of the people of the sprayed area were subjected to a study, it would have revealed the real facts. The lapse of the health department in analysing the data was a conspicuous act even though the department had expert and efficient doctors and auxiliary equipment to conduct such an analysis. It was clear that the health department was well aware of the consequences that such an analysis would reveal the truth that there were not so many patients in the sprayed areas as propagated by the activists.

Further, there were similar diseases as seen in Padre village in the non-sprayed areas also. Similar diseases were reported in Mogral Puthur, Kodom Bellur, Chemnad, Padanna, Chembilode in Kannur district as well as in Amarambalam in Malappuram district. What was the cause for the diseases in the non-sprayed areas?

The census data revealed that morbidity rate in Kasargod district was not more than what it was in other places. Besides, the district has the lowest percentage of people suffering from mental challenges and physical retardation. The morbidity rate was almost the same as in other Malabar districts of Kannur, Wayanad and Malappuram.

The National Programme for the Rehabilitation of the Physically Disabled, NPRPD, a project of the Union Government implemented its programmes in Kasargod, Palakkad and Kollam districts. The door-to-door data collected by the NPRPD coordinators was available in its website. The morbidity status of the ten sprayed panchayats has been compared with that of the non-sprayed panchayats in its website.

The data revealed that out of 11 types of diseases as many as nine diseases including mental retardation were prevailing in the non-sprayed panchayats also. It was also found in the statistical analysis through the Z-test that there was not much difference in the physical and mental retardation in both the sprayed and non-sprayed areas. Now it has become clear that the propaganda that the number of patients hit by physical and mental retardation was the highest in the sprayed area was baseless. It was also clear that in the endosulfan sprayed areas in Kasargod, the number of diseases was not higher compared to other non-sprayed areas.

One of the important findings of the National Institute of Occupational Health, NIOH, based in Ahamadabad was that it could find endosulfan residues in the blood of the residents of the sprayed area even after ten months of the spray. It was not consistent with scientific principles. Studies had further revealed that endosulfan did not bio-accumulate in tropical regions. Even if it entered the blood stream, the residues of endosulfan would dissipate within one month. Therefore, only a small per cent of endosulfan could be seen in blood when compared to its residues in water.

Normally, pesticide residue tests would be conducted in two or three laboratories as per different protocol if any unusual results persisted in the lab test. The NIOH did not test the residues in different laboratories which was the main drawback of its experiment besides being unscientific. The pesticide residue monitoring study by the Delhi-based Centre for Science and Environment, CSE, turned out to be a huge blunder since it published the results without confirming the results in other laboratories.

The same faux pas was repeated in the test of the blood plasma collected by the department of community medicine of the Kozhikode Medical College in its epidemiological study. However, the endosulfan residues in the blood plasma was tested at the Salim Ali Centre for Ornithology and Natural History, SACON. The Government Agricultural College in Vellayani has been regularly monitoring pesticide residues in various fruits and vegetables since 2006. The monitoring study used to detect endosulfan residues in vegetables and fruits. However, it was not the real endosulfan residues which were detected in the test. This was revealed when the studies were confirmed by using Mass Spectroscopy (MS). In other words, there was something which emulated endosulfan in the retention time. This 'endosulfan mimic' would present itself as endosulfan residues if it was not confirmed with MS test.

The first census on disability conducted by the Census Commissioner of India in 2001 exposed the claim of the anti-endosulfan activists that disability rate was the highest in Kasargod district following the spraying of endosulfan. The district-wise disability census report was published in 2005.

According to the report, the number of disabled population was 24 per 1,000 in Kasargod district, but it was 29 each in Pathanamthitta and Thiruvananthapuram districts. As for movement disability, the number per 1,000 was seven in Kasargod, but the ratio was highest in Pathanamthitta and Thiruvananthapuram districts with nine each. When mental disability was three per 1,000 in Kasargod district, it was five each in Kozhikode, Malappuram, Idukki , Pathanamthitta and Thiruvananthapuram districts. When seeing disability was nine per 1,000 in Kasargod district, it was 14 in Idukki, 12 in Alappuzha, 13 in Kollam, 11 in Palakkad districts. However, speech disability was two per 1,000 in Kasargod district and in almost all the districts except Pathanamthitta where it was three per 1,000. Hearing disability was three per 1,000 in Kasargod district which was more or less the same in all other districts.

However, the second census on disability conducted by the Census Commissioner of India in 2011 also confirmed the disability trend as reported in the census conducted in 2001. The census report was released in May 2014 and it was the latest census on disability in India.

According to the data, movement disability was 0.49 per cent in Kasargod while it was 0.64 per cent, 0.59 per cent and 0.58 per cent in the southern districts of Alappuzha, Pathanamthitta and Thiruvananthapuram respectively.

As for mental retardation, the percentage was only 0.19 per cent in Kasargod while for Kottayam, Pathanamthitta and Alappuzha the data was 0.23, 0.22 and 0.22 per cent respectively. (For both Pathanamthitta and Alappuzha the data for mental retardation was the same)

In the case of mental illness, the percentage was only 0.15 for Kasargod while it was 0.25 in Kozhikode, 0.24 in Kottayam and 0.21 in Thiruvananthapuram. Regarding the data under the category 'any other disability', it was 0.32 in Kasargod while the data for both Pathanamthitta and Alappuzha districts it was the same as 0.36. However, Thiruvananthapuram district registered a slight decrease of 0.35 per cent.

The disability census conducted in 2001 and 2011 showed that the number of diseased persons per one thousand of the population in Kasargod district was less than in other districts.

11

ENDOSULFAN : GAS IN THE MEDIA

There was a lot of 'gas' in the media, but fortunately no 'tragedy' ever occurred though it was compared to the Bhopal gas tragedy. For those seeking truth in the media, it was really 'a gas tragedy'. A newspaper even headlined the Endo spray as 'death from the sky'. Everything that the media reported on the endosulfan issue was published on front page which boosted the morale of the reporters. Thrilled by their fantastic stories, more and more media persons, both working for English and local language papers across the country descended on the endosulfan sprayed villages of Kasargod in the early 2000s. The media picked up every detail of the diseases, but failed to investigate whether what they called the strange diseases had previously existed in the villages or the place had a history of such diseases in the past.

The media persons also missed on the cardinal point as to whether the diseases had any link with the spraying of endosulfan. Above all, they failed to verify whether there was any truth in what the anti-endosulfan agitators had been saying. They could have easily solved the puzzle by comparing the data of the disability census conducted by the Census Commissioner of India in 2001.

Thus, media persons who came down to Kasargod were in a state of excitement. Some of them were euphoric that their writings attracted international attention. The attention of the international media was also focused on the issue. A British newspaper of repute reported about the 'endosulfan tragedy' and it was sufficient reason for the Indian media to turn its attention on the non-descript villages in Kasargod.

The media was manipulated and pushed around by a few Non-Governmental Organisations getting foreign money. The veteran media persons who came from the metropolitan cities became mere stenographers of the local anti-endosulfan activists writing down what they had wanted them to do. Since media persons were under the obligation of the NGOs, they had no alternative but to report what the NGOs had suggested.

The media had never before caved in and collapsed as it was in the case of endosulfan reporting. There was, however, only one instance in the past when the media failed miserably to uphold the freedom of the press and media ethics and that was in the days of emergency during 1975-76. Castigating the media in a sarcastic way, the former Jan Sangh ideologue and BJP patriarch L.K. Advani remarked. 'When they asked you to bend you people crawled'. However, the media learnt a good lesson from its earlier pusillanimous ways and came on its own. Media persons started investigative journalism and lately even stink operations to expose the guilty.

But the same media failed once again on another occasion. It was manipulated by a bunch of politicians and police officers of Kerala in reporting what was known as the ISRO espionage case in Kerala in 1993-94. But the media in Kerala failed to acknowledge that its reporting of the ISRO case was thoroughly flawed and that it was manipulated by some political leaders. But it was not ready to acknowledge its mistake and apologise for the campaign it had conducted in the so-called ISRO espionage case. Let alone admitting its mistake, no newspaper ever wrote an editorial expressing the three poignant words- 'we are sorry'. Nambi Narayanan, the victim of the fraudulent media campaign was later given compensation by the court for the mental agony he had suffered.

However, 'Media', the bilingual journal of the Kerala Press Academy wrote an editorial in its October 2012 issue titled

'Was it only the media that was in the dock? 'The Kerala society should hang its head in shame when Nambi Narayanan, a scientist and a victim of the most cruel media hunt stands before us with a clear mind after being absolved of his guilt imposed upon him', the editorial said.

It said that 'the court was influenced or led by the media. The political parties, their leaders and to a certain extent the court formed their opinion on the basis of media reports'. Now the truth came out from the journal of the Kerala Press Academy. The same thing also happened in the case of endosulfan reporting. Mostly it happened that media persons depended only on a single source for news as in the case of the ISRO incident.

The editorial said 'the CPM had played a major role in disseminating untruths in the ISRO case. The party has always criticised the media which published any news which was not to its liking. The allegation of the CPM has always been that a 'media syndicate' was behind all kinds of news against the party'. Significantly, it was the DYFI, the youth wing of the CPM which moved the Supreme Court to ban endosulfan in the country.

The manner in which the media reported the endosulfan issue constituted the real 'media syndicate'. Every media which was at each other's throat and professing different ideology—ranging from religious extremism to right wing politics—joined together and informally formed a media syndicate to spread canards on the endosulfan issue.

The editorial of the 'Media' described how the court was influenced by the media report on the ISRO case. When the CBI submitted in the Kerala High Court that it could not collect any incriminating evidence against former IG Srivasthava in the espionage case, 'the court interrupted to say that it was not true since the court could understand the involvement of the police officer'.

The media depended on the green activists and on some NGOs in reporting the endosulfan story without making an investigation on its own or ascertaining the facts. Even when some of the media persons knew that the so-called victims of endosulfan spray were all frauds, created by the NGOs in collusion with a section of government officials, it did not stop the propaganda. The media showed a slavish mindset from the very beginning on the question of reporting the endosulfan issue.

One of the objectives of the NGOs receiving foreign funds was to form support groups among media persons. The Thanal and the CSE had succeeded to a large extent in foisting such support groups on the media. A section of the media in India was much maligned for what was termed as 'paid news'. It published campaign materials in the garb of news during election after receiving a hefty amount from candidates. The fraud was first exposed by a small and medium newspaper when big newspapers were afraid to expose the scandal.

However, what happened in the case of endosulfan reporting was a sort of disguised paid news. It was disguised because nobody knew whether the editors of newspapers and news channels which supported the anti-endosulfan agitation were influenced by the NGOs.

The Indian media could have exposed the connection between the Delhi-based Centre for Science and Environment, CSE, and the Swedish International Agency, SIDA, which had funded a laboratory to the CSE to conduct the endosulfan residue test in Padre village in 2001. The domination of the European Union countries at the Stockholm convention and the flagrant violation of the rules at the POPRC convention could have been exposed by the media.

The NGOs were also successful in creating a pesto-mania among journalists. When news of diseases on large scale cropped up in Mogral Puthur, a littoral village near Kasargod, the first thing that media persons enquired was whether any pesticide was ever sprayed in the area. A newspaper even blamed a farm research institute of the Union Government located in the area for the diseases. This showed the pesto phobia of the media persons created by the NGOs.

Though the aerial spraying of endosulfan was stopped around 2001, the media projected every death in the area as endosulfan deaths as if there had been no natural deaths in the sprayed area. When an old man of 90 breathed his last and a child of five years died, the deaths would be invariably attributed to endosulfan spray. 'One more endosulfan death' was the heading of the news story. In most cases the reports lacked credibility since the victim was described as born with congenital diseases some 35 or 40 years before when there was no endosulfan spray. The media reported that the effect of the endosulfan spray would last for decades creating panic among the people of the sprayed area. The media had played an obscurantist role in covering up the truth about the pesticide spray.

A six-month-old baby died of hydrocephalus in Ambalathara near Kanhangad in April 2013. The entire media described the event as another endosulfan death. The media said that though endosulfan spray was stopped 13 years before, its residues were still stalking the people causing strange diseases. The house of the deceased child was located far away from the PCK estate where endosulfan was aerially sprayed 13 years before.

The manipulation of the media by the environmental NGOs as happened in the case of reporting the endosulfan story sounded the death knell of media ethics and the freedom of the press. It was rather mystifying that the entire media in the country looked the other way when truth was being suppressed with the clout and money power of the foreign-funded NGOs. It was the pluralistic culture of the media which safeguarded the freedom of the press. There were several cases when the media projected the truth on some popular issues though a section of it carried on wrong propaganda. When the media as a whole bulldozed the truth at the connivance of the NGOs, it constituted the negation of the freedom of the press.

The media across the country had taken a bold stand exposing the action committee of the Kudankulam nuclear plant that the agitation was fueled by foreign funds. Strangely, the same media could not see the foreign strings that pulled the anti-endosulfan agitation in Kasargod.

The media created tremendous disinformation and wrong propaganda on the environmental hazards reportedly brought about by the aerial spray of endosulfan in 11 gram panchayats of Kasargod. The report on congenital disabilities of children were blown out of proportion and there was huge exaggeration in the report on environmental impact of the pesticide spray. The media played a nefarious role in playing up the issue to create scare among the people. In fact, most of the reporters did not visit the sprayed area and they churned out the reports by fabricating stories with their own imagination.

The stories, thus, produced were planted as news reports and the gullible readers believed them all. The media reports about congenital physical deformities, mental retardation, stunted growth, cerebral palsy and cases of hydrocephalus were also reported and attributed to the pesticide spray. It was also reported that there was mass destruction of several fish species and frogs, bees and that of small birds in the area. Miscarriages, bleeding and infertility were also attributed by the media to the pesticide spray.

The media may have some problems in going back and reversing the trend after its ferocious campaign against endosulfan spray spanning more than a decade. But it could still have desisted from reporting fake endosulfan death stories.

Unfortunately, the readers were quite ignorant of the real facts. When endosulfan-related stories appeared in all newspapers with the single theme that the pesticide spray was responsible for all the diseases, the readers had no means of knowing the truth. The electronic media telecast scores of images of deformed and sick children creating a permanent impression among the viewers who included members of the judiciary and the executive.

Generally, it was unfair to use illustrations to depict an invalid child as a victim of endosulfan along with a picture of the insecticide bottle without any proof that the child was indeed a victim of the pesticide. It was known as campaign journalism. But the media has been and is still conducting campaign using all journalistic tools to drive home the point that endosulfan had wreaked havoc in the area. The media acted in a brazen and patently one-sided way in reporting the endosulfan issue. An array of major newspapers vied with one another in reporting false stories.

The media was guided by herd instinct rather than attempting an enquiry on its own. Like a bunch of cattle prodded on by its whip lashing owner, the media browsed contentedly in one direction. All the media followed in the wake of the few newspapers and news channels which first broke the story as 'death from the sky'.

If the endosulfan controversy had broken out in some other countries, the journalists there would have exposed and torn to shreds the whole bunch of untruths. But Indian media has not come of age and it was still being misguided and pushed around because it has not come out of the shell of its commercial interest.

In its eagerness to placate its masters, the media killed its ethics. Electronic media played a major role as even those born with congenital diseases several years before the aerial spraying started was untruthfully projected as the victims of endosulfan. No viewer or reader ever checked the age of the victims. When the same visual of a victim was shown for several times, it became a truth. So the viewers believed that the deformed child was indeed a pesticide victim.

A picture of a child hit by hydrocephalus taken by Madhu Raj, a media photographer became the logo of anti-endosulfan activists the world over. The picture of 11-month old Sainabha was taken from the village of Bovikkanam in Kasargod and the child was not a victim of endosulfan. Yet Madhu Raj was given several awards by anti-endosulfan organisations. His picture of the child hit by hydrocephalus became as famous as the face shot of a partially buried baby taken by Pablo Bartholomew which later became the symbol of the Bhopal gas leak tragedy.

The colour pullout of most of the newspapers devoted lengthy stories on the endosulfan incident cramming the features with half truths and untruths. Though the aerial spraying of endosulfan had no link with the diseases in the sprayed area, as proved by scientists, the reporters published lies that the aerial spray had affected the families living several kilometers away from the sprayed areas. Showing the photos of sick children in border areas of nearby Kannur district, the media carried on the campaign that even those living far away from the sprayed area suffered from various diseases without any proof that the diseased children were the real victims of endosulfan spray.

There was no association of journalists in India that cut across the editorial views. Every journalist was a prisoner of what the editorial policy of his or her paper dictated. The editorial policy, in turn, was not decided by the collective experience of the journalists who were intimately in touch with the ground reality. But on the contrary, editorial policy was decided by editors who were mostly influenced by NGOs and vested interests. Journalists in the field knew the truth in a given situation and they were also well aware of the manipulations created by vested interests.

Media ethics demanded that two views or arguments of the contending parties should be given so that readers could arrive at the right conclusion. But in the coverage of endosulfan issue, the journalists had only one option–to toe the line of the agitators who had a hidden agenda on the issue. When the anti-endosulfan agitation was at its zenith, the media was compelled to write pro-agitation editorials. In some cases, the newspapers complied with the request of the action committee projecting its views in an array of untruths. The views of the Plantation Corporation Protection Council were largely ignored by the media.

There were hundreds of workers and staff employed in the Plantation Corporation of Kerala and they were all readers of newspapers. Though they have the right to know the truth, it was denied by the media by publishing only one-sided and biased version of the entire incident.

How biased and one-sided has been the media on endosulfan reporting was amply proved by the story 'spray of misery' published in the *India Today* magazine in its issue dated June 23, 2001. The National Human Rights Commission had initiated a suo motu action on the basis of the India Today report. But the NHRC closed the suo moto action in April 2005 citing the reason that a case was pending in the Kerala High Court.

The report filed by the magazine's Bangalore reporter Stephen David was thoroughly one-sided apart from being biased. According to the report, six-year old Balakrishna, son of Aithappa Naik was diagnosed for cancer in a Mangalore hospital following high fever. But the reporter had no proof that Balakrishna became a cancer patient because of endosulfan spray. The report was published on the basis of speculation. No study on the issue was conducted by any government agency except by the Delhi-based Centre for Science and Environment. The CSE study was criticised by several experts since it showed high concentration of endosulfan in the blood of the alleged victims.

Another victim in the report was four-year old Nizamudeen of Nettanige in Bellur gram panchayat. Nizamudeen was mentally challenged and according to his mother, there were so many such patients in the village.

Mamata, 17, of Swarga and daughter of Hukkappa Gowda, was both mentally and physically challenged, said the report. Mamata's neighbour four-year old Bharat, son of Ellian Gowda, was another mentally retarded child. The *India Today* report said that there were so many persons affected by physical and mental retardation in the village of Swarga.

Except Nizamudeen in Nettanige, all three victims—Balakrishna, Mamata and Bharat belonged to the Marathi Naik community. I had explained in an earlier chapter how the Marathi Naiks were persecuted by the British following the suppression of the first war of Independence in 1857 and the subsequent rebellion in the Maratha region.

There were a number of patients belonging to the Marathi Naiks in the endosulfan victim's list as well as in the death register. There was a fairly high concentration of Marathi Naiks in the village of Swarga. Their migration and social isolation was the subject of study by anthropologists. But no journalist who visited Swarga in Padre village was inquisitive enough to probe the anthropological angle of how some families of Marathi Naiks became prone to various diseases.

The *India Today* report carried no version of the pesticide industry as well as that of officials of the Plantation Corporation of Kerala, which aerially sprayed endosulfan. The persons quoted in the report were nothing but Dr. V.S. Mohan Kumar and Sree Padre, anti-endosulfan activists. Every journalist who visited Swarga invariably quoted only Dr. Mohan Kumar and Sree Padre and others were virtually ignored by them. The *India Today* report also quoted the version of Padma Venkar, co-author of the CSE report 'analysis of samples from Padre village in Kasargod for endosulfan residues' published in February 2001.

Another report on which the NHRC initiated suo motu action was published in the *Hindustan Times* on November 16, 2010 written by its Kerala correspondent Ramesh Babu. The NHRC said in its website that it had taken suo motu congnizance of the media report.

The report began with the sentence which was rather intriguing. According to the report 'aerial spraying of endosulfan, an insecticide-banned in Kerala since 2005— continues to be used today and poor villagers of northern Kasargod continues to suffer'. Even though the whole issue was controversial, the report did not carry the version of the plantation corporation and the pesticide industry. It was pertinent that there was no aerial spraying of endosulfan at the time of filing the report in November 2010 as it was already banned a decade before.

There were some parties involved in the endosulfan controversy-the pesticide manufacturers, the Plantation Corporation and its workers, the anti-endosulfan action committee and the so-called victims. But except for the victims and the action committee, others were virtually ignored in the media reports blaming them for the alleged pesticide tragedy.

The electronic media in Kerala used to violate all journalistic ethics. When the dispute over Mullapperiyar dam between Kerala and Tamil Nadu was at its peak in 2012, some television channels showed the images of a dam burst taken from a film to give pictorial effect to the impending tragedy. Several children living in the surroundings of the Mullapperiyar dam during the period developed the worst nightmare of a dam burst trembling violently in their sleep. During the thick of the controversy, the television and the media propagated the lie that the dam would burst with devastating effect. But the dam constructed one hundred years ago by the British survived the media reports mocking at the unscrupulous and terrible media campaign.

The way in which the media reported the whole endosulfan stories was a typical case study of media behaviour when it was influenced by powerful lobbies of the NGOs. It has proved beyond doubt that powerful NGOs could take the media for a ride. The whole plan was executed ostensibly to help the poor and hapless patients, but in reality it was to help the NGOs getting foreign funds.

The stories filed by some of the media persons questioning the version of the anti-endosulfan activists were either rewritten at the desk to suit the editorial interest or were out rightly 'killed'. There was an evil design behind the media reporting and it appeared that someone was pulling the strings and influencing the editors. An editor of a Malayalam newspaper purchased land in the sprayed area at cheap prices. His paper was in the forefront of the campaign that the exposed land was highly toxic and that human beings cannot live in the exposed land for long.

The media failed miserably in bringing out the real facts. Journalists should be guided by truth and not by emotion. When the illness in the area was attributed to the aerial spraying of the pesticide, it was but natural that the media would be carried away by emotion, but even then it was morally bound to investigate whether what the activists were saying was all true.

In the case of endosulfan reporting, all the opposition views were ignored and those who expressed doubts were branded as agents of the pesticide manufacturers. There were many people, both in the media and outside who were skeptical whether all the diseases were caused by the pesticide spray. Many of them became silent fearing that they would be maliciously linked with pesticide manufacturers and isolated from the mainstream. The agitators thus got a level playing ground where there was none at the other end to defend the blows. Since the field was left without any rival players, what the anti-endosulfan agitators said shaped the public opinion. They were winning the game in the absence of anyone who could defend the blows at the other side. Even though those living in the sprayed areas knew the truth, they also kept quiet.

Even when agriculture scientists tried to establish the truth that there was no link between the aerial spray of endosulfan and the disease, they were ridiculed by the media and the anti-pesticide lobby. Two scientists of the Kerala Agriculture University had presented a joint paper at the Swadeshi Science Congress held at the CPCRI in Kasargod rebutting point by point that the endosulfan spray had no role in causing the diseases. But the media criticised the scientists and wanted the government to initiate action against them. This showed the sheer arrogance and lack of tolerance of the media. Even the democratic option of the experts to use a scientific forum to air their views was threatened by the media.

The tendency among most of the newspapers was to invite the opinion of anti-endosulfan activists if anyone happened to say that the whole endosulfan controversy was a fraud. Media persons would seek the opinion of the activists on the issue. The dissenting opinion would be published insignificantly overwhelmed by a full page devoted to the views of the activists. Finally, the lone voice would be silenced through the combined media attack. This very often created severe pressure on those holding the opposite views. It was also intended to act as a warning to others to keep aloof from criticizing the activists or the NGOs.

Kerala has an aggressive media culture. As a result, there was fierce competition among the media creating many undesirable and disturbing trends. It was the media which normally decided on the agenda and the politicians exploited the situation to activate its cadres and expand its base. But in the endosulfan issue, it was the NGOs which had set the agenda, and the media and politicians were carried away by its campaign. It was the media which formed public opinion in the state since people of Kerala were addicted to newspaper reading. For them newspapers formed part of their life. When a public opinion was formed on an issue based on media reports, it would be difficult to change the public perception. Everything that was printed in newspapers would be taken as gospel truth.

The socio-cultural movement in the state had exerted a strong influence on the people. The media had played a pivotal role in the state's renaissance movement. So the awareness created by the media on all issues concerning social life was exploited by Environmental NGOs under the influence of the European Union.

All efforts had been made to eradicate different views on endosulfan spray in the early phase of the agitation. The representatives of the pesticide manufacturers had tried to project their views in the early 2000s through media conference, but their views on the issue were not given prominence. So the media had played an influential role not only in projecting the endosulfan issue as a pesticide tragedy, but also to play down the opposite views. This was because of the fact that environmental activists working in the media acted as both reporters and activists at the same time. No wonder, many of the media reporters in Kerala acted as environmental activists also. Far from being the watch dog, the media looked the other way when environmental NGOs surreptitiously tried to enslave it.

The aerial spraying of the pesticide over plantation crops and people falling sick as a result of the spray constituted a romantic concept of the media which was normally starved of such sensitive issues. No doubt, the issue attracted the media from far and wide and even those who contributed to the foreign television pitched their camp in the sprayed area to give it a global splash. Even artists and singers took advantage of the situation. Those mediocre artists and singers craving for fame and recognition tried to attract the media attention by organising music programmes and display of street paintings. Some media activists made documentaries and sent them for award committees. The real intention of such activists was fame and beyond which they never cared for the so-called victims whom they had made the characters in their video films and documentaries. Some of them sold the videos to foreign television companies which telecast the 'horrible plight of the denizens of Kasargod hit by the aerial spray of endosulfan'.

12

SOCIAL IMPACT OF A RUTHLESS CAMPAIGN

The relentless and systematic propaganda carried on by anti-endosulfan activists and the media adversely affected the sprayed villages. The people became panic-stricken due to fears of genetic defects that would be transmitted through generations resulting in mentally and physically challenged offspring. There were people haunted by the phobia that their land, water, soil and air were all polluted because of the hell of a propaganda mindlessly carried on by the activists. The unscientific report by the department of community medicine of the Kozhikode Medical College which was projected by the media to frighten the people added fuel to the fire. Though it constituted the real misery of the people, no media persons, except a few, turned up to report on the fear and panic gripping the villages and the district administration kept a studied silence. It was much more cruel that the plight of the so-called victims of endosulfan.

The newly-married couples became panic-stricken. When married women in the villages became pregnant, they started visiting the hospitals for scanning with many of them eventually opting for terminating the pregnancy. Parents of brides and grooms insisted for blood test to ensure that the prospective brides and grooms did not carry endosulfan residues in their blood. A marriage proposal for a girl, belonging to the Enmakaje gram panchayat was cancelled as the bridegroom insisted that the girl should be subjected to blood test. But the bride's party turned down the suggestion which broke the marriage proposal. There were several instances like this in the sprayed areas.

Fear turned into panic and then into consternation when parents of young girls found it difficult to get suitable matches for their daughters. Parents from educated families outside the sprayed area and in Karnataka gave the whole exposed area a wide berth because of the widespread media coverage of endosulfan poisoning in the blood of the residents. The study by the Centre for Science and Environment heightened the fear as nobody from outside ventured into the sprayed villages seeking marriage alliance. First, the propaganda was confined to the village of Padre and then spread to the entire Enmakaje gram panchayat. But some parents found a solution in the midst of mounting odds against their families. They temporarily settled in the houses of relatives in Karnataka as well as in other non-sprayed areas.

Members of families especially women suffered from social stigma and ostracism. Brides and grooms already proposed to each other backed out from the marriage deal as they feared that the next generation would also be affected by strange diseases. There were cases when parents married off their daughters to relatives when they found it hard to get bridegrooms from outside the villages. Some of the families constructed comfortable houses taking loans from banks expecting that their daughters would get good matches. But the result was rather disappointing.

Mothers panicked and worries became their constant companion if there was any delay in their daughters attaining sexual maturity. The constant refrain of the activists that endosulfan would delay sexual maturity for teenage girls caused them to worry about their growing daughters. Those who had watched the helicopter spraying the pesticide started worrying even when they suffered from slightest fever. According to a doctor working in a sprayed village, patients who visited him would tell at the first consultation itself that they used to watch the helicopter spraying endosulfan. This was to clear the lingering doubt in their mind whether the disease had anything to do with watching the helicopter. All this happened because the activists instilled fear among the whole generation of people about the impending diseases awaiting them. The simple and innocent people of Enmakaje believed the propaganda since the campaign was conducted by educated people, sometimes by doctors who turned into activists. There was no reason to disbelieve them as they were highly respected people in the area. Since the Padre village was a compact society with no floating population, any rumour or propaganda travelled fast triggering panic among the people.

The people of the sprayed villages lost their self-esteem. When they moved to other places from the sprayed areas they introduced themselves as those living outside the sprayed area. They feared that people in non-sprayed areas such as in district headquarters and in big towns would isolate them if they revealed that they belonged to the sprayed areas.

Many of the people were against the propaganda in the beginning since they feared that it would result in their social isolation and they would become pariahs in their own land. But they kept quiet as the propaganda gained momentum fueled by NGOs which planted fraudulent scientific reports in the media on endosulfan pollution in Enmakaje. The miseries of the villagers increased following the declaration of the entire villages as endosulfan affected by the government. But the government failed to supply eco-friendly bio pesticides in the place of chemical pesticides even though it banned all pesticides. This forced the farmers to take recourse to cross-border transportation of pesticides from Karnataka. When the anti-endosulfan campaign reached its peak, the government even banned the copper sulphate which was commonly used to prevent diseases affecting coconut and areca nut trees.

The couples who have deformed children were given a rude shock when their families described the diseases as born out of family curse. The tendency to describe the birth of every deformed child as divine curse was the popular belief among the people. The belief was that the couple having deformed children got just retribution for their past actions and misdeeds. The belief in one's karma in previous births added to the sufferings of the families.

As the campaigns intensified, the villagers conjured up visions of strange diseases stalking them and feared that they would become bed-ridden for the rest of their life. And adding fuel to the fire, the NGOs working in the field conducted propaganda on the deleterious effects of endosulfan in various countries of the world.

A couple in Karadka decided not to have any more children since the second child was also born with hydrocephalus. The first child was born with the same disease, but died after a few years of its birth. The picture of the second child was widely used in the electronic and the print media. The mother of the child belonged to Karnataka, and his father belonged to another non-sprayed village of Kasargod. The distraught father of a deformed child said the belief by members of his ancestral family that he got an invalid child because of divine curse was too much for him to endure.

Rich couples in the sprayed areas frequented the multi-specialty hospitals in Mangalore. Parents from outside the district also made frantic enquiries whether the prospective grooms belonged to the affected villages. A study conducted in the eastern hill areas showed that the marriage proposals from south Kerala to the villages in the eastern areas of Kasargod came down after the endosulfan issue started engaging the media headlines. The villagers in the eastern area were mostly of those who had settled there from south Kerala. The study had highlighted that couples had opted for divorce fearing that their offspring would also develop diseases later. A man in Kanhangad divorced his wife after she gave birth to a deformed child. He suspected that the child was a victim of endosulfan and thought that the people would isolate the family. In several families 'endosulfan poisoning' or the birth of a deformed child was enough reason for the husband to divorce his wife.

As a result of the virulent campaign, mothers were afraid to feed their babies with breast milk since they believed that it contained poison. Even normal children were deprived of breast milk because of the strident campaign by anti-endosulfan agitators. For the sake of foreign money, they unleashed fearful campaigns and the victims happened to be innocent babies whose right to be born on the Mother Earth was taken away by the activists as couples thought it prudent to terminate pregnancies.

But the action committee never came to the help of the so-called victims. No amount was paid to the victims till the government formed the Endosulfan Remedial Cell and prepared a list of the patients through medical camps. Nor did the agitators build up confidence among the families; the purpose of the campaigners was only to create panic and take maximum advantage out of the situation. Surprisingly, even the district administration did not take any confidence building measures to assuage the mental agony of the families.

Even the monthly pension of ₹ 1,000 to 2,000 given to the patients' families created problems. In the families where there were more than three deformed children, there was a steady income of ₹ 6,000 per month. In some cases, the bread winners of the family used to go for work to feed the children. After the pension was sanctioned, parents became lazy and they confined themselves in their houses without doing any work. In some of the families, the heads of the family were alcoholics spending their hard earned income on cheap country liquor creating disquiet and domestic quarrel. Mothers were often blamed for giving birth to disabled children. In some cases, the constant blaming of mothers ended up in divorce. In a society where women played the gender role of looking after their children, fathers very often kept aloof from the responsibility of feeding their children. They sought easy divorce.

There were several families in the sprayed area in which women lived alone with one or two of their disabled children since they were either divorced or deserted by husbands. There were cases in which men who deserted their wives developed live-in relationship with other women without legally divorcing their wives.

Actually it was poverty and malnutrition which caused the diseases. Marriages among blood relatives also created diseases. Among many of the castes and sub-castes in the area, there existed the custom of marrying the blood relatives. Adolescent marriages also led to diseases among teenage mothers and their babies.

Generally, the government did not take any poverty alleviation measures in the sprayed area. Financial help by the government would be given only to those having deformed children who were included in the endosulfan victims' list. But majority of the families lived in poverty and they were made to fend for themselves or survive on their own. Poor families lived in make shift dwellings; there were several houses without latrines and women and grown up girls had no privacy in their homes.

In most of the cases, the money given as compensation by the government to the dependents of the alleged victims was squandered away on liquor. In most cases, a relative who died more than ten years before was rarely mourned. But the amount of ₹ one lakh given as compensation to the families was considered as easy money and it was soon squandered away. A major portion of the compensation was cornered by local political leaders or social workers who helped the families to get the victims included in the endosulfan death list. A social activist said that local political leaders would accompany the postman to the houses of the victims carrying money order of the monthly pension. They collected their commission at the spot itself since it was the local political leaders who helped the families to get the patients enrolled in the endosulfan list.

The anti-endosulfan agitation created social isolation among the people in the villages where the pesticide was sprayed. A vast population was forced to remain isolated from the rest of the society which violated their human rights because of the mindless campaign of the activists. But surprisingly, no human right activists raised their voice against the social stigma suffered by the people in the sprayed area. Anti-endosulfan agitators who created the problem did not stop their ill-motivated campaign. The worst affected were the families of the workers of the plantation corporation who were selectively isolated by the activists with the propaganda that they were really responsible for the diseases in the area.

But the National Human Rights Commission could not think of assuaging the mental agony of the villagers, especially those of the families of the plantation workers. It instilled fear among the people saying that endosulfan incident was next only to the Bhopal gas tragedy. But for the NHRC only the so-called victims of the pesticide spraying had their human rights violated. The propaganda that endosulfan residues would remain in the soil for a long period forced them to dispose their lands at cheap prices.

Following contrived reports of high rate of cancer in the sprayed area, panic-stricken people suspected any disease to be the beginning of cancer. When children suffered from normal headaches, their panic-stricken mothers suspected the symptom to be the beginning of hydrocephalus. Even if a few decided to flee the area they had to do so by selling their property at throw away prices. Irresponsible activism and a fierce propaganda made the people refugees in their own land. School going children in the sprayed areas became dull in grasping lessons as they could not concentrate on their studies.

When the propaganda reached its peak, a group of youths demolished the make shift venue erected by anti-endosulfan activists in Peria. They feared that the propaganda would isolate the villagers and they did not want a repetition of the plight of their counterparts in Enmakaje.

If this kind of propaganda was conducted in any other country the perpetrators would have been hauled before law and landed up in jails. But not in India which is rather lax when it comes to implementing laws. The bureaucrats and the administrators were reluctant to give replies to the questions sent under the Right to Information Act. The legal system, magistracy and the lawyers failed to rise up to the expectation of the people. Propaganda against a community, sect or ethnic groups denying their existence was unlawful. The right to life guaranteed under the constitution of the country was also denied to the people of the sprayed area. The anti-endosulfan activists including the media which created fear among the people were responsible for the isolation of the people.

The land sharks in collaboration with the activists funded and encouraged the agitation. Some unscrupulous elements approached the villagers and convinced them that endosulfan residues would linger in the land for more than one hundred years and tried to negotiate the sale of lands at throw away prices.

The social isolation of the people in the villages became intense as the anti-Endo campaign reached its crescendo in the run up to the POPRC convention in Geneva in April 2011. There was none to tell them after all that it was a high drama played by some NGOs and the district administration in collusion with the media. Citing some scientific reports, a few of them by the State Pollution Control Board, the media reported that the endosulfan residues could be still found in the soil of the exposed area heightening the fears of the people.

Janu Naik, a cancer patient in the endosulfan list committed suicide when he came to know that he would not get the compensation of ₹ 5 lakh ordered by the National Human Rights Commission. The Endosulfan Nodal Cell had pared down the list of the endosulfan victims removing cancer patients from the list. The National Human Rights Commission had ordered the compensation to be paid only for the bed-ridden and the disabled, leaving out cancer patients. Some of the victims in the endosulfan list were expecting compensation from the government which could be used for the marriage of their daughters. They became crestfallen when they came to know that cancer patients were not in the list of the victims eligible for compensation.

The agitation in Kasargod had its fallout in nearby Karnataka villages across the border where endosulfan was used in private cashew plantations. The anti-endosulfan activists in Karnataka contacted their counterparts in Enmakaje and wanted to conduct a joint agitation. The activists in Karnataka were also influenced by some NGOs to start similar agitation there.

However, the Karnataka government constituted a health committee which probed the disease across the border. It was alleged that as many as 15 children in Panaje in Puttur Taluk were blind and it was attributed to the aerial spraying of endosulfan in Perla division of the Plantation Corporation, located 1.5 km from Panaje. But the probe by the health department of the Karnataka government found that there was no link between the aerial spray of the pesticide in Perla division of the plantation corporation and the diseases in Panaje. The prompt action of the Karnataka government saved its people from social isolation unlike what happened in Kasargod villages.

The people in the sprayed area finally formed an organisation to free themselves from the humiliation and insult heaped upon them by the anti-endosulfan activists. The natives wanted an end to the exploitation by land mafias who tried to purchase their lands at cheap prices on the fallacious propaganda that their lands were all polluted with endosulfan residues. They were also keen to get suitable matches for their sons and daughters from outside the sprayed areas. Above all, they wanted to put an end to the hell of a propaganda unleashed by anti-endosulfan activists for the sake of foreign money. They formed an organisation at a meeting held in Perla on May 1, 2013 and demanded that the government address their grievances.

13

DOCTORS UNDER PRESSURE IN PESTICIDE SPRAYED AREA

It was an exercise in futility. The valuable time of officials and so much of government money was spent on medical camps for the suspected patients in the pesticide sprayed areas. The unceasing propaganda by the media and its orchestration by political parties created a situation in which the government found itself in a piquant situation. Wilting under pressure, special medical camps were arranged for the patients in the sprayed areas. Though they were not the 'victims' of endosulfan spray, there was not much opposition from any quarters in holding the medical camps since everyone sympathised with the sick and the infirm. After all, they were patients hit by various diseases.

But the government soon faced a dilemma. Supported by the media, which claimed that there was no border for endosulfan diseases, the number of patients spilled on to the neighbouring district of Kannur as well as to the villages beyond the state border. But medical camps were held only in the sprayed areas despite the media campaign.

Thus, the patients in the sprayed area ultimately benefitted from the medical camps following the long-drawn agitation of the anti-endosulfan votaries while others in non-sprayed areas whose numbers came almost double that of the sprayed areas suffered their agonies in silence. As a result, the patients in the sprayed area got the best medical attention with chronic cases being referred to Mangalore and Pariyaram medical colleges. As several such types of diseases were everywhere in Kasargod, the patients in the sprayed area were more lucky since their problems were attended by the government while others had been left in the lurch.

The CPM ruled District Panchayat which held a Study Congress in 2005 suggested the setting up of a special purpose cell in the district for coordination of the efforts in the field. The CPM apparently wanted to use the endosulfan issue to garner votes during elections. The 'Study Congress' was another exercise in futility since no attempts were made to study whether the patients were the real victims of endosulfan or there were more patients in the non-sprayed areas.

A consultative workshop was held in Kasargod in the first week of August, 2005 with the participation of 'experts in the field', officers of the various departments and social workers. A Vision Document and action plan for intervention in the pesticide sprayed area was prepared in the workshop and submitted to the government. The event was sponsored by some Non-Governmental Organisations though the funds for organising such workshops were given by the government. The organisations exerted pressure on the District Panchayat which was a willing tool in the hands of the NGOs.

However, specialty medical camps were conducted from December 2010 to January 2011 in all 11 gram panachayats where the pesticide was sprayed, as part of the phase one camp. As many as 17 medical camps were held in the sprayed area attended by 125 specialist doctors from government medical colleges and 175 doctors from the state health service department.

As many as 15,698 persons attended the camps and 3,434 patients were identified as suspected 'victims' of endosulfan. People from 36 gram panchayats participated in the medical camps including 11 gram panchayats where pesticide was sprayed, according to government records produced in the Kerala High Court.

At the phase two camp, 738 patients attended the specialty camps and 257 of them were identified as suspected 'victims' of endosulfan. This along with the already identified 3,434 patients and others 'through field verification by medical officers and para medical staff' were added taking the final tally of suspected patients to 4,182.

However, in the third phase specialists from medical colleges examined the cases screened by doctors at the Public Health Centres, PHC, as well as at the Community Health Centres, CHCs. The total number of patients screened in phase three camps were 3,692 and this together with the patients at the phase four camp had not been included in the total list of the 'suspected victims'. But the government records presented at the court did not either specify the number of patients who were screened at the phase four camp.

Looking back, one could see the sheer waste of money and the efforts of the officials and their lack of forethought on the issue. A number of government vehicles were pressed into service to ferry the officials to conduct meetings and medical camps. Significantly, the list of 4,182 patients in 11 sprayed gram panchayats prepared with such hectic efforts after several medical camps were re-categorised to just 1,613 persons in October 2012.

The report of the medical camps was sent by the District Collector to the Executive Director of the Social Security Mission in the state capital. Though the District Collector had informed the Social Security Mission that the list containing the names of 4,182 persons with personal and disease details was sent, such details of diseases were deliberately deleted from the list. It was a bogus list since the doctors who attended the camp could not certify that as many as 4,182 persons were the victims of endosulfan spray. The details regarding the diseases were deliberately withheld from the total list of the victims.

Most of the addresses of the patients were mentioned as 'changed' in the remarks column of the report indicating 'address changed'. The pesticide industry which obtained the list under the Right to Information Act questioned the fraudulent list, but there was no response from the District Collector and the Social Security Mission. Though the families of the victims were contacted in the telephone numbers provided in the list, they said there was no change in their residential address and were still residing in the same premises.

The details of patients prepared by the Endosulfan Cell appeared bogus since it contained several names recommended by local political leaders. The LDF and the UDF Governments gave away a total of ₹ one lakh each to the dependents of the dead without any post mortem report and medical certificates. What was needed was only the oral version of the local political leaders or a newspaper report carrying the death report.

The bogus patients belonged to non-sprayed areas also. According to the families of the patients, the diseased persons had stayed in the sprayed area at the time of the endosulfan spray, but later changed their residence to no-sprayed areas. This was the reason why the final column in the patients' list carried the remark 'address changed'. But the Endosulfan Nodal Cell had not collected any details about their stay in the sprayed area—not even the details of the ration card or the taxes they had paid to the local bodies. The whole list appeared bogus since the officials of the Endosulfan Nodal Cell and the district administration connived with the anti-endosulfan agitators while preparing the list.

Parents of an eight-year old girl rejected the monthly amount of ₹ 2,000 given to the family. Nandana who was suffering from periodic crack of skin on her heels had attended the endosulfan patients' camp held in Cheemeni. Her father Chandran was surprised to receive ₹ 10,000 from the government. Although he received the money, he did not know why the amount was sent. It was then that he realised that his daughter's name had been included in the endosulfan patients' list (Serial No. 2658) in Kodombelur gram panchayat, a non-sprayed area. Later, Nandana recovered from the crack on her heels and she started going to school. Her family did not want her name to be permanently included in the endosulfan list because of the stigma attached to such diseases. The family got the amount through money order of ₹ 2,000 in the first month.

Though the parents returned the money order, the same amount was sent the next month also. They rejected the amount, but surprisingly, the family got the amount for the third time. Then the parents of Nandana informed the authorities in writing to delete her name from the endosulfan list. Though there were no plantations in Kodom Bellur gram pachayat and, therefore, no endosulfan spray, as many as 89 persons in the gram panchayat were getting regular monthly doles. Since it was a CPM stronghold, there had been strong political pressure to include the gram panchayat in the endosulfan list.

The monthly pension to the patients was paid from the government exchequer squandering public money. The plantation corporation was forced to give ₹ 5 crore to help the patients in 2010 during the rule of the Left Democratic Front led by the CPM. The PCK Protection Council managed to get a copy of the beneficiaries of free ration from a civil supply outlet in Muliyar. The diseases as entered in the list were rather funny; there were patients who suffered from tooth ache, skin diseases, vision problem and other silly diseases and yet they were getting free ration and monthly doles.

The Plantation Corporation Protection Council obtained the list of persons who allegedly died due to the aerial spray of endosulfan. Those who died some years before the officials prepared the list were posthumously described as victims of endosulfan and their names were added to the list. Those who died in motor accidents were described as victims of endosulfan and a total of ₹ one lakh was given to the family. The government had given a total of ₹ one lakh each (₹ 50,000 each given by both the LDF and the UDF governments) to the families of the 734 persons who reportedly died following the aerial spray of endosulfan. The number of endosulfan deaths steadily increased as patients included in the list were dying frequently.

In many cases the date of death of the victims was not mentioned and even then relief was granted to the next of kin of the dead. There were complaints that the compensation was given not to the real dependents of the victims. Though the Endosulfan Nodal Cell was asked to give a copy of the death register of the victims, the terse reply received was that there is no death register. Endosulfan death list appeared highly false since nobody had died of the use of the pesticide. It was all a fictitious story; those who died due to heavy drinking of alcohol were all included in the list. Similarly, those who died of cancer due to the excessive use of tobacco were also in the list. Now there was no natural death in the sprayed area since everyone who died was described as a victim of endosulfan.

It was the CPM led district panchayat which started preparing the death list. The details of the death were collected separately by various government departments. The Endosulfan Nodal Cell had claimed that the list was scrutinised by a joint meeting of the officials of various departments and the deceased were identified at the meetings.

There were so many unanswered questions. How the officials certified that a victim had died because of endosulfan spray in the absence of any medical proof? No post-mortem of the victims was ever conducted and there were no medical certificates either showing that the victims had died because of the endosulfan spray.

The Endosulfan Nodal Cell could at first identify only 400 victims when the question of paying compensation to the next of kin of the victims came up for implementing the recommendations of the National Human Rights Commission. The nodal cell could not find nearly half of the next of kin of the deceased. Then who received the payment of ₹ 50,000 each announced by both the LDF and the UDF government?

But the government version as submitted in the High Court said that there was transparency in preparing the death list of the victims. In 2006, it was the district panchayat which initiated the process of preparing the list of those who died in the endosulfan sprayed area and that of their dependents. The district panchayat convened a meeting of officials of the departments of health, social welfare, agriculture and local bodies. The lists of victims separately collected by various departments were consolidated at the joint meeting of the officials. As many as 133 deceased were identified at the meeting and ₹ 50,000 each was given to their dependents from the Chief Minister's Distress Relief Fund.

During 2007-08, the district panchayat president convened the meetings of heads of different government departments to identify the deceased. The process was the same as initiated in 2006 also. But the health department objected to the preparation of the victims' list by the district panchayat, a civic body ruled by the CPM. The District Medical Officer of Health prepared the new list and sent it to the District Collector. Later, ₹ 50,000 each was given to the dependents of 45 victims from a list of 353 persons. In 2011, the UDF government decided to give ₹ 50,000 each to the families of victims and for this all the lists were consolidated.

Those families who were already given ₹ 50,000 each during the LDF rule was given the additional amount of ₹ 50,000 by the UDF government taking the total compensation to ₹ one lakh each. The families of the so-called victims were given ₹ one lakh each in August 2013 as part of implementing the recommendations of the National Human Rights Commission which ordered a total of compensation of ₹ 5 lakh each to the 'endosulfan victims'.

However, endosulfan patients' list was prepared by the district panchayat during 2006-07 and 2008. The list contained the names of persons in CPM families triggering allegations of nepotism. The patients' list was prepared from an earlier list prepared by the district panchayat which contained several persons who suffered from silly diseases.

The endosulfan medical camps were held only from December 2010 to January 2012 and out of which a list of 4,182 patients was compiled. But the patients' list was prepared even before conducting medical camps to identity them. The officials were at pains to explain this incongruity since the list included the names of those given by local political leaders.

The death lists obtained by the Plantation Corporation Protection Council carried several 'surprises'. Those who died in their ripe old age were described as endosulfan victims. For instance, Keshavan Namboodiri in Puliyanur in Kayyur-Cheemeni gram panchayat (Serial No. 49) died on October 2, 2011 at the age of 94. Kesavan Namboodiri lived up to the ripe old age though he was an alleged victim of endosulfan when even healthy people could not live up to the age of 94; Kunhikrishan Agasa of Bithody in Bellur died on September 16, 2011 at 85 (Serial No. 44); Nagamma of Enmakaje died on September 29, 2011 at the age of 93 (Serial No. 46). There were several persons in the list who died between 70 and 90.

What were the diseases from which the endosulfan victims suffered which led to their death ? Seventy two year old Mutha (Serial No. 37) in Enmakaje gram panchayat died because of cataract. But eighty-year-old Chana (Serial No. 189) of Kallar gram panchayat died on November 9, 2009 due to 'general weakness' ! According to the affidavit filed by the government in the High Court, each and every death was subjected to 'death audit' by a committee of government officials!

Strangely, a new disease not in the medical dictionary and not recognised by modern medicine, however, emerged in Kasargod—'endosulfan disease'. It was a word coined by the Endosulfan Nodal Cell and the media. The medical camp held for the victims in Badiadka in January 2011 turned out to be a sham following the heavy turnout of patients.

Hundreds of patients attended the camp. But each patient was examined within a few minutes. Each discipline of medicine such as neurology, orthopedics, ENT, dermatology, ophthalmology, gynecology and surgery was headed by an Assistant Professor and three medical students studying for their first year Post Graduate course.

The number of patients who attended the gynecological camp was far below other categories. The patients were mainly drawn from four gram panchayats including Enmakaje where the aerial spraying had reportedly wrought more havoc. The media and the anti-endosulfan activists had described that gynecological problems were more acute in the sprayed areas, but the number of women who attended the gynecological camp was below 80.

Nevertheless, reproductive health events were found significantly higher in the affected areas according to a paper on 'gender and sociological concerns in the endosulfan affected area' prepared by Dr A.K. Jayasree, professor of community medicine at the Pariyaram Medical College, Kannur, for the National Workshop on Rehabilitation of Endosulfan Victims.

According to the paper, 'the reproductive health events including infertility, precocious puberty, abortion, intra uterine death, neo natal child birth and genitor urinary disorders are found significantly higher in this population when compared to other affected areas. In adolescent population, reproductive disorders are higher. There is history of menstrual irregularities for girls, more reported before ban on endosulfan'.

But media persons who visited Badiadka medical camp could find that doctors were sitting idle at the gynecological section of the medical camp chatting to their colleagues while other sections witnessed large number of patients. If there had been serious gynecological problems among women in the pesticide sprayed area, the medical camp would have been crowded with women and young girls especially because the medical camp was held for patients drawn from four gram panchayats.

Most of the elder persons who had eye problems had come there in large numbers. Several patients with mouth cancer queued up before the cancer counter. However, the doctors remained tight-lipped when asked about the parameters they used in categorising suspected endosulfan patients. They remained silent on the questions of media persons since no specific guidelines were issued by the authorities. According to doctors, there was no clinical, biochemical or other criteria for diagnosing a patient as endosulfan victim. Dr Mohammed Asheel, Assistant Nodal Officer of the Endosulfan Victims Relief and Remedial Cell had admitted that no guidelines were issued by the Government. So the list of 4,182 patients were categorised as endosulfan victims without even a guideline!

The doctors in the Public Health Centres were asked to conduct preliminary screening of patients. In the absence of any clear cut guidelines, doctors found it hard to classify the patients. Doctors at the medical camps were also hit by the lack of back up facilities since the camps were held in schools which lacked even the basic facilities.

The Kerala Government Medical Officers' Association, KGMOA, demanded that the Government should issue a guideline for doctors regarding the diseases to be categorised as endosulfan diseases. Dr M. Muralidharan, state secretary of the KGMOA said that government doctors working in the sprayed area were facing a dilemma in the absence of such a guideline.

Dr Muralidharan said that doctors were compelled to recommend even diseases such as piles, polio, diarrhea, scabies, traumatic amputation, mongolism and even cataract as endosulfan related disorders. Citing an instance, he said a polio patient was brought to a PHC by social workers and local political workers. The duty doctor told them that the child was hit by polio, but the doctor was threatened and the patient had to be referred to the medical camp. He said doctors were forced to work against medical ethics and morality. Since all patients in the sprayed area were classified as endosulfan victims, they were getting a monthly amount of ₹ 1,000 to ₹ 2,000 each.

The media persons and newspapers had no compunction in describing even ordinary deaths as caused by endosulfan. The age of the patients in the report would be given as 60 or 70 and it would say that the victims suffered from the disease by birth which meant that they suffered from congenital diseases. Endosulfan was started spraying only in the late 70s and it was stopped around 2000 after 20 years of spray. It meant that the 'victims' were born with genetic defects even before the aerial spray of the pesticide started in the area.

Government doctors in the sprayed villages faced acute pressure from patients suffering from various diseases. They insisted that they be included in the patients' list. Patients with chronic ailments beseeched the doctors to include them in the endosulfan list. Doctors faced the dilemma since the Endosulfan Nodal Cell added as many as 300 diseases in the endosulfan category. Bronchial asthma which is common in any population was included in the endosulfan list. Similarly, chronic obstructive pulmonary disease, commonly found in smokers, too, was in the list.

Further, various types of connective tissue disorders like rheumatoid arthritis, osteoarthritis which were common in any population were also included in the list. Besides, different types of joint pain, chronic skin disorders like eczema, various fungal infections and decreased vision due to refractive errors also found in the long list of endosulfan diseases. Again, dementia and the Alzheimer's disease which were common in the age group above 60 were also listed as endosulfan diseases.

Menstrual irregularities, mental retardation, cerebral palsy, peripheral neuropathy, vertigo, uterine fibroid, varicose vein and even head ache such as migraine were included in the 300 types of diseases in the list. Besides, all types of cancers were also there in the endosulfan list. Thus, all diseases which were found common in any population were included in the list with the result that the number of patients burgeoned to more than 6,000.

According to doctors working in the pesticide sprayed area, about 2,000—3,000 persons applied for entry in the endosulfan list. About one lakh persons suffering from the 300 odd types of diseases made a clamour to get entry into the coveted endosulfan list. Once their names were included in the list, a steady income of ₹ 1,000 to ₹ 2,000 per month was assured for them from the government exchequer. Who was responsible for squandering government money? The culprits were nothing but the anti-endosulfan activists and officials in the Endosulfan Cell who colluded with NGOs like Thanal.

As a result of the waywardness of the officials of the Endosulfan Nodal Cell and the district administration, the government faced a dilemma following the directive by the National Human Rights Commission to pay compensation of ₹ 5 lakh each to the deceased and the same amount to the bed-ridden patients. If ₹ 5 lakh each was to be paid to the so-called victims, the government had to shell out ₹ 38 crore to pay the compensation as the number of victims crossed more than 700.

According to Dr Mohammed Asheel, Endosulfan Assistant Nodal Officer, no doctor can certify that a patient was hit by endosulfan spray since there was no proof. The word that can only be used was suspected victim of endosulfan spray. The District Medical Officer also expressed the same opinion. He said that no doctor can certify that the diseases were caused by the pesticide effect in the absence of any proof. He said it was a team of doctors from the Kozhikode Medical College who decided whether a person was an 'endosulfan patient' or not. Classifying a person as an endosulfan patient was very easy. The doctor has only to tick the column which said 'whether the patient was a victim of endosulfan or not'.

It was the Endosulfan Nodal Cell which was responsible for classifying 300 types of diseases, most of them being common diseases, as having been caused by endosulfan. It was rather strange to say that the aerial spraying of a pesticide caused 300 types of diseases, and that too twice a year, with a limited quantity of 1.37 litre per hectare ! It may be a world record of sorts.

The Nodal Cell officials had confessed to media persons that in the initial stage persons suffering from common diseases such as hearing loss, epilepsy, ear ache, jaundice, depression and strangely even amputees were included in the patients' list.

But questions on how the doctors classified whether a person was an endosulfan 'victim', asked under the Right to Information Act, brought only vague answers. What were the clinical parameters used to determine whether a patient was an endosulfan victim or not? The expert doctors of the medical colleges in the state who attended the camp had no answer.

But doctors working in the sprayed areas complained to the district authorities that the Endosulfan Cell was dominated by vested interests and that it was not taking them into confidence. Doctors working in the rural areas complained that the district officials have not been inviting them to the meetings where crucial decisions had been taken and refused to hear what they had to say on the issue. Doctors in the pesticide sprayed rural areas said the Endosulfan Cell was not taking any confidence building measures and instead it was adding to the worries of the people by including more diseases in the list. Doctors complained that as a result the people lived in perpetual panic.

Doctors who worked in the endosulfan sprayed villages said medical camps had been held in the area after the controversy attracted the media limelight. But the patients who attended the camps in the beginning were limited in numbers. None of them were the victims of endosulfan, but they suffered from ordinary diseases. When medical camps were held at their door steps, several patients availed the opportunity of free medical care. But now people were vying with each other to attend the camps because of the monetary benefits they would get when included in the coveted endosulfan list.

There were doctors who toed the political line. If the policy of the government was that there were so many endosulfan patients in the area, they had no alternative but to support the official view. They feared disciplinary action such as punishment transfer or suspension from service.

But there were doctors who revealed the truth. According to them, the diseases such as hydrocephalus, cerebral palsy, cancer and such other diseases were not abnormal in the district over and above the national or state average.

A team of doctors of the Indian Council of Medical Research had held discussions with the doctors working in the sprayed area in Kasargod before the Stockholm convention. Doctors from the sprayed area told the ICMR team that they found no unusual diseases in the area. The diseases were the same as those prevailed in other non-sprayed districts where some of the doctors had worked previously, they said. But the higher district officials pulled up the doctors who said at the meeting that they found only ordinary diseases in the sprayed area which can be found anywhere in the state.

Following the 36-day long fast organised by the Endosulfan Peeditha Janakeeya Munnani, EPJM, in Kasargod town in February 2013, the government had agreed to hold a series of medical camps for the so-called endosulfan patients. One of the demands of the action committee was to conduct fresh medical camps to identify the victims living in other parts of the districts 'who had been staying in the affected area while endosulfan was aerially sprayed for 20 years'. Thus, four medical camps were held in different places from August 22 to 25, 2013.

There was an influx of patients at the medical camps as their numbers crossed more than 6,000. People suffering from even silly diseases thronged the venue of the medical camps. The Endosulfan Nodal Cell had arranged ambulances and vehicles to ferry the bed-ridden to the camp. Experts from all medical colleges in the state examined the patients at the medical camps.

Interestingly, patients from Mogral Puthur gram panchayat, a non-sprayed area, where there were large number of patients than those found in the pesticide sprayed villages also attended the medical camps. There was demand from political parties to consider the patients in Mogral Puthur similar to those in the sprayed areas. So the patients of Mogral Puthur—located on the coastline where there was no cashew plantation and, therefore, no pesticide spray—were finally approved as those hit by endosulfan.

14

NHRC INITIATES SUO MOTU CASE

The National Human Rights Commission, NHRC, initiated a *suo motu* action on the basis of a report published in the *India Today* magazine in its issue dated July 23, 2001 captioned 'spray of misery'. The report related to the sufferings of the people of Swarga in Kasargod district in North Kerala following the aerial spraying of endosulfan for 20 long years from early 1980s. However, the report lacked credibility since it failed to prove authentically that the diseases were really caused by the aerial spray of endosulfan.

However, on April 25, 2005 the NHRC took the significant decision to close the case it had taken suo motu on the basis of the *India Today* report since proceedings were pending in the Kerala High Court. The Commission said 'since the proceedings are pending in the High Court of Kerala concerning the same issue and the matter being sub-judice, no further action is needed to be taken by the Commission at this stage. The case is closed accordingly'.

Though the National Human Rights Commission had closed its proceedings, it once again initiated suo motu action on the basis of another media report. This time it based its action on the report "Crippled Kerala villagers crying for Endosulfan ban" published in *Hindustan Times* on November 11, 2010. The NHRC said in its website that the Commission took the suo motu cognisance of the media report alleging that the aerial spraying of endosulfan was still being continued in the area. The suo motu petition was based on the factually incorrect report which stated that 'aerial spraying of endosulfan was still being used in the area'.

The NHRC chaired by Justice K.G. Balakrishnan, however, failed to note the old files of the Commission which had closed and 'weeded out' the case since it was sub-judice. The revival of the case by the NHRC was against the Human Rights Act. According to the Human Rights Act 1993, the Commission 'shall not inquire into any matter after the expiry of one year from the date on which an act violating the human rights was alleged to have been committed'.

The NHRC held its sitting for a day in December 2010 in Kasargod and interviewed the parents of some suspected victims at the Collectorate Hall. In fact, the Commission spent very little time and visited only a few houses in the sprayed area. The Commission told the media that the aerial spraying of endosulfan had seriously affected the health of the people and they needed compensation, asserting that it was a grave problem on the lines of the Bhopal gas tragedy.

Justice K.G. Balakrishnan, Chairperson of the NHRC stated in its proceedings. ' In 2001, taking cognizance of reports in the media that the aerial spraying of endosulfan in the district of Kasargod in Kerala had led to severe health hazards, the Commission asked the Indian Council of Medical Research for a report which was submitted in July 2002 by one of its constituent institutions, the National Institute of Occupational Health after a thorough environment epidemiological study, conducted to rigorous scientific standards, and which took into account earlier investigations and surveys'.

The NIOH study had said that there was significantly higher prevalence of neurobehavioural disorders, congenital malformations in female subjects and abnormalities related to male productive system in the study group (Padre village, Enmakaje panchayat) as compared to the reference group (Miyapadavu village of Meenja panchayat).

The report found that the two groups differed mainly with respect to aerial spray of endosulfan. Therefore, the most probable cause for the problems in the study area could be relatively high and continued exposure to endosulfan through various environmental media such as food, water, soil and air.

The Commission held that the possibility of the disruptive effect of endosulfan observed in the study had great relevance to the health of the future generations. It suggested that considering the potentiality of the grave consequence, the Principle 15 of the Rio declaration of the Earth Summit should be followed. This related to the precautionary principle and emphasised that lack of scientific certainty was no reason to postpone action to avoid potentially serious harm.

The Commission strongly criticised the Union Government for its claim that there was no scientific basis for the action recommended by the experts of the Stockholm Convention for the ban already imposed by other nations.

'The Commission is at a loss to understand the logic of this stand. The countries that have banned endosulfan are those that have access to the most advanced scientific research. They included the US, the EU, Japan, the Republic of Korea, Australia and New Zealand which had taken their decision on the basis of scientific data and studies', the Commission observed.

The Commission said 'the Government of India indeed have independent but similar scientific evidence. The comprehensive scientific study carried out by the NIOH confirmed well before this was accepted in some other countries that have now imposed a ban that endosulfan has serious and long term effects on health and on the environment. When it claims a lack of scientific evidence, the Government of India is either being disingenuous or disowning the work of the premier institute of medical research that it has set up'.

The Commission further said 'Its directives to the ICMR to review the study means that the Government finds its conclusions inconvenient. The Commission is as deeply troubled by the implications of this stand as by the consequences it has already had on human rights in India and quite possibly in other countries to which Indian companies have exported endosulfan.'

The NHRC reiterated that the present stand of the government has led and would continue to lead to grave violations of human rights. Since endosulfan was a persistent organic pollutant, the dangers it posed would linger and multiply through the generations, causing harm on a scale that cannot presently be fully quantified.

Taking cognisance of fresh reports received in November 2010, the Commission sent a team of its officers to Kasargod to conduct an independent investigation. This team of officials were not scientists, but according to the NHRC, the team confirmed a continued high incidence of medical disorders recorded by the NIOH. But the NHRC solely depended on the NIOH report demanding ban on endosulfan. The NHRC stated in its proceedings that the comprehensive scientific study carried out by the NIOH confirmed that endosulfan has serious and long term effects on health and on the environment. The NHRC, therefore, recommended to the Union Government to take administrative and legislative action to ban the use of endosulfan all over the country.

The NHRC directed the state government to pay at least ₹ five lakh to the next of kin of those who died and those who were fully bed-ridden or unable to move without help as well as to the mentally retarded. The Commission recommended ₹ three lakh to the other disabled persons. 'A panel of doctors should assess the extent of physical disability to classify the category of victims. The Union government should give adequate financial help to the State government', it said.

The NHRC also wanted a survey of other populations that might also have been affected by the use of endosulfan including Palakkad where there were reports of similar problems faced by villagers. The Commission called for increase in the quantum of relief and rehabilitation for the victims and their families and that it was paid regularly and in full. The NHRC also wanted the government to improve the facilities for diagnosis, treatment and therapy available at hospitals and health centres that tend to the victims while ensuring that one of them was equipped and staffed to offer advanced care. All Primary Health Centres in the eleven villages which were seriously affected should be upgraded to Community Health Centres. The Commission directed the government to implement its recommendations within eight weeks.

Though the NHRC had recommended to the Union Government that it should take administrative and legislative action to ban endosulfan, the government did not take any steps though the Commission issued the directive as early as December 31, 2010. But endosulfan was temporarily banned in the country by the Supreme Court on May 13, 2011 following a writ petition filed by the Democratic Youth Federation of India, DYFI, youth organisation of the Communist Party of India (Marxist).

Another recommendation of the NHRC to the Union Government was to conduct a nation-wide survey of population that have been affected by the use of endosulfan, particularly sprayed from air, to determine the scope of relief and rehabilitation that may be needed. This survey was not conducted by the government.

The NHRC also directed the Union government to supplement the efforts of the government of Kerala and of other State governments where victims of endosulfan use could be found in order to provide them relief and rehabilitation .

Another suggestion of the Commission was to start a palliative care centre or hospital in the district for the treatment and rehabilitation for the victims. The Commission said 'As the victims are in large number of about six thousand in a small locality of eleven villages-namely, Kayyur-Cheemeni, Ajanur, Pullur-Periya, Kallar, Panathady, Muliyar, Karadka, Kumbadaje, Badiadka, Bellur and Enmakaje, a

Centrally sponsored Palliative Care Centre should be established for Kasargod district and effective ambulance services be provided to all physically handicapped or mentally retarded victims with adequate trained staff. The state government should render all help to establish the said Palliative Care Centre or Hospital'.

However, the 'small eleven villages' which the Commission had mentioned were actually gram panchayats with a total population of 2.95 lakh and they were not small villages. Though the Commission had said that there were about six thousand victims in a small locality of eleven villages, the State government whittled down the list of the total endosulfan victims of 4,182 to just 1,613 in November 2012 after scrutinising the list with the help of medical officers and gram panchayat authorities.

But most of the recommendation of the NHRC to the State government also remained unimplemented which included the conduct of a survey of other populations in the state that might also have been affected by the use of endosulfan including Palakkad.

However, the Pesticide Manufacturers and Formulators Association of India, PMFAI, filed a petition in the Kerala High Court challenging the directions of the National Human Rights Commission. When the case came up before the High Court it ordered that the case be posted along with similar cases on the subject.

The PMFAI said the National Human Rights Commission depended heavily on the report of the National Institute of Occupational Health, NIOH, which allegedly falsified the scientific data. The pesticide industry obtained the data under the Right to Information Act. Further, the two expert committees appointed by the Union government to review the NIOH report had found inadequacies and various flaws in the report.

'The Commission report had made it clear that it had appointed a core group of health personnel in December 2010 and it had unanimously expressed the view that endosulfan should be banned in India. But there was no reference in the Commission report about the names of the members and their expertise or the terms of reference given to the core group. Moreover, the Commission's report skipped any reference on the core group or it was discreetly silent on the earlier intervention of the Commission on the same issue which was subsequently closed and weeded out since it found the matter sub-judice', said the PMFAI.

The petitioner stated that the Protection of Human Rights Act 1993 defined human rights as the rights relating to life, liberty, equality and dignity of the individual guaranteed by the Constitution or which embodied in the international covenants and enforceable by courts in India.

According to the PMFAI, the mandate of the National Human Rights Commission was limited by the rights enshrined in the Constitution of the country and it has no mandate to advise or recommend on international trade and conventions. The NHRC should have taken cognisance of the expert committee report chaired by Dr Dubey which had reviewed the NIOH report. The NHRC should have sought explanation from the NIOH scientists.

A scientific report considered by the Commission should be of impeccable scientific integrity. But the report produced by the NIOH and solely relied upon by the Commission was scientifically erroneous and falsified, said the PMFAI.

Since two writ petitions were then pending before the Kerala High Court, the NHRC report was very much sub-judice. Besides, the Kerala Human Rights Commission had also taken up the matter of unusual diseases in Padre village and as per rules the NHRC cannot inquire into any issues pending before the State Human Right Commission. But the NHRC kept a studied silence on the issue which was earlier taken up by the Kerala State Human Rights Commission.

The Commission had served notices to the secretary of the ministry of environment and forest, ministry of agriculture as well as to the Chief Secretary of the State. But the Commission report did not make any reference about the response from the recipients of the notices. 'The Commission's report was unlawful, arbitrary, without jurisdiction and, therefore, not maintainable', the PMFAI said in its writ petition to the Kerala High Court.

The PMFAI submitted in the High Court that endosulfan was not responsible for causing public health problems in a few villages in Kasargod as alleged by environmental NGOs. It said that the International Agency for Research on Cancer, IARC, under World Health Organisation had not listed endosulfan as a cancer causing substance. The US Environmental Protection Agency, US-EPA, had also found that endosulfan was not a cancer causing substance.

The association said that diseases attributed to endosulfan in the sprayed area were also found in the non-sprayed villages located far away from the sprayed areas. Therefore, the alleged diseases in some villages in Kasargod would not be addressed by taking recourse to regulatory action as ill-advised by the Commission.

As per the procedures, the NHRC should have taken evidence from the pesticide manufacturers who were affected by the action of the Commission. In other words, the Commissions enquiry was not inclusive, did not pass the test of equality, fairness and natural justice. Though the Commission was informed about the errors and flaws in the NIOH report more than a month before it produced the report, the NHRC failed to acknowledge and respond to the letter. The Commission held a sitting at the Kasargod Collectorate in December 2010 without even informing the various stake holders and totally ignoring the past procedures of the Commission.

The PMFAI urged the Commission to withdraw its report dated December 31, 2010. It also sent a copy of the submission to the Prime Minister, Union Ministry of Health and Family Affairs, minister of Environment and Forest, Ministry of Law as well as to government of Kerala.

But the National Human Rights Commission did not file any response petition in the High Court. Though the Kerala government had also been given a copy of the submission, it demanded a huge amount from the Plantation Corporation of Kerala to pay compensation to the alleged victims of endosulfan.

According to the counter affidavit filed by the State government in the High Court in February 2013 in response to a writ petition filed by the Plantation Corporation Protection Council, the government admitted that it required ₹250 crore for fully implementing the NHRC recommendations. Besides, it needed ₹ 235. 33 crore to set up more relief and rehabilitation centres for the victims. Thus, a total amount of ₹ 485.33 was required to meet the expenses.

The State government then made three proposals to the Union Government to fully implement the rehabilitation package as well as compensation to the victims. The government on March 23, 2011 sent a letter to the Joint Secretary, Union Ministry of Health and Family Welfare. Another proposal was made to Prime Minister Manmohan Singh on April 22, 2011 by an all party delegation from Kerala. Chief Minister Oommen Chandy also made a proposal before the Prime Minister seeking help for the victims. Meanwhile, the principle secretary (Health) of the state government made a new proposal to the Union government on August 1, 2011.

However, the Union government was not in a mood to oblige the State government. The State government again sent a letter on August 8, 2011 to Gulam Nabi Azad, the Union Minister for Health and Family Welfare for an assistance of ₹ 485.33 crore. The Union government, however, informed the NHRC that 'there was no scheme under which it can pay to support the compensation and that it was the responsibility of the State government'.

Meanwhile, the state cabinet took a decision on May 18, 2011 to implement the proposal of the National Human Rights Commission. In pursuant to this, the principal secretary of the Health and Family Welfare attended a review committee meet of the National Human Rights Commission on August 26, 2011 regarding the issue of the rehabilitation of the victims. Though the representative of the State government tried to convince the NHRC of the efforts already taken by the government to rehabilitate the victims, the Commission sharply pointed out the failure of the State government in implementing the directives of the NHRC.

The NHRC said that it fixed a low amount to the victims compared to the rate of compensation awarded by the courts. The NHRC pointed out that since the pesticide was sprayed by a government owned company, the refusal of the State government to pay the compensation was unacceptable and the government was bound to implement it. The NHRC also cautioned that if its order was not complied with within four weeks, the matter would be referred to the Supreme Court. The State government then approached the NHRC seeking more time and requested the Union Government for financial help.

Meanwhile, the NHRC asked the State government to submit explanation for non-compliance of its order by December 13, 2011. The state government requested the NHRC to grant two month's time to implement its decision. Subsequently, the NHRC extended the time up to March 13, 2012.

However, as per a decision on January 12, 2012, the government decided to give ₹ three lakh in two instalments of ₹ 1.50 lakh each to the bed-ridden patients. The first instalment would be given with the money that the Plantation Corporation of Kerala would give before March 31, 2012 and the next instalment by the State government after providing sufficient budget allocation in the next financial year ending March 2013. (But there was no budgetary provision in the 2013 budget to pay compensation to the so-called endosulfan victims). The balance of ₹ two lakh would be considered as deposit and the interest of ₹ 2,000 accrued for five years would be given to the victims every month as pension. The fixed deposit in the name of the victims would be returned to them at the end of five years. The government also took the decision to pay a total ₹ three lakh each to the disabled persons.

Though the director board of the Plantation Corporation affirmed that it would fulfill its social obligation, it however, sought the help of the government in paying the amount. On the basis of a meeting held by the managing director of the PCK with the Chief Minister and the minister for agriculture, the state cabinet took the decision on February 2, 2012 to exempt the Plantation Corporation from the liability of paying the compensation.

In the meantime, the NHRC informed the State government in a letter on April 26, 2012 that if its order was not implemented by June 4, 2012 it would summon the Chief Secretary before the Commission on June 6, 2012. Thus, driven to the wall, a state cabinet meet on May 24, 2012 decided to fully implement the NHRC recommendations. The director board of the Plantation Corporation was forced to take a decision to disburse an amount of ₹ 27 crore to the government by crediting the amount to the account of the District Collector, Kasargod, by June 4, 2012 based on the cabinet recommendations.

Since the government order covered only the bed-ridden persons, it however decided to give ₹ five lakh each to the families of the deceased also. An amount of ₹ 20.88 crore was then given to 1,602 victims and another ₹ six crore was deposited in the names of next of kin of the deceased, numbering 400, to implement the direction of the National Human Rights Commission.

15

DUBEY PANEL FLAYS NIOH REPORT

The National Human Rights Commission asked the Indian Council of Medical Research to conduct an epidemiological study relating to the alleged diseases in some Kasargod villages following the aerial spray of endosulfan. The ICMR, in turn, directed the National Institute of Occupation Health, NIOH, to conduct the epidemiological study. The NIOH submitted its report to the government in two phases in December 2001 and January 2002.

Dr O.P. Dubey, the then Assistant Director General (Plant Protection) of the Indian Council of Agriculture Research, ICAR, was directed by the Union Government to review the epidemiological report of the National Institute of Occupational Health. The expert group chaired by Dr O.P. Dubey visited Kasargod on two occasions. It invited experts for peer review of the NIOH report and the residue data. It received valuable data from the Kerala Agricultural University. The District Medical Officer of Health in Kasargod provided data on health of local population.

The Dubey committee which held its sittings in Kasargod flayed the media for publishing pictures of the alleged pesticide victims. The pictures were used by the print and the electronic media without verifying the truth. The committee lashed out at the newspapers which repeatedly published the picture of a girl hit by hydrocephalus claiming that she was a victim of endosulfan. The Dubey committee held that hydrocephalus was not associated with the spraying of endosulfan.

The workers of the Plantation Corporation of Kerala, PCK, also testified before the Dubey committee. They told the committee that they were healthy even though they were exposed to the pesticide by preparing its compound for aerial spray. The PCK workers told the committee that they did not even take any precaution while handling the pesticide by covering their face or wearing gloves.

But the media alleged that the workers were ferried in vehicles by the PCK management to depose before the commission. The media reports said that the PCK even ferried its workers from Mannarkkat in Palakkad district where endosulfan was aerially sprayed for several years.

The Dubey committee studied the use of endosulfan in PCK plantations covering about 4,696 hectare in 20 villages. The committee also examined the details furnished by the Plantation Corporation as to the methods adopted for using endosulfan. The Dubey committee blamed the PCK after detailed hearing of its officials that it had not taken necessary precautions both in the case of pre and post aerial spray of endosulfan in its plantations.

Dubey committee found serious design flaws, selection bias and selective and inadequate presentation of data in the NIOH report. The expert group categorically stated that the NIOH study report was not in conformity with the known and accepted properties of chemistry and toxicology of endosulfan.

The study lacked scientific validity, said the Dubey committee. The NIOH study was conducted to investigate the disease pattern in the affected villages and control population. The ICMR had stated that the study would be carried out in villages, among school children and plantation workers. But the scope of the study was only confined to a small group of school children. But the NIOH did not study about the health condition of the villagers and the plantation workers who should have been the main subjects of study since they were directly exposed to the pesticide. Though the

NIOH was known as the National Institute of Occupational Health, the PCK workers who were subjected to occupational hazards were not studied by the commission which again exposed the bias of the NIOH.

The primary objective of the NIOH was to confirm the reported disease pattern in the exposed populations and evaluate the magnitude of the problem in comparison with reference populations (non-sprayed villages) through a well designed epidemiological study. Epidemiology related to the comparative study between exposure to suspected toxicant and the presence of adverse health effects in a given group of people. Therefore, selection of the reference population and the control population was most crucial in any epidemiological study. The NIOH selected 619 students of Government Higher Secondary School in Vaninagar in Padre village (exposed group) and 416 students from two schools in Meenja gram panchayat.

The selection of Padre village as exposed population and Meenja as control population was not justified. The NIOH stated in its report that three small rivers separated Meenja from the village of Padre thereby excluding any possibility of cross contamination of water resources. The report said that it was ensured through repeated enquires that in the areas of sample collection there was neither previous aerial spray nor manual spray of endosulfan on the crops or plantations in the area.

The claim by the NIOH that Meenja was a totally non-exposed area was a travesty of truth. The agriculture department had supplied pesticide including endosulfan to farmers for several years. Therefore, several pesticides, including endosulfan had been in use in Meenja for several years together. Therefore, it was not a true unexposed area. So the NIOH has not achieved its basic objective of evaluating the magnitude of disease pattern in exposed population by comparison with control population.

The Dubey committee found that while the report gave levels of endosulfan residues in drinking water samples taken from Vaninagar—exposed area—it did not give similar data for the samples taken from Meenja. A total of as many as 262 samples were taken for analysis by the NIOH, but the report did not give complete results and raw data of the findings. Criticising the NIOH report the Dubey committee stated that the definition of any study report should begin with the common characteristics of both the exposed and control population. But the NIOH has not clarified the common characteristics that all the students of the study group shared to qualify themselves to be the real exposed group. The Dubey committee alleged that the epidemiological study carried out by the NIOH did not achieve its primary objective of the reported disease pattern in the exposed populations and in evaluating the magnitude of the problem by comparing it with the control population through a well-designed epidemiological study.

The Dubey committee also pointed out the selection bias. The report said that selection bias could occur when those selected happened to be different from those within the study area. Padre village has two schools—one in Vaninagar and the other in Swarga. The ICMR team which had visited the area on August 11, 2001 had stated that while in Vaninagar school there were many mentally or physically abnormal children, there were no physically abnormal children in the school in Swarga. This was an important difference, pointed out the Dubey committee. For, if the study was to be unbiased, students from both the schools should have been selected for the exposed study group. Another important thing was that the Swarga school was closer to the PCK plantation than the Vaninagar school.

The study also suffered from selection bias of another kind. It did not cover areas or groups where endosulfan was used and where people were normal and healthy. For instance, the Dubey committee pointed out that the NIOH study did not cover the farm workers and their families who had been exposed to endosulfan spraying.

Prior to the commencement of the study, the NIOH had written to the PCK about its intention to include the PCK farm workers in the study. The NIOH had written to the plantation Corporation that 'we also wish to carry out complete medical check-up of the workers as part of our detailed environmental epidemiological study which we plan to begin soon.' Thus, NIOH report had failed to address the primary objective as mentioned in its report as well as the one mentioned in the ICMR report.

The NIOH report had stated that 'a well planned epidemiological study was, therefore, necessary to confirm the high incidences of diseases in the villages near cashew plantation in Kasargod district and evaluate exposure to endosulfan and find out its relationship with endosulfan, if any.'

The Dubey committee report said that the NIOH study had not covered all or at least a sizeable number of villages near cashew plantations. Though PCK plantations covered 19 villages, the NIOH study was confined only to a school in Vaninagar which was not directly exposed to the aerial spraying of endosulfan. No attempt was made by the NIOH to conduct a cross-sectional study covering other villages from among the 19 villages. The NIOH study had, therefore, only a narrow focus and it failed to address the stated objectives of the study. Further, the NIOH report had not brought out certain facts and information concerning endosulfan use in the area taken up for the study—Padre village.

During the visit of the expert committee, it was noted that Vaninagar was only three-four kilometers away from PCK plantations and only 24.1 litres of endosulfan were sprayed there in December 2000. The pre-monsoon showers were received only in April 2001. Though the NIOH report extensively quoted from open literature, it has not taken cognisance of the reports published by the Food and Agriculture Organisation, FAO, and the World Health Organisation, WHO, concerning the eco-toxicological properties of endosulfan.

The expert group found that environmental factors such as solar radiation, temperature, soil moisture and soil microbial activity directly influenced the duration of the chemical in the environment. For instance, the half life of endosulfan in temperate climate would last as long as 365 days, but in tropical climate it would last only for 20 days. There were several scientific reports that established the fact that endosulfan degraded rather fast in Indian environmental conditions. Therefore, the persistence data generated in a temperate country like Canada as quoted in the NIOH report has no validity in India which is a tropical country.

Besides, further studies on pesticide residues showed that endosulfan did not persist for long in Indian environmental conditions. Under the circumstances, it was highly improbable that endosulfan residues may have persisted for more than five months. It was also improbable that the residues moved along with run-off water to a distance of three-four kilometers to Vaninagar from the exposed area and that too in an undulating land full of vegetative cover.

The Dubey committee also pointed out a fallacy in the NIOH report. It stated that 'since the water is used for irrigation purpose there is likelihood of exposure through food'. The committee said that endosulfan was not a water soluble system enabling it to move from irrigation water into crop plants.

Under the caption 'limitations of study' the NIOH in its first report expressed apprehension that all children in Vaninagar school may not have come from the affected areas where endosulfan spray has been carried out. This limitation was highlighted by the NIOH itself.

Further, the NIOH report has not considered the No Observable Adverse Effect Level, NOAEL, or Acceptable Daily Intake, ADI, which stands for the threshold limit or measure of a quantity of a chemical that can be consumed on daily basis over a life time without harm. The WHO has fixed an ADI of 0.006 mg for endosulfan in 1998. This reinforced the fact that for everything there was a threshold limit.

The Dubey committee made the recommendation and findings that there was no link between the use of endosulfan in PCK plantations and health problems reported in Padre. In consideration of the recommendations given by various other committees, it recommended that aerial spraying of the pesticides may not be allowed at all in any situations including in the PCK plantations to ensure full safety. It suggested that application of all pesticides including endosulfan was to be done adhering to regulatory stipulations in force from time to time. The pesticide manufacturers should take necessary steps to promote and educate sellers and users to ensure correct and safe use of all pesticides.

Most importantly, the committee recommended that since the relationship between the alleged illnesses with endosulfan in Padre could not be established, it was recommended to conduct a comprehensive, well-designed and detailed health and epidemiological study in the entire cashew plantation area of Kerala. This was to ascertain the incidence of diseases in Padre vis-a-vis the state average in case there was evidence of unusual health problem to investigate and pinpoint the most probable factors responsible for the problems.

The pesticide manufacturers had charged the NIOH with denying information regarding its scientific study on the 'unusual diseases' in Padre though the demand was made under the Right to Information Act. The terse reply of the NIOH was that the information was not available with the NIOH; scientists who produced the report left the NIOH and that the study and data were the intellectual property of the scientific institution.

But on an appeal filed by the industry the Central Information Commissioner directed the NIOH to give required information. Subsequently, the NIOH gave over 1,800 pages of data which it had earlier claimed was not available. The initial refusal of the NIOH to allow access to analytical data was an act of concealing the scientific fraud.

The pesticide industry found after analysing over 1,800 pages of the data obtained under the Right to Information Act that it provided unmistakable evidence that the report had plenty of falsified data and that it was fundamentally erroneous and fraud.

The pesticide industry alleged that NIOH report suffered from alteration of data, incorrect presentation of facts and inconsistency in calculating methods. There was mismatch between the number of samples taken and the number of samples reported as analysed. Besides, the scientists of the NIOH in their report submitted to the Commission misrepresented facts, falsified the data to reach an erroneous conclusion that showed endosulfan as a causative agent for certain health problems in Padre village.

The NIOH scientists made material misrepresentation of facts to the NHRC, expert committee appointed by the government, policy-makers, and media and to the general public with the full knowledge of their falsity and in reckless disregard of the truth, it said.

The NIOH while supplying information under the Right to Information Act chose to 'mask' certain vital data regarding some soil sample analysis. This was yet another example that evidently showed the desperate attempts by the NIOH to suppress erroneous data.

The NIOH, a government-funded institute under the Indian Council of Medical Research has an obligation to the government policy-makers to ensure that its scientific study was accurate, complete and reliable. But the data collected under the Right to Information Act showed that the NIOH scientists surreptitiously indulged in a range of scientific misconduct and manipulation of the data. It was also revealed that the NIOH report was not critically examined or checked for scientific correctness and validity by experts within the NIOH or the ICMR before submitting it to the NHRC.

But the anti-endosulfan activists rejected the Dubey committee report alleging that Dr Dubey who had worked as director of the Central Plantation Crops Research Institute,

CPCRI, in Kasargod absolved the pesticide industry and the Plantation Corporation of Kerala from the charges leveled against it by the activists for allegedly causing diseases in scores of villages in Kasargod.

However, in view of the lack of consensus among various experts on the issue, the department of Agriculture and Cooperation of the Union Government decided to revisit the issue. Thus, a committee was constituted under the Chairmanship of Dr C.D. Mayee, the then Agriculture Commissioner of the Union Government to review the safety of endosulfan in 2005.

First of all, the expert group reiterated the earlier view of Dr Dubey committee and said that there was no link established between the use of endosulfan by the Plantation Corporation of Kerala and the health problems reported in the village of Padre in Enmakaje gram panchayat. The expert group recommended that aerial spraying may be allowed only in case of national exigencies after getting the nod from the Central Insecticides Board and that application of pesticides including endosulfan to be done adhering to regulatory stipulations in force from time to time.

The expert group recommended that the pesticide manufacturers should take necessary steps to promote and educate sellers and users to ensure correct and safe use of all pesticides. Another recommendation of the expert group was that since the country had adequate pre-registration data and post-registration review processes concerning use of pesticides, science-based responses be made available to all stake holders and general public by registration authorities.

The committee also recommended to conduct a comprehensive, well-designed and detailed health and epidemiological study in the entire cashew plantation of the state to ascertain the incidences of diseases in Padre village vis-a-vis other relevant locations in other parts of the state to investigate and, if possible, pin point the probable factors that were responsible for the alleged health problems in Padre village. The same recommendation was also made by the Dubey committee.

Even though the use of endosulfan was not clearly linked to the alleged health problems in some villages in Kasargod, the Committee recommended that it would be better if use of endosulfan was kept on hold in Kerala. Finally, after considering all factors and available reports, the Committee recommended that the use of endosulfan be continued as per provisions of the Insecticides Act, 1968.

The scientists of the ENVIRON International Corporation based in Florida in the USA also conducted a review of the NIOH report. The NIOH report was reviewed by Robert P. DeMott, principal toxicologist, Environ International who was the corresponding author of the review.

The report evaluated the scientific methods, conduct, interpretations and conclusion of the report titled "*Final Report of the Investigation of Unusual Illnesses Allegedly Produced by Endosulfan Exposure in Padre Village of Kasargod District (N. Kerala)*" conducted by the National Institute of Occupational Health (NIOH).

The NIOH report had studied the environmental and human health conditions in an area near cashew plantations in Kasargod where there has been a history of aerial application of endosulfan. The NIOH report covered environmental sampling of soil, water, sediment and other materials.

According to the Environ review report, the NIOH report concluded that endosulfan was the "most probable" cause of the diseases documented in the report. But the NIOH study was conducted to evaluate human health conditions, termed a survey study. It cannot, therefore, reach the conclusions regarding the causes of effects noted. The method used by the NIOH was generally accepted as suitable solely for generating preliminary hypothesis. Since it was based solely on the study design selected, ascribing endosulfan as the most probable cause of the conditions recorded, it was not a scientifically valid report, the Environ study said.

'When the analysis were considered and also its interpretations, serious limitations and inadequacies, however, emerge. There were serious omissions and errors in the computation and presentation of the analytical results for endosulfan in environmental samples', according to the Environ review.

The review report said: 'in fact there was not even confirmation that the measurements made were actually endosulfan. Lack of confirmation, calibrations and quality assurance, quality control information are such that these results would commonly be rejected by environmental regulatory agencies and would not be considered reliable for characterising human health risks for any type of regulatory or judicial action'.

Criticising the NIOH study, the Environ analysis said 'the survey method as conducted to obtain information regarding human health conditions does not confirm to the generally accepted requirements for epidemiological studies and is insufficient for reaching a conclusion that endosulfan effects are observed in Padre village'.

According to the Environ review report, the effects reported to be linked to endosulfan were not biologically plausible as toxicological responses to the low background levels of endosulfan were found. 'The congenital conditions highlighted for male reproductive effects, in fact, were not even found in excess among the boys from Padre village. And the measurements characterised to reflect neuro-behavioural disorders were not generally accepted as direct markers of such effects'.

Further the review said 'the interpretations stretch highly uncertain and highly subjective tests into such serious terms "disorders", "abnormalities", and "malformations". The results do not support the presence of elevated rates of such conditions in Padre village. The analysis and interpretations do not meet generally accepted scientific standards for establishing chemical exposures as an explanation for purported health effects'.

The Environ report, therefore, said 'the NIOH report cannot be used to draw a causal connection between generally accepted scientific standards of endosulfan exposure and various reported symptoms and outcomes because of the limitations of the design, the uncertainties and inadequacies of the analyses, and the lack of concordance between the reported findings and actual adverse health conditions'.

According to the Environ study, the NIOH report presented the results of analytical chemistry testing used to measure endosulfan concentrations from samples of soil, sediment, water and human blood. The report used these results to make comparisons between the environmental conditions in Padre village, hypothesised to be impacted by aerial spray of endosulfan, and a reference area (Meenja panchayat village) approximately 25 km away where this type of spraying was reportedly not used. The report used the results from blood samples to make comparisons between children from the study versus references areas. The analysis said that these analytical data were, thus, the critical foundation upon which the comparisons attempting to link endosulfan to the observations in Padre village depended.

However, the Environ review made the serious charge against the NIOH report that selected data had been excluded from the NIOH report without explanation. The information obtained from NIOH under the Right to Information Act revealed inconsistencies between the raw data compared to the summary results presented in the NIOH report.

Exposing the wrong interpretation of the test, the Environ report said that the reporting of endosulfan in water and soil at concentrations well below the minimum detection limit of one to three ppb and the large number of "peaks" reported in the blank and standard reference samples suggested that random peaks due to electronic noise were routinely misinterpreted as endosulfan peaks.

Another important finding of the Environ analysis was that the total endosulfan concentrations in top layer of soil—

which was the layer where the greatest potential exposures would occur—were reported inaccurately. According to the raw data provided by the NIOH through the Right to Information Act, the mean total endosulfan concentration in the upper soil layer in the study area (pesticide sprayed area) was 0.242 ppb compared to a mean concentration of 0.303 ppb in the reference area (non-sprayed area). Again, the concentration found in the study area for total endosulfan was lower and not higher than that found in the reference area. This, however, contradicted the NIOH study.

Interestingly, it was the results from the reference group that appeared unusual compared to other studies. Because of its wide usage in parts of the world, the background level of endosulfan were routinely found in human blood even in the absence of specific exposures such as the aerial spraying being investigated around Padre village.

The most important finding of the Environ review report was the results from the Padre village group appeared to be within the range of routine background endosulfan levels found in other populations. The reported values for this village did not stand out as being obviously elevated due to exposures from the aerial spraying patterns on the plantations in the area.

The Environ International also pointed out the obvious bias in the NIOH study. According to reporting by teachers of the 619 school children in Padre village, 1.8 per cent of them were "arrogant", 1.3 per cent were "aggressive" and 0.3 per cent were "restless". This was compared to 416 school children in the reference area (non-sprayed area) and among them not even a single child was found restless and aggressive, except that one child was reported arrogant. The behaviour of the children in Padre village was described as being aggressive, arrogant and restless to show the 'neuro-behavioural disorders' among the children.

According to the Environ report, the reporting bias occurred on the part of the teachers of the Padre village since they were aware of the endosulfan issue. But the teachers in the reference village (non-sprayed village) who were also well aware of the endosulfan issue chose to under report about the problems of their children.

The Environ said that the NIOH report came to a series of conclusions that there was a significantly higher prevalence of neurobehavioural disorders, congenital malformations in females and male reproductive abnormalities in Padre village. Further, the NIOH report also concluded that endosulfan exposure from aerial spraying in the cashew plantation was the 'most probable' cause of the health conditions documented in its report.

The Environ scientists, however, remarked that those conditions were not supported by the study design and methodologies or results of the investigation that was completed. The conclusions reached by the NIOH outreached the stated objectives of the study which had specified that the survey approach was intended to serve to generate a hypothesis regarding potential etiological factors. Though this was theoretically attainable, the survey method employed could not as a matter of generally accepted epidemiological science serve as the basis for determining causation from a single environmental factor.

The Environ study said that the design and methods adopted by the NIOH were suitable only for generating preliminary hypothesis. Therefore, the survey could not in the first place support the conclusion reached regarding endosulfan as the probable cause.

It said 'review of the final report, the first report and the information provided subsequent to an RTI request and available scientific literature lead us to conclude that this investigation is impacted by analytical limitations; computational errors; reporting of documentation errors and omissions; and inadequate substantial interpretations to such an extent that it is not scientifically reliable. The uncertainties are sufficient that results from this investigation would frequently be rejected by environmental regulatory agencies and excluded from consideration of regulatory or judicial actions.'

The Environ study said 'we recognised serious limitations in the analyses for endosulfan conducted on environmental and blood samples. The survey approach used to document health conditions is subject to substantial sources of potential bias and did not include steps to either eliminate or specifically recognise the impact of biases.'

Finally, the Environ review report said that the conclusions presented in the NIOH study that endosulfan application was the most probable causative factor for the conditions reported amounted to stretched and selective interpretations of the results obtained. The study was not, therefore, a valid means to support such a conclusion. Besides, the report was not an appropriate or complete scientific representation of the study conduct and findings.

It said that 'substantive corrections, expanded disclosures and further analyses are necessary before the report would meet the expected standards for scientific reporting'.

16

EPIDEMIOLOGICAL STUDY BY KOZHIKODE MEDICAL COLLEGE

The department of Community Medicine of the Kozhikode Medical College, KMC, conducted a three-part epidemiological study in the endosulfan sprayed villages during 2010-11. The study was supported by the department of Health and Family Welfare of the Kerala Government. The first study was titled 'epidemiological study on the health status of the population in endosulfan affected areas in Kasargod district, Kerala'. The second one was a school- based epidemiological study 'on the health status of adolescents in areas exposed to endosulfan spraying in Kasargod district of Kerala'. The third one related to the 'estimation of endosulfan residues in human blood in Kasargod district'.

The department of Community Medicine of the Kozhikode Medical College selected Banam, a village located in the eastern areas of the district and not exposed to the pesticide spray for conducting the epidemiological study. The other village selected to conduct the comparative study was Muliyar, a sprayed village. If the community medicine department of the KMC had selected Mogral Puthur gram panchayat, the entire fake story on endosulfan diseases would have been exposed. Mogral Puthur, a non-sprayed village has more number of patients suffering from the same sort of diseases than in the sprayed areas. But the study prepared by the Kozhikode Medical College assumed significance since the epidemiological study was altered and presented by the DYFI in its writ petition to the Supreme Court.

The study by the department of Community Medicine of the Kozhikode Medical College was an exercise in futility. The study, despite its contradictions and design flaws, revealed that the non-sprayed village of Banam which was selected to compare with the sprayed area of Muliyar had more or less the same number of diseases. In some cases the unsprayed Banam had more number of patients than the sprayed village of Muliyar.

The study by the KMC suffered from several inherent contradictions. First of all, it was a weak study which failed to assume professional standards. A cursory glance at the study report would reveal that those who had conducted the study had made painful efforts to make it appear that the sprayed village of Muliyar had more number of patients.

The epidemiological study began in 2010 following a government order on April 9, 2010. The investigators of the study team were headed by Dr C. Prabhakumari, Professor and Head of the Department of Community Medicine and Dr T. Jayakrishnan, Assistant Professor and Dr Thomas Bina, professor of the same department. The study was completed in 2011.

Dr T. Jayakrishnan was known for his anti-endosulfan views from the very beginning. Addressing a seminar on endosulfan issue in Kasargod he had stated that many of his colleagues had told him that the diseases in the sprayed areas were as common as in all other parts of the state. But according to him, the diseases found in the villages were all caused by the spraying of endosulfan since the entire area was exposed to the pesticide spray for 20 long years. Therefore, it was apparent that he had begun his work not with a clear mindset devoid of any bias.

Meanwhile, tempers had been building up in Kasargod to use the place as a springboard for the campaign for a worldwide ban on endosulfan. The LDF government headed by Chief Minister V. S. Achuthanandan was under tremendous pressure from the anti-endosulfan lobby to carry out another epidemiological study in 2010. The Democratic Youth Federation of India, DYFI, youth wing of the CPM was toying with the idea to move the Supreme Court for a ban on endosulfan in the country in the run-up to the assembly election in Kerala in 2011.

With the blessing of the health department and the school teacher-turned health minister P.K. Sreemathi of the CPM, the preliminary work on the epidemiological study began in August 2010 in order to present a pre-conceived report on endosulfan spraying and its alleged adverse fallout on the people of the region. A team of doctors from the Indian Council of Medical Research had held discussions with Chief Minister V.S. Achuthanandan a few months before the completion of the study.

Dr K.M. Sreekumar, Associate Professor of the College of Agriculture in Padannakkad and Dr K.D. Prathapan, an entomologist of the Vellayani Agriculture College conducted a critical study of the report of the department of Community Medicine of the Kozhikode Medical College in 2011.

They said that the KMC study was a comparison of the health problems of 1,000 families in Bovikkanam in Muliyar gram panchayat, an endosulfan sprayed village and 850 families of Banam in Kodom Bellur gram panchayat, a non-sprayed area. However, the people of Bovikkanam and Banam were not comparable as they were dissimilar socially and economically. The population of Muslims in Banam was only 15 per cent while their percentage was 45 in Bovikkanam.

This difference was reflected in the food habits as well as in the educational and health status of the people in the area. It was reported that eleven gram panchayats in the district were affected by the aerial spraying of endosulfan. However, the medical college report said that Muliyar gram panchayat with a large number of victims was selected randomly. A well-designed study based on adequate number of representative samples would have produced conclusive and better results. Evidently, no effort was made in this direction, they said in the study.

The various parameters of health studied in the report were not properly defined. For instance, there were many types of liver diseases including infective jaundice. It was not clear which types of liver diseases were included. Without providing working definition of a parameter, the study would become unclear, they said in their critical study.

The study team of the Kozhikode Medical College had analysed endosulfan residues in the blood plasma of 43 subjects in 11 grama panchayats where the pesticide was sprayed. However, no attempt was made to compare these values with those from the non-sprayed area. It was important to make comparisons and draw valid conclusions in regard to this main parameter under study.

Though Gas Chromatography (GC), was used for the analysis of the pesticide residues, Mass Spectroscopy, MS, was not done to confirm the results. The Government of India had made it mandatory to confirm the analytical values with MS in laboratories under the All India Network Project on pesticide residues, said Dr. Sreekumar and Dr. Prathapan in their critical study.

Simply put, all analytical laboratories used an instrument called Gas Chromatography, GC, to estimate chemicals in test samples consisting water, soil, soft drinks, milk and blood. GC is a chemical analysis instrument used for separating and estimating chemicals present in a sample. The GC used a narrow capillary tube known as 'column' through which various chemicals of an injected sample passed in a gas stream.

As the chemicals existed at the end of the column, they would be detected electronically. The GC produced a graph known as chromatogram. Peaks on the chromatograms represented analysed or captured chemical compounds. In order to produce accurate and reliable measurements, the GC has to be properly calibrated before any sample was analysed.

The conclusions of the KMC study were largely based on subjective parameters. The information gathered was mainly based on memory recall by the subjects. No efforts were made to cross-check the information with other easily available documented facts. For example, death and birth data were accurately documented in gram panchayat offices which was a fairly good source of information to study any possible changes in the demographic pattern. Similarly, local veterinary hospitals recorded unnatural death of cattle. Banks and insurance companies, too, have a data base of morbidity and mortality of cattle as they were legally bound to pay compensation to the cattle owners. The study was conducted at the peak of the propaganda by local clubs and the media. Hence it was highly probable that the responses of the subjects were biased and hence the inferences of the study were erroneous and misleading, said Dr Sreekumar and Dr Prathapan.

The reproductive health events in women above 30 years whose reproductive period started during the period of aerial spraying have been compared with those aged below 30 years whose reproductive period started after the cessation of the aerial spraying. This study was designed to assess plausible improvement in the reproductive health of women following the winding up of endosulfan spraying. The study report has specified that data on the reproductive health events in all married women in the study area had been collected by the medical college study team. However, it gave rise to a problem since married women normally moved into the family of their husbands after their marriage.

This showed that at least a section of the women studied by the KMC researchers were living outside the study area with their parents during the period of spraying. Similarly, many housewives in the unsprayed area of Banam moved to their husbands' houses from the neighbouring sprayed area.

This simple social reality was strong enough to falsify the whole data and inferences on reproductive health events in women as evidently the study was based on a mixture of subjects from both exposed and unexposed areas.

According to the agricultural scientists, a high proportion of young married men in Muslim families of Muliyar would be generally working in the Gulf countries. As a result of the long spell of separation of the couples, chances of conception would be less and it was common that such couples sought infertility treatment. This, again, was a strong factor that would distort the results of the study on the reproductive health of women as well as their infertility rates. Moreover the data on reproductive health problems during the period of pesticide spray (1980-2000) was never statistically compared with the same during the decade after the pesticide spraying was stopped.

Endosulfan residues in the blood plasma of 43 subjects from the affected areas were sent for chemical test and all samples contained pesticide residues varying from 2.51 to 170.40 ppb (parts per billion) with an average of 41.65 ppb. However, the level of endosulfan residues in blood serum nine months after the last spray was only 0—12.77 ppb according to the NIOH study conducted in 2001. This showed more than fourfold increase of endosulfan residues in the blood serum of affected people over 10 years. No endosulfan was ever applied in Kasargod during the past decade following its ban.

According to the study conducted by the Centre for Water Resources Development and Management, CWRDM, no detectable endosulfan residues were observed in drinking water in the sprayed area. As there was no endosulfan in drinking water, it was surprising that such extremely high levels of residues were observed in human blood. Data on the pesticides residues in the blood serum of 43 subjects were given in the published report of the medical college. After statically comparing the data on pesticide residues in the blood serum of 43 subjects with the health status of each individual as shown in the report, it was found that the health status of each individual was not related to the endosulfan content in the body of the victims.

On analysing the chromatograms obtained from the Salim Ali Centre for Ornithology and Natural History, only values of the four samples mentioned in the KMC report agreed with the chromatogram readings. This revealed that serious lapses had crept into the analysis of endosulfan residues, said the critical study.

A parameter that was objectively assessed was physical disability. The prevalence of physical disabilities in the age group of 1-9 years in Bovikkanam, a sprayed village was 0.5 per cent while the same data on Banam, a non-sprayed area was 1.4 per cent. The reason for the increased incidence of physical disability in the unsprayed area was not clarified in the report. None of the parameters studied were compared with the state average or the national average. Without comparing the prevalence of every health parameter, it was impossible to establish the epidemiological evidence of the ill-effects of endosulfan.

The sex ratio in Bovikkanam was 957 females for 1,000 males while the ratio was 1,016 for the same number of males in Banam. The study team attributed it to the male biased sex ratio to the spraying of endosulfan. There was no empirical evidence that endosulfan would tilt the sex ratio in favour of males. On the other hand, some studies had suggested that the organochlorine pesticides might reduce the proportion of male births. However, many studies in this regard remained inconclusive.

As per the 2001 census data, out of the 11 sprayed grama panchayats, as many as five had a female biased sex ratio. However, boys outnumbered girls in the age group of 1-6 years in most of the panchayats in the district. The sex ratio of Muliyar panchayat that included Bovikkanam was 10:12 which meant ten males for every 12 females. Deriving conclusions without examining available facts and figures clearly indicated the bias of the study team, noted the critical study.

The study stated that the reproductive health events such as abortion, intrauterine death, stillbirths and child deaths were found to be reduced to 50 per cent among the age group of 20-29 years indicating a reduction in reproductive health problems following the cessation of spraying 10 years before. This inference was not based on any statistical analysis.

A comparison of data on abortion and neonatal infant child deaths of the sprayed area against that of Banam, a non-sprayed area, would prove this inference to be totally baseless. For instance, the rate of abortion in the unsprayed Banam in the age group of 20-29 was 4.3 per cent and the same in the age group of 30-39 years was 7.4 per cent. The percentage of rates of fall in both the sprayed and unsprayed areas was roughly the same (42 per cent) which may be due to better access to improved medical facilities.

The data on objective parameters generated by the KMC study team that reflected the reality of the health status have not been made public. For example, 10 out of 6107 individuals (0.16 per cent) in the pesticide sprayed area were cancer patients. However, the number of cancer patients in the unsprayed area of Banam was 11 out of 3742 (0.29 per cent). The rate of incidence of mental retardation was equal in both the populations. The prevalence of skin diseases in the unaffected area was 2.19 per cent while that of in the pesticide sprayed area was only 1.8 per cent. Asthma, seizure and psychiatric problems too were less in the insecticide sprayed area. Death due to old age was proportionally higher in the affected Bovikkanam. However, kidney and liver diseases and the history of infertility were more in the sprayed area.

The proportion of individuals who had undergone various surgeries were more in the unsprayed area (5.85 per cent) compared to that of Bovikkanam, i.e., 4.49 per cent. Surgical rectification of hand or foot anomaly was less in the sprayed area. Endosulfan was known as an endocrine disruptor (the latest toxicological review of the pesticide disputes this argument) and was linked to cryptorchidism (undescended testis) in boys. However, according to the unrevealed data, more surgeries were performed in the unsprayed area to correct cryptorchidism.

Sub-lethal doses of the pesticide were likely to affect the fetus during the first three months of pregnancy. However, as per the report the rate of congenital defects was similar in both places.

'It was clear from the KMC report that the unsprayed and sprayed areas did not differ much in terms of the occurrence of diseases or disabilities. The disability census data in 2001 showed that Kasargod did not have an increased rate of any of the mental or physical disabilities compared to other districts in the state. There was no reliable data to prove that there was a higher occurrence of any disease or disability in the sprayed area compared to the unsprayed area. The allegation that there were increased health issues in the endosulfan sprayed areas in Kasargod was not proved conclusively by any study till date', concluded the critical study of the KMC report by the two scientists.

Data on pesticide residues in the blood plasma of 43 subjects were provided in the report. However, it was shocking that the column on the health status of each individual was deleted in the original document submitted to the Supreme Court. But according to the full 53 page report of the KMC study obtained under the Right to Information Act, it was found that the health status of an individual was not related to the endosulfan content in one's blood. Fearing that this would be exposed, the entire data on the health status of individuals subjected to analysis of pesticide residue was deleted from the published report. Out of 43 persons as many as 21 were found healthy in the health status report.

For example, the total endosulfan residues in the blood of a person was given as 88.42 ppb in Kakkar (serial number 16), but in the health status column it was shown that the same person was healthy. How can it be true when a person carrying a total of 88.42 ppb of endosulfan including alfa, beta and endosulfan sulphate in his blood be healthy? There are so many examples in the report on endosulfan residues in human blood plasma of persons carrying large percentage of endosulfan in the blood and still the persons were described as being healthy. Another instance was a sample from Enmakaje with a total of 117.18 ppb of endosulfan found in a person. But the health status column of the person was shown as healthy.

Yet in another instance, a female patient in Badiyadka (Serial No. 29) has 110.18 ppb of endosulfan. Her diseases were described as epilepsy and valvular heart disease. Therefore, the blood plasma report of the Kozhikode Medical College lacked consistency and was contradictory to each other. A person with 117.18 ppb of endosulfan was described healthy, but another with 110.18 ppb was described as epileptic and a heart patient.

However, the principal of the medical college replied to the Plantation Corporation Protection Council that the report prepared by the community medicine department was extensively reviewed by the Central team, the Supreme Court expert committee on Endosulfan headed by Dr. Viswa Mohan Katoch, Director General of the ICMR along with other scientists during their visit to the medical college on May 24, 2011.

The letter said that 'a second team including Prof. Aravind Pandey, Director of the National Institute of Medical Statistics, New Delhi, reviewed the raw data of the studies on July 5, 2011 in Kozhikode. The data was again reviewed by the National Institute of Medical Statistics in July 2011 along with a number of the research team'. How was it that the flawed report of the Kozhikode Medical College was declared error free after its review by an expert team?

The pesticide industry slapped a legal notice on secretary of the department of Health and Family Welfare informing that the industry had found fundamental and serious flaws in the residue analysis report in the study conducted by the

Kozhikode Medical College. The industry questioned whether the study was reviewed for its scientific rigour and data integrity by the Institutional Research Committee, IRC, or the Institutional Ethics Committee, IEC.

The pesticide industry said in the legal notice that the endosulfan study by the Kozhikode Medical College was riddled with methodological and analytical flaws and errors. It alleged that the principal of the medical college had failed to rigorously examine the raw data and methodology of the residue analysis before accepting them for inclusion in the report.

The pesticide industry said in the legal notice that the principal and a few scientists of the Kozhikode Medical College stubbornly and intentionally refused to respond to the communication sent by the industry to 'explain in detail the fundamental flaws, errors, omissions, materials alteration and fabrication egregiously present in the scientific report funded by the Kerala Government'.

According to the industry, when evidence of serious scientific errors was brought to the notice of the institutions, there should have been immediate response and corrective measures. Further, any scientific report funded by Government organs and produced before the Supreme Court should be of impeccable quality and devoid of errors and misrepresentation of facts.

The blood plasma samples collected by the Kozhikode Medical College were tested at the Salim Ali Centre for Ornithology and Natural History, SACON, Coimbatore. But the pesticide industry alleged that the SACON had used a flawed method to analyse the blood plasma samples. It said that the initial expert view of the data analysed by the SACON and submitted to the Kozhikode Medical College was thoroughly invalid because of several reasons. Though this was informed to the principal scientist of the SACON, with copies marked to the director of SACON and principal of the KMC, no reply was received by the representatives of the pesticide industry. The industry, therefore, submitted an application under the Right to Information Act and the SACON provided raw data and other relevant information to the question asked under the Act.

The pesticide industry alleged that the major flaw in analysing the blood plasma samples was the failure to confirm the Gas Chromatography-Electron Capture Detection (GC-ECD) results using the GC-Mass Spectroscopy, (GC–MS). The industry said that confirming the GC-ECD data using the GC-MS was both scientific and a statutory requirement in getting the correct answer. The Joint Parliament Committee, JPC, on pesticide residues had said that the GC-ECD test alone cannot identify chemicals.

The JPC had expressly stated in its report that the methods based only on chromatographic analysis without invoking the spectrometric detection were not suitable as confirmatory methods. Therefore, the data generated without confirmation by GC-MS was to be considered invalid. Similarly, the residue data reported was far below the Linear Calibration Range. The LCR represents the range of a chemical concentration in a sample that can be reliably and reproducibly quantified with accuracy and precision.

But the SACON remained firm in its decision to not withdraw the report of the Kozhikode Medical College. In a reply to the legal notice sent by the pesticide industry the SACON Director Dr P.A. Azeez said that withdrawal of the report would not in any way promote scientific reasoning, analysis and growth of scientific knowledge. However, the pesticide industry said that it was unfortunate that SACON which was functioning with government funds had sent such an evasive reply. The pesticide industry said that instead of addressing its queries, the SACON Director evaded the real issue which was about the flawed methodology used in detecting endosulfan residues.

17

GOVERNMENT KEEPS A STONY SILENCE

The State government acted in stony silence refusing to respond to scores of letters sent by the Plantation Corporation Protection Council demanding action against the erring officials of the district administration for creating scams after scams by doling out largesse to the fake victims of endosulfan; as a result, it had to ultimately move the High Court for justice.

The workers and staff of the Plantation Corporation of Kerala, PCK, formed an organisation called the PCK Protection Council in 2010 when the anti-endosulfan action committee demanded a sizable area of the PCK land in Kasargod to rehabilitate the suspected endosulfan victims and their families. The workers who convened a meeting decided to strongly oppose the move. The meeting felt that if the land was to be given for rehabilitation, it would affect the financial prospects of the company and thereby the future of the workers. They feared that its land would be grabbed by the mafia which has set its eye on the fertile land of the PCK. The land mafia was supporting the agitation solely to grab the land.

At the meeting an organisation called the Plantation Corporation Protection Council was formed with M. Gangadharan Nair, a supervisor of the PCK in Muliyar division as its secretary. Gangadharan Nair on whom the endosulfan had fallen while filling it in the helicopter tank was elected as the secretary since he was regarded as a suitable candidate to lead the movement.

He had strongly criticised the endosulfan action committee stating that the agitation was fueled by pumping European Union funds received by some NGOs. He had challenged the anti-endosulfan action committee that he was ready to take a bath in endosulfan before the glare of television cameras and media persons after covering his mouth and eyes. He demanded that once he could demonstrate in public that nothing would happen even if he was drenched in endosulfan, the action committee should call off the agitation. This was intended to make it clear that even though endosulfan had fallen over him, he was still keeping good health and was not scared of the pesticide. But the action committee did not accept his challenge.

The PCK Protection Council sent several letters to the government demanding probe into the endosulfan controversy including the origin of foreign funds. Alleging corruption the PCK Protection Council also wrote a letter to the director of Vigilance and Anti-Corruption Bureau to enquire about the foreign money received by the NGOs. But there has been no response from the government on the demands raised by the organisation. This explained the pervasive influence wielded by the anti-endosulfan lobby in the bureaucracy.

The organisation's secretary sent the letters to the government in exercise of his fundamental duty enshrined in the Constitution of the country. He had been supervising the spraying of endosulfan from 1980 onwards and as such he considered it as his fundamental duty under the Constitution to expose a series of scientific frauds propagated and perpetuated by some politicians, land mafia and NGOs in the guise of helping the victims.

In his letter to the President and the Prime Minister of the country he narrated several instances of fraud and scams committed by the NGOs and a section of government officials. As per the data collected from the government under the Right to Information Act, those who suffered from common diseases were enlisted as endosulfan victims. They were getting monthly financial assistance, free medical treatment, free ration and special age relaxation for government jobs. Most important, the PCK Protection Council said that no patients were subjected to individual medical check-up clinically certifying them as endosulfan victims.

Giving instances of such fraud, the PCK Protection Council said Girija from Iyyathadka suffered from hypertension; Pushpa of Vaninagar from asthma; Muralidharan of Kottodi from piles; Kumba of Pettikundu from diabetes and blood pressure. Other patients namely, Rajan of Periya was hit by tuberculosis, Subba Pattali of Swarga suffered from jaundice and Mana Pattali from heart disease. The glaring examples of other victims were Ramakrishnan of Jinnadkam who became handicapped after falling into a well and Balakrishnan of Panathur who suffered fracture following an accident in a Gulf country where he was working before. The anti-endosulfan activists had alleged that strange diseases were stalking the exposed area following the aerial spraying of endosulfan.

Questioning the entire endosulfan list and terming it bogus, the PCK Protection Council informed the constitutional heads that there were so many bogus names in the endosulfan list. The organisation said most of the victims were born before the spraying of endosulfan started in the area and their diseases were congenital by nature and yet they were included in the endosulfan list. It wanted to know the questionable criterion and procedures adopted in classifying them as endosulfan victims. The council demanded that since it was a government-sponsored scandal, it should be thoroughly investigated by the vigilance department, Comptroller and Audit General of India and the Central Bureau of Investigation.

The PCK Protection Council quoted a relevant observation of the Supreme Court in this regard which said that 'holders of public office are accountable for their decisions and must submit themselves to public scrutiny. Any deviation from this must be severely dealt with instead of being pushed under the carpet'.

The organisation had earlier submitted a memorandum to the Chief Minister demanding probe into the incident, but the letter failed to elicit any reply from the government. The PCK Protection Council said that as a politician it was convenient for Chief Minister Oommen Chandy to distribute largesse to the victims, but a Chief Minister of the State was elected by the people and elevated to a position wherein he held a trust on behalf of the people. Chief Minister Oommen Chandy has to deal with people's money in a fair and just manner. He cannot commit breach of trust reposed on him by the people and cannot act in an arbitrary manner, said the PCK Protection Council.

Invoking the physical disability census data published by the Census Commissioner of India, the organisation said that the often repeated allegation that thousands of people in Kasargod district had suffered physical and mental disabilities on account of endosulfan spraying by the PCK was not at all true. The door-to-door survey provided the most authentic information about physical and mental disabilities present in every district in India. The first report of disability taken by the Census Commissioner of India in 2001 showed that Kasargod district has the lowest number of disabled person for every 1,000 population. Other districts of Kerala such as Kollam, Idukki, Thiruvananthapuram, Pathanamthitta, Kottayam, Kozhikode, Alappuzha and Ernakulam have far higher disabled population than in Kasargod district. In fact, the prevalence of physical disability of 24 per one thousand in Kasargod district was much less than the Kerala average of 27 per 1,000. Similarly, the mentally disabled population was the lowest in Kasargod district in entire Kerala. These vital and authentic facts were willfully ignored or suppressed.

The Kerala government had sanctioned ₹ 10 lakh in 2010 to the Kozhikode Medical College to conduct a health survey and study in the exposed area in the district. This study showed that the population living in endosulfan sprayed area was relatively healthy than those in the non-sprayed area.

The health survey and study by the department of community medicine of the Kozhikode Medical College incidentally brought to light another contradiction. According to the medical college study, the Kodom Belur gram panchayat was not exposed to aerial spraying of endosulfan and hence it was selected to compare the diseases in the sprayed area in the epidemiological study of the medical college. But, strangely, there were as many as 89 persons from Kodom Belur gram panchayat in the endosulfan list prepared by the government.

The PCK Protection Council said that several experts had pointed out the serious scientific flaws and errors in the report by the Kozhikode Medical College. Some of the opinion of the experts had also been published by the media. But the Kozhikode Medical College maintained silence on the scientific flaws and errors.

The letter sent to the Constitutional heads by the PCK Protection Council had also invoked another order of the Supreme Court which said that 'it is high time that public servants should be held responsible for their malafide acts in discharge of their function as public servants. When the elected government decides to spend public money the decision cannot be founded on scientific deceit, shrouded in secrecy and kept beyond public scrutiny'. The Kerala government has failed to scrupulously respect the fundamental duty enshrined in the Constitution.

In the circumstances, the Plantation Corporation Protection Council demanded a thorough investigation into the whole episode in which enormous amount of money from public exchequer was spent on a section of people who reportedly suffered from exposure to endosulfan. The organisation demanded that accountability must be fixed on erring public servants and doctors who prepared the bogus list of the victims with the false intention without medical evidence and misled the public, policy-makers and the judiciary. The government must prove that there was strong element of scientific integrity.

The PCK Protection Council also demanded that the funds received by local NGOs from foreign sources in the guise of helping the endosulfan victims should be made public. They should be tried under the relevant provisions of the Foreign Exchange Management Act and the Indian Penal Code after suitable investigation and auditing to find if there were any offences of embezzlement or misappropriation.

It requested the President and the Prime Minister to provide similar monetary benefits to all physically and mentally disabled persons in all districts of Kerala considering the data provided in the disability report by the Census Commissioner of India. But the PCK Protection Council made it clear that the help should not be falsely linked to the Plantation Corporation or to the spraying of endosulfan.

After a few weeks of sending the letters to the President and the Prime Minister, both the offices responded to the letters by the PCK Protection Council. The letter from the President dated January 4, 2012 addressed to the Kerala Chief Secretary wanted him to take action on the petition and communicate it to the petitioner. The letter from the Prime Minister, also addressed to the Chief Secretary, wanted appropriate action to be taken on the petition. Both the offices informed the PCK Protection Council that it can take up the issue directly with the Chief Secretary on the strength of the letters.

It, therefore, sent a letter to the Chief Secretary on February 4, 2012 demanding some more investigations following the reply received from the offices of the President and the Prime Minister. It wanted the Chief Secretary to provide the names, designations and addresses of government doctors, including those from the Kozhikode Medical College who prepared and approved the bogus list of persons as victims of endosulfan to provide them financial compensation from the government. Similarly, the council also wanted the name, address and designation of government doctors who certified deaths as caused by endosulfan spray without any post-mortem and clinical evidence. It stated that the deaths had occurred several years before and the blame was posthumously put on the Plantation Corporation.

The PCK Protection Council urged the Chief Secretary to initiate action against Thanal, an NGO which carried on false campaign against the PCK. There were reports that the Thanal had received huge foreign funds from 2001 claiming to help the victims. The government should enquire whether the Thanal was a registered association or it was permitted under the Foreign Contribution Regulation Act to receive foreign funds and whether it had submitted proper accounts.

Though several letters voicing the same demands were sent to the District Collector, Kasargod, and other higher ups, no reply was received from any of the officials. The Chief Secretary chose to keep a discreet silence and the entire bureaucracy remained secretive in providing the right answers.

Even though there was no reply from the bureaucrats for the questions asked under the Right to Information Act, the organisation sent another petition to the Public Information Officer of the District Collector seeking more details. The petition sent on May 14, 2012 sought the details of the persons in the government list who died from exposure to endosulfan including their names, age and full address. The questions also related to the copies of the post-mortem or death certificates of the victims specifying the cause of the death including details of the compensation already paid or proposed to be paid to the families of the deceased as well as the names of the recipients.

But the reply received by the PCK Protection Council was rather amusing. According to the reply, the details sought by the PCK Protection Council were confidential in nature and so it could not be given to a third party. The Plantation Corporation had given ₹ five crore in 2011 and ₹ 27 crore in 2012 to pay compensation to the victims, but the reply that the details of endosulfan deaths were confidential in nature was highly evasive and was meant to hush up the entire fraud.

Frustrated at the inaction and lethargy of the Chief Secretary who consistently refused to reply to the letters of the Plantation Corporation Protection Council, it finally decided to move the High Court against the state administration. The council slapped a legal notice on the Chief Secretary on August 23, 2012 under Section 80 of the Civil Procedure Code 1908, in the light of various Supreme Court judgments.

The PCK Protection Council said in the legal notice to the Chief Secretary that the Kerala government was doling out huge largesse to a sizable number of population in Kasargod district allegedly died or suffered health problems from exposure to aerial spraying of endosulfan over the cashew plantations owned by Plantation Corporation of Kerala.

The Chief Secretary was informed that 'If exposure to endosulfan really caused a host of health problems, the primary victims should have been the workers of the Plantation Corporation in Kasargod district. There were about 2,000 persons living inside cashew plantations while endosulfan was aerially sprayed. There was also a school functioning within the cashew plantations and none of them had any health problems. Even workers who regularly sprayed endosulfan were not affected'.

'The anti-PCK and anti-endosulfan campaign was engineered by politicians, land mafia and certain NGOs receiving huge foreign funds. It was not clear if the Ministry of Home Affairs had permitted the NGOs to receive foreign funds under the Foreign Exchange Management Act. Investigation must include this also', said the legal notice.

The state government had given huge funds even diverting the amount from the National Rural Health Mission to some NGOs to work in Kasargod and help the alleged victims. The PCK Protection Council also wanted to conduct a probe into the alleged manipulation of the blood samples of endosulfan victims in the residue analysis by the Coimbatore-based Salim Ali Centre for Ornithology and Natural History.

According to the legal notice, the Chief Secretary was informed on February 22, 2012 that some doctors of the Kozhikode Medical College intentionally ignored and suppressed scientific data to mislead the judiciary, policy-makers and the general public into believing that aerial spraying of endosulfan had caused health problems in Kasargod.

The PCK Protection Council which later filed a writ petition in the High Court made the plea to issue a writ of mandamus or any other appropriate writ to the government to reply to the letters sent by the PCK Protection Council. The counsel of the petitioner wanted to investigate the irregularities in selecting the victims and demanded action against the officials who prepared the bogus list. It also wanted the government to investigate the involvement of the NGOs in collecting foreign money and prayed for an interim order to stall all further proceedings to disburse compensation to the alleged victims.

The petitioner submitted in the court that several letters to the authorities had stated that the officials in Kasargod had failed to follow any guidelines for scientifically and clinically identifying the persons who claimed that they were the victims of the aerial spray of endosulfan. The officials were colluding with the NGOs to disburse monetary compensation on the strength of bogus claims, the court was informed.

But the state government was not at all responding to the detailed representations submitted by the PCK Protection Council. The victims' list was burgeoned with persons having political affiliation who were not suffering from any ailments or diseases. The victims were suffering from common diseases as found everywhere. It was detrimental to the interest of the PCK since it was made liable to contribute money to the government to help the suspected victims.

The PCK had already shelled out ₹ 32 crore to the government without holding any adjudication regarding the liability of the corporation in paying the so-called victims. The counsel of the organisation said in the writ petition that there has been a massive financial scandal in paying compensation to the suspected victims.

Though several expert committees had conducted studies regarding the alleged health problems in certain villages in Kasargod, none of them has been able to scientifically prove that the diseases were caused by endosulfan spray. Even cases of natural deaths were reported as deaths caused due to endosulfan for the purpose of collecting monitory benefits. The victims' list was crammed with political workers of both ruling and opposition parties. Doctors were forced to enroll political activists and influential persons of the villages in the list. Doctors were coerced to certify them as victims of endosulfan spray. There was no verification of the diseases by any government hospitals or by any medical expert body before enrolling them as pesticide victims. Huge amounts were disbursed to persons enrolled in the list.

There were illegalities in preparing the list and also in the disbursement of compensation amount among persons who had died due to other ailments which could not be attributed to endosulfan. The government did not take any action on the letters sent from the offices of the Prime Minister and the President of India despite repeated reminders from the PCK Protection Council. Despite specific directions from the office of the President and the Prime Minister, the Chief Secretary failed to conduct any probe into the collection of foreign funds. Though Dr. Mohammed Asheel, an employee of the state government was sent by an NGO working for the ban on endosulfan to attend the Stockholm convention, no probe was conducted by the government into the incident. The Chief Secretary was duty bound to respond to the letters sent from the offices of the President and the Prime Minister of the country.

The Supreme Court had in several cases held that a public servant was a trustee of the society and in all acts of public administration the person has to be honest, sincere and faithful in matters of public administration. The inaction of the government on the issue was causing huge loss to the exchequer. The Supreme Court had held in one of the cases that 'it is high time that the public servants should be held responsible for their malafide acts in discharge of their function as public servants'.

Showing the bogus list of the victims, funds were obtained by government agencies and NGOs both inside and outside the country. There was no mechanism to oversee such funds raising or auditing the account as to how the funds were utilised. There was also an attempt to keep alive the 'endosulfan tragedy' by using the media to collect foreign funds. Some of the vested interests also worked to keep the PCK closed as the plantation corporation possessed 5,000 acres of land which was an attraction for the land mafia.

The disbursement of compensation to persons who were not entitled to get any benefit was causing huge loss to the exchequer and the burden was thrust upon the PCK and ultimately it affected its employees and their families. If any compensation was to be given to anyone it must be clinically proved that the person was a real victim of the pesticide use.

There was serious apprehension among the people regarding the involvement of various stake holders in the process of disbursement of compensation to the victims. The process has to be made transparent and accountable. The government was, therefore, duty-bound to respond to the petitions submitted by the PCK Protection Council. Though the representations to the government were made as early as on December 8, 2011 there has been no response from the government and there was no justification for the inaction.

But a single bench of the High Court directed the Advocate General to file relevant papers following the petition filed by the PCK Protection Council. But the office of the Advocate General filed a counter petition in the High Court giving reply to all writ petitions filed in the case by various parties by combining all the earlier writ petitions. Some of the petitions were filed by anti-endosulfan action committee demanding the formation of a tribunal to give compensation to the so-called victims.

But there has been no answer to the specific points raised by the Plantation Corporation Protection Council in the response petition filed by the Advocate General in the High Court. The PCK Protection Council, therefore, filed another petition seeking answer to the specific questions it had raised in its earlier writ petition.

18

DYFI MOVES THE SUPREME COURT

The Democratic Youth Federation of India, the youth wing of the CPM filed a writ petition in the Supreme Court on April 25, 2011 with a plea to ban endosulfan all over the country. The petition was filed in the run-up to the assembly election in Kerala in May 2011. It was ostensibly regarded as a political decision to file the writ petition since it was expected that a ban on endosulfan would help the CPM-led LDF to get mass support and win the election as it was a popular issue in Kerala. But the fact was that the DYFI filed the petition due to pressure from the European Union, EU, and also from some NGOs getting funds from the EU. The European Union has been using Left organisations all over the world to achieve its objectives of pushing its products as a market strategy.

T.V. Rajesh, state president of the DYFI filed the writ petition on behalf of the youth organisation. According to him, he was compelled to move the court 'under Section 32 of the Constitution of India under compelling circumstances in which the valuable lives of a large section of people were directly affected by the use of endosulfan', a pesticide which, according to the petitioner, was already banned in 81 countries of the world and was not permitted for use in another 12 countries). 'All developed countries including European Union banned this killer pesticide and most of other nations were not permitting its use', said the DYFI in the writ petition.

Elaborating the principles of the DYFI as its locus standi for the writ petition, T.V. Rajesh said the Democratic Youth Federation of India was formed in 1980 and the 'whole gamut of activities of the organisation revolved around service to the humanity by documenting the applicable skills, stating clearly what we are doing and capable of doing.'

'The DYFI is demonstratively upholding the cause of humanity taking active part in rescue, relief and rehabilitation in almost every natural calamity. The DYFI is always with the downtrodden, stands for the rights of women, the backward and weaker sections of society', it said.

According to the petitioner, 'the DYFI as a responsible youth organisation is of the opinion that nature belongs to the future generations too. The coming generations would require just institutions, basic energy and material resources, a functioning atmosphere, flourishing ecosystem and an unpolluted and unpoisoned environment'.

The writ petition said that 'chemicals, besides food, air and water have always been part of man's environment in some measure. The ecosystem has become imbalanced by uncontrolled use, abuse and misuse of natural resources and manufacture of hazardous products and chemicals resulting in the endangering of the very existence of human race'.

The petitioner said the excessive use of chemicals and pesticides for optimising agricultural production created alarming danger to health and safety of living beings in general and agricultural workers in particular. 'The impact of use of pesticides on global environment may vary in magnitude, and exhibits a variety of behavioural patterns and modes of action. Pesticides affect man's ecosystem and their residues can get into the food chain. The amount of pesticides consumed by people depends on the manner of use of pesticides particularly on farm crops, its storage and processing'.

In most of the developed countries the use of hard pesticides of agricultural crops has been either banned or restricted and other pest control programmes were adopted in order to maintain the ecosystem. But the developing countries are still using these pesticides without caring for the side-effects on environment, said the petition.

Recently, the Central Government has set up the Pesticides Environment Pollution Advisory Committee in the Ministry of Agriculture to review from time to time the environmental repercussions. 'It is a fact that pesticides considered hazardous in rich countries remain in use in developed countries. In India, pesticides have been used over the past four decades for crop protection and control of diseases like malaria. One will have to weigh the benefits of use of pesticides and the adverse effect that is produced on human health on account of use of pesticides'.

According to the DYFI, several studies had documented that endosulfan could affect human development. 'Researchers studying children in an isolated village in Kasargod district in Kerala, India, have linked endosulfan exposure to delays in sexual maturity among boys'.

It said that endosulfan was the only pesticide applied in cashew plantations in the hills above the village for 20 years contaminating and polluting the village environment. The researchers compared the villagers to a 'control group' of boys from a demographically similar village that lacked a history of endosulfan pollution. Compared to the 'control group', the exposed boys had high levels of endosulfan in their bodies, lower levels of testosterone and delay in reaching sexual maturity. Birth defects of the male reproductive system including cryptorchidism (undescended testis) were also more prevalent in the study group'.

The researchers concluded that 'our study results suggest that endosulfan exposure in male children may delay sexual maturity and interfere with sex harmone synthesis.' Increased incidents of cryptorchidism have been observed in other studies of endosulfan exposed populations, said the petitioner.

'Endosulfan is an off-patent organochlorine insecticide and acaricide. This colourless solid has emerged as a highly controversial agri chemical due to its acute toxicity, potential for bioaccumulation and role as an endocrine disruptor', said the DYFI.

According to the petitioner, 'endosulfan has been used in agriculture around the world to control insect pests including whiteflies, apids, leahoppers, Colorado potato beetles and cabbage worms. Because of its unique mode of action, it is useful in resistance management. However, since it is non-specific, it can negatively impact populations of beneficial insects. It is, however, considered to be moderately toxic to honey bees and it is less toxic to bees than organophosphate insecticides'.

Highlighting the hazards of endosulfan, the DYFI said in its writ petition that all over the globe the countries were becoming aware of the hazards posed by this toxic pesticide and had forwarded suggestions for its ban in various international conferences and had already decided to campaign for its ban in the entire globe. 'But due to unknown reasons the government of India has not banned this potentially hazardous pesticide in India, except for some states which have on their own banned its sale and use. This outdated and potentially hazardous pesticide was still in use despite serious attempts made by various human rights organisations'.

The DYFI said the Insecticides Act, 1968 regulated the import, manufacture, distribution and use of insecticides with a view to preventing risk to human beings and animals. This statute specifically provided a regulatory system of insecticides, but in the case of endosulfan the government machinery completely failed to protect valuable human life from the hazardous effect of endosulfan. The failure of the government violated the fundamental rights of the victims affecting their health.

Expressing his grievances, the petitioner said that on April 22, 2011, an all party delegation from Kerala met with the Prime Minister requesting him to ban endosulfan all over the country. But the response received by the delegation was negative. The petitioner expressed shock and dismay that the Union Minister of Agriculture and the Minister of Forest and

Environment had not even studied the scientific report submitted by the expert committee in 2002.

The petitioner claimed that the various non-government organisations had studied at their own level and most of the studies revealed the hazardous effect of endosulfan use and its impact on food, water and beverages. The Kerala government and the Union Government had appointed 11 various commissions to enquire about the issue. Those enquiry reports, in one way or the other, inferred that endosulfan was responsible for hazardous mutations and ailments of the people of Kasargod villages.

The petition was filed under Article 32 of the Constitution praying for a writ of mandamus directing the government to follow the principle 15 of the Rio Declaration of Earth Summit, considering the potentiality of grave consequences.

The Principle 15 of the Earth Summit has said that 'in order to protect the environment, the precautionary approach shall be widely applied by states according to their capabilities. Where there are threats of serious or irreversible damage, lack of full scientific certainty shall not be used as a reason for postponing cost effective measures to prevent environmental degradation'.

The petition was filed, according to the DYFI, since the right to life guaranteed under Article 21 of the Constitution of the country was infringed upon by spraying the pesticide. On December 31, 2010, the National Human Rights Commission initiated suo motu proceedings on the basis of media reports regarding aerial spraying of endosulfan in Kasargod district in Kerala which led to severe health problems.

The petitioner said that he was seeking the ban 'because the Government of India has chosen to turn a blind eye towards the report of the Food and Agricultural Organisation, FAO, of the United Nations which had concluded that long term intake of residues of endosulfan from uses that have been considered by the JMPR (Joint Monitoring of Pesticide Review) was 'likely' to present a public health concern'.

The petitioner further said that endosulfan was one of the most toxic pesticides in the market today responsible for many fatal pesticide poisoning incidents around the world.

The DYFI, therefore, prayed before the Supreme Court to issue a writ to prohibit the sale of endosulfan in its present form or any other derivatives in the Indian market.

The DYFI also wanted the court to direct the chief secretaries of all state governments to explain their stand on the ban of endosulfan. The petitioner wanted the court to issue a writ to the Union Government to provide appropriate and sufficient rehabilitation facilities for the victims affected by the application and use of endosulfan.

Another important prayer of the DYFI was to identify the manufacturers of endosulfan in the country and recover compensation from them and to pay sufficient and adequate amount to compensate the families of all victims who had died and all those who were suffering adverse effects from the use of endosulfan.

However, the writ petition filed by the DYFI in the Supreme Court to ban endosulfan contained several half truths and untruths. Moreover, it had also played some tricks to mislead the court. For instance, what the DYFI mentioned as research studies were the ones conducted by the Centre for Science and Environment, Delhi, the National Institute of Occupational Health, NIOH and the department of community medicine of the Kozhikode Medical College. The NIOH report had been criticised by the ENVIRON International of the US which termed the study 'unreliable and full of errors'. The flawed study conducted by the CSE which made a mockery of science had been rubbished by scientists. Similarly, the critical studies conducted by two scientists of the Kerala Agricultural University had found that the epidemiological study by the department of community medicine of the Kozhikode Medical College was not worth publishing in any scientific journal. The O.P. Dubey Committee and the C.D. Mayee Committee which reviewed the NIOH report had noted its design flaws and opined that the endosulfan spray had no link with the alleged diseases in the area.

According to the DYFI writ petition as stated earlier, 'the organisation was formed in 1980. The whole gamut of activities of the DYFI revolves around service to the humanity by documenting the applicable skills stating clearly what we are doing and capable of doing'.

However, the truth was just the opposite. The DYFI, youth wing of the CPM had conducted an active campaign against the verdict of the Kerala High Court by Justice K. Narayana Kurup banning smoking in public places on June 12, 1999, a popular verdict which was followed by other state governments. The CPM and CITU, its trade union wing had organised a march to the High Court following the verdict. The CPM fought against the verdict since it felt that it would affect the livelihood of hundreds of *beedi* workers especially in Kannur district of Kerala, a party stronghold. Almost all beedi workers were the sympathisers of the CPM and, therefore, the active workers of the DYFI.

The World Health Organisation, WHO, had given the warning that smoking caused cancer, lungs problems, heart diseases and such other chronic diseases and that about nine lakh people fell victims to tobacco use every year in India. Besides, each cigarette and beedi packet contained the statutory warning that 'smoking is injurious to health'.

The DYFI, or for that matter the CPM, cannot explain how its march to the High Court and campaign against a pro-people and progressive verdict by the Kerala High Court became 'a service to humanity' as stated by the organisation in its writ petition to the Supreme Court. Moreover, the DYFI activists were involved in a number of cases of political murders in Kannur district. Such an organisation cannot have a humane face.

The Pesticide Manufacturers and Formulators Association of India, PMFAI, challenging the writ petition said that it was not maintainable under Article 32 of the Constitution of the country and it should be dismissed totally since the petitioner had 'falsely stated that he has no personal or political interest of any kind'.

According to the counter petition, the petitioner T.V. Rajesh was a politician belonging to the Communist Party of India (Marxist) and that he has filed the writ petition in the guise of Public Interest Litigation, PIL, to further his own political interest and that of his party's self-serving needs and publicity. The petitioner was elected as MLA of the CPM from Kalliassery assembly constituency, Kannur district of Kerala in the election held in April 2011. The DYFI, the organisation of the petitioner was the youth wing of the CPM, it said.

According to the counter petition, T.V. Rajesh was involved in organising street protests in Kerala against endosulfan prior to the April 2011 election to the Kerala assembly. It was widely believed that the CPM selected him as a candidate for assembly election for the first time only after seeing his ability to politicize the endosulfan issue in Kerala. Therefore, it was clear that his writ petition, styled and camouflaged as Public Interest Litigation, PIL, was in fact a political interest litigation to foster his own personal interest as well as the political interest of his party.

The PMFAI said in the counter petition that T.V. Rajesh had willfully misrepresented crucial substantive information. He had distorted the report of the Joint Monitoring of Pesticide Review, JMPR, changing the crucial word 'unlikely into 'likely'.

Besides being completely false, the statement amounted to willful misrepresentation of material facts. The report of the Food and Agriculture Organisation, FAO, of the United Nations had in fact observed in its report that 'long term intake of residues of endosulfan from uses that have been considered by the JMPR is 'unlikely to present a public health concern.' But the DYFI changed the world 'unlikely' into 'likely' in its writ petition to the Supreme Court.

Moreover, it was the falsified report of the department of community medicine of the Kozhikode Medical College that was presented in the Supreme Court which resulted in the temporary ban on endosulfan. The most striking fact about it was that the entire report of the department of community medicine of the Kozhikode Medical College was not presented in the Supreme Court, but instead only 16 pages of the report were presented in the court.

T.V. Rajesh, CPM member of the state assembly who filed the petition in the Supreme Court had stated on Page 22 of the writ petition that the annexure filed in the court along with the writ petition were true of its respective originals. Further, not only that many tables in the original report of the epidemiological study by the Kozhikode Medical College were missing in the writ petition, but many tables which were not in the original report were inserted in the petition.

For instance, Tables 1 to 6 were missing in the petition as well as Tables from 10 to 12. The entire column on the health status on Page 51 of the original study report was missing in the writ petition. All these missing tables showed that there was not much difference in the status of diseases in both the endosulfan sprayed and non–sprayed areas and that those carrying heavy concentration of endosulfan in their blood were reported healthy.

Significantly, Section 193 of the Indian Penal Code says that 'whoever intentionally gives false evidence or fabricating false evidence for the purpose of being used in a stage of judicial proceedings shall be punished with imprisonment which may extend to seven years', said the counter petitioner.

However, it is mandatory for the court's registry to carefully scrutinize all affidavits, petitions and applications and reject those which did not conform to the requirements of order XIX of the civil procedure code. The Supreme Court in the Amar Singh vs. Union of India and others case had directed in 2011 that 'the registry must henceforth strictly scrutinize all the affidavits, all petitions and applications and will reject or note as defective all those which are not consistent with the mandate of order XIX of the code of civil procedure.' But in the case of the writ petition filed by the DYFI, there has been no scrutiny by the court's registry even though it was mandatory.

It was the CSE which conducted the first study on the issue after getting sufficient funds from the European Union. Details of CSE study was discussed at length in an earlier chapter. In fact, the Supreme Court banned endosulfan for eight weeks on the basis of the report submitted by the community medicine department of the Kozhikode Medical College which was manipulated by the DYFI and also on the strength of other documents falsified by the DYFI. It made the whole thing murkier by withholding the relevant parts of the report of the medical college study. However, the Pesticide Manufacturers and Formulators Association of India, PMFAI, said that it was a grave offence to mislead the Supreme Court by submitting a fraudulent report.

After the Supreme Court imposed an eight week ad-interim ban on endosulfan, the counsel of the DYFI was compelled to file the full report in the Supreme Court. The fresh petition incorporating the complete report of the Kozhikode Medical College was filed by Meena C.R., counsel of the petitioner, in the Supreme Court on August 27, 2011. However, the fresh affidavit stated that what was filed earlier was a 'relevant extract' of the study report.

Challenging the DYFI, the Pesticide Manufacturers and Formulators Association said that the DYFI had falsely stated that the right to life guaranteed under Article 21 of the Constitution was infringed upon by the pesticide manufacturers. The DYFI provided no cogent evidence in support of the core allegation that endosulfan was responsible for death of numerous persons. All that the DYFI had produced were photographs of alleged victims of endosulfan from Kasargod which were doing the rounds in the media since 2001 without any scientific and medical evidence. Information received from the government in 2007 under the Right to Information Act said that there were only two deaths allegedly due to the aerial spraying of endosulfan from 1980 to 2006. Even these two deaths in 26 years turned out to be in no way clinically related to the endosulfan use. This information has disproved the contention of the DYFI that endosulfan had caused deaths of numerous persons.

The petitioner had sought to invoke the precautionary principle of the Rio declaration of the Earth Summit to ban the production, sale and use of endosulfan throughout the country only on the basis that the aerial spraying of endosulfan in the cashew plantations of the PCK that allegedly caused diseases in the village of Padre in Kasargod.

The petitioner also filed disturbing photographs of children suffering from health problems allegedly due to use of endosulfan. The DYFI has not been able to establish that the health problems of the people of Padre and of the children whose photographs have been filed in particular were due to the use of endosulfan.

According to the counter petition filed by the Pesticide Manufacturers and Formulators Association, the DYFI has relied on the report of the National Institute of Occupational Health, NIOH, and the epidemiological study conducted by the department of the community medicine of the Kozhikode Medical College which, however, failed to establish a causative link between the use of endosulfan and alleged health problem in Kasargod district.

The counter petitioner said that while the report 'Endosulfan – the Kerala story' prepared by the health department of the Kerala Government highlighted several adverse health effects allegedly caused by the use of endosulfan relying on certain international studies and papers, there have been various other scientific studies by international agencies which were ignored by those who prepared the report of the Kerala health department.

These international agencies were the WHO, the Food and Agriculture Organisation, FAO, of United Nations, US-EPA and California EPA. The studies had concluded that 'endosulfan was not carcinogenic and mutagenic'.

It was not even genotoxic, not a dermal sensitiser and not a neurotoxic agent, said the studies. It would not cause adverse effects on reproductive organs and was not an endocrine disruptor either. 'In the case of endosulfan, there is in fact strong scientific certainty that it does not cause the host of health problems', the studies noted.

A remarkable submission by the pesticide manufacturers in the counter petition was that precautionary principle of the Rio Earth Summit could not be invoked on the alleged health problems in one area alone where there was no direct link established between the use of endosulfan and the alleged health problems. Further, no health problems had been reported from the rest of the country where endosulfan had been in use for over 40 years.

The words 'lack of full scientific certainty' in the precautionary principle of the Rio Earth Summit could be applied only in large number of cases where endosulfan was found to be causing health problems. However, in a small per cent of such cases where the causative link between endosulfan and the health problems have not even been proved conclusively, the precautionary principle cannot be applied, said the counter petition.

According to the PMFAI, the documents submitted by the DYFI particularly the NIOH report was under challenge by the pesticide manufacturers. The first report was submitted in January 2002 and the final report in July and August 2002. The first report of the NIOH was discussed at the meeting of the Inter Ministerial Committee, IMC, formed under the directive of the Supreme Court. The IMC after studying the report sought the views of the Registration Committee of Pesticides. It constituted an expert group under the chairmanship of Dr O.P. Dubey, (ADG plant protection) of the Indian Council of Agriculture Research, ICAR.

The expert group chaired by Dr O.P. Dubey said the NIOH report suffered from serious design flaws, selection bias and selective and inadequate presentation of data and selective suppression of facts. The committee observed that 'there is no link established between use of endosulfan in PCK plantation and health problems reported in Padre village'.

Another expert committee appointed by the Union government under the chairmanship of Dr C.D. Mayee in 2004 had also upheld the expert views of the earlier committee under the chairmanship of Dr O.P. Dubey.

Following specific complaints in 2010, the Union Minister of Health and Family Welfare informed the Indian Council of Medical Research and the National Institute of Occupational Health to examine the report. Consequently, the ICMR invited the chairman of the International Treaties Expert Committee of Indian Chemical Council and other experts to a meeting in Delhi in January 2011 to discuss and understand the errors in the NIOH report.

At a meeting convened by the ICMR, a comprehensive presentation was made explaining with empirical evidences of various errors and flaws in the NIOH report. It was agreed at the end of the meeting that NIOH scientists would explain the errors, flaws and discrepancies within two weeks as recorded in the minutes of the meeting. However, there was no response from the NIOH in this regard even after it was given a number of reminders.

The pesticide manufacturers said that 'analysis and reprocessing of over 1,800 pages of raw data obtained under the Right to Information Act provided unmistakable evidence that the NIOH report contained plenty of falsified data and it was fundamentally erroneous and flawed. In fact, the NIOH report was an end product of laboratory fraud and it had liberally used falsified data in preparing the report. The report suffered from alteration of data, incorrect presentation of facts and inconsistency of calculation methodology. The NIOH scientists in their report submitted to the National Human

Rights Commission misrepresented facts, falsified data to reach an erroneous conclusion that showed that endosulfan was a causative agent for certain health problems in the village of Padre in Kasargod'.

Another industry association called the Endosulfan Manufacturers and Formulators Welfare Association, EMFWA, served a legal notice on Dr P.K. Nag, director of NIOH on January 22, 2011. The legal notice demanded the NIOH to withdraw its report. However, the NIOH failed to reply to the legal notice.

The DYFI had relied on the suo motu proceedings initiated by the National Human Rights Commission, NHRC, in December 2010 on the basis of the NIOH report submitted in July 2002. But the NHRC had closed the former *suo motu* proceedings initiated on the basis of a media report in 2001. A writ petition was also filed in the High Court of Kerala challenging the recommendations of the NHRC on December 31, 2010.

According to the counter petitioner, the Parliament passed the Insecticides Act, 1968 and the Insecticides Rules, 1972 which vigorously enforced both scientific and regulated use of pesticides in India. Even the use of the product was well regulated in as much as the Registration Committee approved the crop wise, pest wise and dose wise usage including pre-harvest interval of each registered product. This was done after careful evaluation of data and in fact gave specific approval to the product label and leaflet which were legally required to be attached to each container in which the product was sold.

The PMFAI said in the counter petition that the recommended use of registered products did not in any way infringe the right to life guaranteed under Article 21 of the Constitution. 'Endosulfan was one of the insecticides registered for use in India by the Central Insecticides Board. Use of endosulfan in the country was reviewed by three expert committees in 1991, 1999 and 2003 and its use was, therefore, legal', said the PMFAI.

19

SUPREME COURT IMPOSES *AD-INTERIM* BAN ON ENDOSULFAN

On May 13, 2011 the Supreme Court passed an *ad-interim* order to immediately ban the production, use and sale of endosulfan all over the country and ordered the seizure of permit given to the manufacturers till its further orders. The Supreme Court order came as a bolt from the blue for endosulfan manufacturers. The DYFI moved the petition 'in public interest' alleging harmful effects of the pesticide following the aerial spray of endosulfan in some gram panchayats in Kasargod district.

The court said in the order that endosulfan was being used in paddy, sugarcane, cotton, mango and cashew and the studies conducted in the area where endosulfan was used had revealed adverse affects on human health and environment. 'Some of the studies also indicated that endosulfan is significantly associated with neuro-behavioural diseases, cognitive disorders, hydrocephalus, mental retardation, cortical blindness, seizure disorders and Parkinson's disease'.

The court noted, 'it was pointed out that its effects have been felt in the state of Kerala and its use has been completely banned in that state. We have gone through the report published by the Government of Kerala and the photographs appearing therein are highly disturbing', observed the court.

The Kerala Health Department had published a booklet titled 'Endosulfan–the Kerala story'. The booklet was prepared by officials of the health department. But the alleged victims of endosulfan whose pictures had been published in the booklet had nothing to do with endosulfan spray. They were children who suffered from some common diseases.

Media persons who had visited the villages of the victims— whose pictures were published in the booklet— were convinced that the pictures were not of the victims of any pesticide spray. If an impartial probe was ordered on the incident, it would have exposed the fraud committed by the Kerala health officials who prepared the booklet 'Endosulfan— the Kerala story'.

The booklet was highly false since children suffering from various diseases were projected as victims of endosulfan. These highly disturbing pictures got the stamp of authenticity and credibility because it was published by the department of Health and Family Welfare of a state government under its official insignia. But politicians can manipulate anything by using officials to serve their political agenda. The booklet in English which was a highly fabricated publication was used in the anti-endosulfan agitation worldwide.

The Supreme Court had stressed in its order that some studies indicated that endosulfan caused some diseases. The study in question was the report of the National Institute of Occupational Health, NIOH.

The court observed in its judgment 'Right to life, guaranteed under Article 21 of the Constitution of India, is the most fundamental of all human rights, and any decision affecting human life, or which may put an individual's life at risk, must call for the most anxious scrutiny'.

After hearing the counsel of the DYFI, the pesticide manufacturers as well as the Solicitor General of India the Supreme Court said that it was of the considered opinion that a detailed study on all India basis has to be undertaken by an expert committee so that its ill-effects on human health could be better addressed.

The court, however, directed the committee to be headed by the Director General of the Indian Council of Medical Research, ICMR, and the Commissioner of Agriculture to conduct a scientific study on the question whether the use of endosulfan would cause serious health hazards to human beings and cause environmental pollution.

The committee was directed to submit the report within eight weeks from the date of the order and also to suggest an alternative to endosulfan. The court then passed the ad-interim order banning endosulfan for eight weeks.

In its subsequent sitting on August 8, the court asked the joint expert committee to enquire about the total quantity of the manufactured endosulfan remaining in various companies in the country. The court also wanted details about the manufactured stock of endosulfan which could be exported in terms of the pending export orders.

The court sought the details from the expert committee to which countries the exports could be made and on the conditions under which it could be exported. The court also wanted to know the steps that government could take to dispose of the balance quantity and at what stage the material could be destroyed. The court directed the Joint Expert Committee to keep in mind the environmental norms whether the destruction of the balance quantity would result in ecological degradation.

The court, however, received the answer in its sitting on September 30, 2011. According to the Joint Expert Committee, the available stock with the manufacturers was 1,734 metric tonnes. The accumulated quantity of endosulfan technical was 1090.596 metric tonnes.

The court then observed that 'having heard the learned counsel on both sides, we are of the view that 1090.596 metric tonne of endosulfan be permitted to be exported on conditions enumerated below to those countries from whom export orders of endosulfan have been received by the manufacturers in India so that the manufacturers are able to fulfill their contractual obligations and, to that extent, the alleged pollutant stands eliminated from this country'.

The court, however, issued a direction to prevent pollution along the way in the course of the export. The court made it clear that the order was strictly confined to the manufactured quantity which was accumulated to the extent of 1090.596 metric tonnes and no manufacturer should produce it in any form. However, the counsel for the DYFI opposed the export of endosulfan abroad.

The court took up the case again on December 13, 2011. The Joint Expert Committee in its report in August 2011 indicated that a quantity of 2698.056 KL of endosulfan formulation was lying unsold as an inventory. The Pesticide Manufacturers and Formulators Association of India had made a plea before the court to export the existing stock of 2698.056 KL of endosulfan.

The court permitted 34 units of manufacturers and formulators in the country to export the existing stock. The court directed that three endosulfan manufacturers-the government owned Hindustan Insecticides, Excel Crop Care Ltd and Coramandal Int'l should decide the existing quantity of endosulfan and then dilute, repackage and export the pesticide. The court, however, said that the permission for dilution should not be treated as permission to manufacture endosulfan formulation in any form.

In continuation of its orders dated September 30 and December 30, 2011 the Supreme Court observed 'the time has come for the Central Government to inform the court as to what step it intended to take in the matter of disposal of raw material, which is Hexa Chloro Cyclo Pentadiene (HCCP) lying with the three companies, one of which is a public sector company. The court directed the Central Government to submit its report on the disposal of HCCP and the final product and the period within which it was either to be disposed or phased out.

The court in its order on October 9, 2012 noted that by its earlier orders on May 13 and August 5, 2011, the committees constituted under these orders were required to make specific answers to the queries raised in the order. However, no satisfactory answer has been furnished to the court.

It noted that 'the committee constituted consisted Director General of the Indian Council of Medical Research, ICMR, and the Commissioner of Agriculture who was required to conduct scientific study on the question whether the use of endosulfan would cause any serious health hazards to human beings and would cause environmental pollution. Again there is no specific answer provided by the committee in its report filed before.'

The court observed that one of the issues raised was that the committee did not represent all relevant stake holders and hence it could not examine all the facts and provide complete answers with certainty.

Because of this, the court asked the Joint Expert Committee represented before the court to add more members to the committee from relevant and specialised fields who would help to come to a more definite conclusion.

The court wanted the committee to be expanded with additional members such as the Director General of Health Services, two scientists—one from the ICMR and the other from the Union Ministry of Agriculture—as well as the member secretary of the pollution control board. The court put five questions before the committee and wanted it to submit the report within six weeks.

The questions were: 'what is the exact quantity of endosulfan formulation, form or any other form or raw material as available in India as of today; whether use of endosulfan should at all be remitted or will it be in the greater human and environmental interests to ban the use of endosulfan in its entirety.

Another question was: 'if the use of balance endosulfan, available as of now, is not permissible, in that event how much endosulfan can be exported to other countries on the lines as was permitted by this court vide interim order passed earlier by the court.

The court also enquired whether it was possible to destroy the entire balance of endosulfan in any form or raw material and what would be the cost of destroying endosulfan. The court wanted the joint expert committee to take into consideration the views expressed by different state governments. The court also directed that if it was found appropriate, it may hear the stake holders who were present and represented before the court.

The Centre for Environment and Agrochemicals, CENTAGRO, an organisation of farmers, agriculture scientists and agrochemical manufacturers based in Mumbai which was a stake holder represented before the Supreme Court appointed Expanded Joint Expert Committee, EJEC, on November 10, 2012.

The CENTAGRO said the disputed fact related to the health problems arising out of the aerial spray of endosulfan by the Plantation Corporation of Kerala in its cashew estates in Kasargod for 20 years. T.V. Rajesh, MLA from Kallaissery assembly constituency and DYFI leader filed his writ petition before the Supreme Court seeking total ban on endosulfan on the basis of three scientific studies.

The first study was conducted by the National Institute of Occupational Health, NIOH titled 'investigation of unusual illness in Padre village of Kasargod district (North Kerala) in 2001-02. The study was conducted by Dr. Sayed and Dr. Aruna Dewan, scientists of the NIOH. This report was later submitted to the National Human Rights Commission.

'An unauthorised, altered and scientifically fabricated version of the same report was subsequently published by a few scientists of NIOH and scientists of Kasturbha Medical College, KMC, in Mangalore in a US-based web magazine called Environmental Health Perspective, EHP, in 2010 and in the subsequent year'.

'Another document relied by the DYFI was an epidemiological study conducted by the department of the community medicine of the Kozhikode Medical College. The CENTAGRO said in its representation that even before the DYFI filed its petition before the Supreme Court in April 2011, the scientific errors and fabrication in the NIOH study had been challenged in legal forums'.

The CENTAGRO further said 'a civil case was filed in the principle civil court, Padri, in Gujarat in September 2007 against Dr Aruna Dewan. Despite repeated notices from the court for cross-examination, she failed to make an appearance during the past five years.

The Pesticide Manufacturers and Formulators Association of India had filed a writ petition in the Kerala High Court against the National Human Rights Commission. Though the writ petition was filed in February 2011 much earlier than the DYFI petition in the Supreme Court, the NHRC did not file any response petition.

A meeting was held at the ICMR office in Delhi on January 24, even before the DYFI filed the petition to discuss and address the identified flaws in the NIOH report. Though a comprehensive presentation was held to highlight all the serious flaws in the NIOH report at the meeting chaired by ICMR Director General Dr V.M. Katoch, the fundamental flaws so glaring and prominent were not corrected by the ICMR. A subsequent letter sent to the ICMR still remained unanswered for the past 20 months.

A legal notice was sent to Dr V.M. Katoch, Director General of the ICMR on February 17, 2012 urging him to report about the material facts in his possession, but there has been no response from the ICMR.

In March 2012, the US-based ENVIRON International Corporation, a scientific organisation reviewed the NIOH report. The ENVIRON which made a 62-page report reached the conclusion that there were serious discrepancies between the raw data and the NIOH report.

The CENTAGRO's representation before the Supreme Court expert committee said that the silence and inaction from both ICMR and the NIOH was certainly a cause of concern. It called for investigation into scientific misconduct by the premier research institute such as the ICMR and the NIOH functioning under the Union Ministry of Health and Family Welfare.

'The widespread and unchecked growth of scientific misconduct in government-funded research institutes (IIT, Kanpur, NIOH, Kozhikode Medical College included) is deeply alarming. Equally alarming is the apathy shown by the apex authorities managing these institutes to the well founded complaints of scientific misconduct,' said the CENTAGRO in its petition to the response committee.

The Expanded Joint Expert Committee headed by Dr V. M. Katoch, Director General of the Indian Council of Medical Research started its proceedings from October 16, 2012. The committee in its first sitting reviewed the reports of the National Institute of Occupational Health, NIOH, and the epidemiological study by the Kozhikode Medical College. The committee decided to collect the relevant national and international data and information on endosulfan. It also decided to review the report of the registration committee of the Central Insecticide Board which permitted the continuous use of endosulfan.

The committee also decided to collect the views of the Rotterdam Convention which considered the persistent nature of endosulfan as well as toxicological data from international literature about different pesticides including endosulfan. It also decided to collect the available data on the existing stock of endosulfan and its raw material along with the recommended methods of disposal.

The second meeting held on October 26, 2012 decided to collect data related to the toxicity of all other pesticides registered for use in the country. The committee was of the view that toxicity data should be related to common health hazards generally related to endosulfan such as carcinogenicity, endocrine disruption, congenital anomalies, reproductive dysfunctions and neurological manifestations.

This was considered essential to compare the toxicity of other pesticides being used with that of endosulfan. The committee also decided to study the phasing out plans used by different countries which have already banned or phased out the pesticide. This was decided to suggest a rational plan for disposal of endosulfan and its raw material. The Central Pollution Control Board was requested to provide information on the estimated cost and modalities of disposal of the present stock of endosulfan and its raw material so that feasibility and appropriate economic viability analysis can be done.

All the collected data was reviewed at the third meeting of the joint expert committee held on November 5, 2012. Interestingly, the committee noted that many of the pesticides currently in use also have been reported to have health and biological effects similar to endosulfan in varying degrees.

Based on the deliberations at the meetings, the Expanded Joint Expert Committee submitted its report to the Supreme Court on November 17, 2012. Replying to the first query by the Supreme Court on the existing stock of endosulfan, the joint expert committee said a total of 2,658 MT of Hexa chloro cyclo pendadine, HCCP, was lying in the country. The other stocks are : endosulfan formulation (liquid) — 1,786 KL – and endosulfan (dust)—128 MT.

The committee made a detailed response on the question by the Supreme Court whether the use of endosulfan at all be permitted or would it be in greater human and environmental interest to ban the use of endosulfan in its entirety.

The committee observed that endosulfan has important health hazards and biological effects related to endocrine disruption, carcinogenicity, congenital anomalies and reproductive and neurological abnormalities. However, the committee noted that 30 to 35 per cent of the registered pesticides were also known to have the above mentioned health and biological effects to varying degrees as published in the peer reviewed journals from various parts of the world.

The most prominent observation of the joint expert committee was that given the situation endosulfan alone cannot be singled out for such potential risks agreeing that all pesticides by nature were toxic compounds and most of these may have some unwanted effects which have been well documented. However, the committee noted that before registration of any pesticides in the country for commercial use, health risk assessment was carried out by the Central Insecticide Board.

The committee said that appropriate use of pesticides and precautions in consonance with good agriculture practices was essential to ensure adequate production and availability of agricultural commodities for the food security of Indian population. Considering the benefits and potential risks the committee felt that the continued use of pesticides was desirable for India. Since India was a signatory to the Stockholm Convention and Rotterdam Convention, it was committed to discontinue the use of endosulfan over the next five years. The committee noted that almost all the countries which banned endosulfan had a phase out plan by its use in agriculture over a period of 2-6 years. Such a phasing out plan would ensure that all the stocks available in the countries would be utilised and exhausted completely in a desirable time frame.

The expert committee conveyed the views of the Union Ministry of Agriculture that if no further raw material was allowed, the existing stock would be depleted within a period of two years. The committee, therefore, made the suggestion that to exhaust the available stocks of the raw material, manufacture and use of endosulfan may be permitted for a total period of two years. Further, the committee said that the manufacturing and marketing companies should be asked to ensure to completely exhaust the available raw material during the period and ensure that the pesticide was fully utilised in accordance with label claim and good agricultural practices for pest control.

Moreover, many other pesticides which were being used in the country showed some similar health and biological effects as with endosulfan. Therefore, phasing out of endosulfan appeared to be the most viable plan. During this phasing out period, the information about alternative pesticides for the prevention of damages to crops should be widely disseminated by the Union Ministry of Agriculture.

Further, the labels on the endosulfan packing and containers should clearly mention that these products were not to be used beyond the period of two years with date of expiry clearly marked. The states which permit the use of endosulfan would keep detailed inventory control and ensure strict monitoring of the persons and places where endosulfan was being used and keep a vigil on the unwanted health effects, if any.

The expert committee said that since it was suggesting the international practice of phasing out plan and, therefore, allow its use for a limited period of two years, the proposal to destroy endosulfan did not arise. This recommendation was also in agreement with the fact that it was not feasible to destroy the large quantities of raw materials with the manufacturers and the pesticide formulations lying with the various agencies. Disposal of existing stocks of endosulfan in existing incinerators may take long duration due to the limited capacity and the cost of disposal would be exorbitant and also prohibitive as per Dr Gajbhiye committee. The same view was also expressed by the Central Pest Control Board which estimated the cost to the tune of ₹ 1,189 crore for incineration and would require several years of dedicated operations. The expert committee took into consideration the views expressed by different state governments, but they reported no adverse effects of endosulfan.

The DYFI in its counter affidavit filed with permission of the Supreme Court demanded the rejection of the response of the expanded joint expert committee. T.V. Rajesh, MLA, DYFI leader and petitioner in the case said that the committee decided the whole issue in a predetermined manner and it abdicated its function. He alleged that the expert committee clearly avoided recalculating and reconciling the amounts of endosulfan stock in the country. Further, the committee chose not to answer questions of the Supreme Court objectively and truthfully. The DYFI reiterated the allegation saying that the answers of the expert committee were meant to placate and suit the interest of the pesticide industry. The committee has been evasive in its reply to the Supreme Court questions and, therefore, the report appeared vitiated.

Most importantly, the DYFI counsel said that the committee recommended the restart of the use of endosulfan even after concluding that the pesticide has known adverse effects on human life and environment. It was also against the catena of decisions of the Supreme Court observed earlier.

Alleging that the deliberation and meetings conducted by the earlier expert committee and then the expanded committee was a total sham, the DYFI said that the whole issue was not considered in its seriousness and was handled in a very casual and callous manner.

The DYFI counsel said that no serious debates and dialogues were held at the committee meetings abdicating its function assigned by the court. The expert committee did not give a scientific expert view on the issue even though the committee was expanded. The counsel said that certain members who were expected to contribute significantly did not even participate in the meeting.

Though the expert committee was expanded to give the court a deeper insight into the issues relating to the continued use of endosulfan, the report produced by the committee turned out to be a futile exercise despite the court directing the committee to provide an analysis and a final scientific report on the issue.

Regarding the first question of the Supreme Court, no effort was made by the committee to collect or to ascertain the exact quantity of endosulfan other than the industry feedback. Further, no statement or affidavits were filed with regard to the total quantity of endosulfan exported with the permission of the court, the DYFI counsel said.

According to the DYFI, the expert committee supported its contention by saying that endosulfan has important health hazards and biological effects. But at the same time the committee recommended the use of endosulfan for two more years to exhaust its existing stock in the country and for its final phase out. The committee also noted that 30-35 per cent of other registered pesticides have also similar biological effects.

The DYFI petition said that the committee did not identify or disclose the other pesticides having 30-35 per cent adverse effects which were still being used in India. It stated that it was pertinent to mention that every other pollutant or pesticide had not been banned under the Stockholm convention, but endosulfan has been specifically banned. This showed the hazardous effects of endosulfan which has been completely overlooked by the expanded committee.

Coming down heavily on the expanded committee, the DYFI said that the committee should have suggested the ban on endosulfan for the greater human and environmental interest taking into consideration its adverse effects on health. But the committee only considered its financial aspects. The response of the committee regarding its disposal was to continue its use threatening health and environment. The temporary ban on endosulfan for the past one and half year has not impacted on the growth and production of agriculture.

Further, the DYFI said the expanded committee has not given any appropriate response on how much of endosulfan could be exported to other countries if the surplus stock of endosulfan was not permitted in the country.

On the question regarding the issue of destruction of endosulfan the expanded committee chose to remain silent, said the DYFI. The response of the committee in this regard showed the predisposition of the committee. 'Its response on the question of destroying endosulfan stock was over exaggerated completely against the safety and interest of human beings on earth. While the expanded committee had to decide on the cost and economic ramification of destroying the endosulfan stock, it unnecessarily suggested the reuse of endosulfan for two more years', alleged the DYFI.

The DYFI petition against the response of the expanded committee said that 'it was difficult to control the manner in which endosulfan was used by farmers and farm workers. The notion of phase out period for endosulfan was wholly inappropriate in a developing country such as India where innocent residents, flora, fauna and environment in surrounding areas were vulnerable to pesticide threat'.

The DYFI said that the committee could have availed the support and technical knowledge of the National Rural Health Mission in Kasargod district. However, the scientific committee failed to consider the material evidence placed before the expanded committee.

According to the DYFI, 'the response of the committee was vague and failed to understand the views expressed by various state governments. No proper study was conducted by various state governments except Kerala and Karnataka. No opinion of other stake holders was considered as directed by the court.

Criticising the response of the committee, the DYFI said that it endorsed the view of the pesticide manufacturers when it said that the continued use of pesticides was desirable in India since the recommended dosage and methods of use were also mentioned on the label and in the inside leaflets of endosulfan containers. Since most of the farmers in the country were illiterate they could not understand the harm or benefits of using or applying a certain pesticide to their crops.

The DYFI said that 'even if it was considered that the cost of disposing harmful pesticides was prohibitive, the unrepairable hardship or damage it would cause to the environment or human beings could have been considered in the first place'.

'It was obligatory on the part of the expanded committee to weigh the options and come to a conclusion that as to whether the cost of disposal or the sufferings of the people was of paramount considerations. Though the committee was expected to fairly analyse the situation, the committee supported the views of the pesticide manufacturers', said the DYFI.

Further, the committee failed to search for study reports on endosulfan overlooking the safe techniques and best practices adopted by other developing countries which had banned endosulfan as early as 1998. Discussion on best technique for detoxification and disposal of endosulfan was taking place all over the globe and India can play a significant role in developing low cost methods to detoxify endosulfan.

Finally, the DYFI said in its counter affidavit that it was clear that the expanded committee has not been of adequate assistance to the court in regard to its queries even though a serious responsibility was devolved on the committee in view of the threat to human life and environment.

It was also a violation of the consistent obligation assured by the government under international human rights treaties to take effective measures for realising the concept for right to food without pesticides which created serious health problems. The counsel for the DYFI, therefore, made the plea before the Supreme Court to reject the recommendations of the Expanded Joint Expert Committee.

The case subsequently came up before a bench headed by the Chief Justice and consisting of other judges. Having heard the counsel of the opposing parties, the court expressed the view that the writ petition demanding ban on endosulfan be heard and disposed as expeditiously as possible. The court called for taking up all pending applications for consideration along with the writ petition on February 19, 2013. The Supreme Court also directed various states to file their response to the writ petitions by February 11, 2013 through the respective department of health if they had not already filed it. The court said that the Central Pollution Control Board be added as a party to the proceedings and that the board be represented for the final hearing on February 19.

The court suggested that the contempt case filed by the DYFI against CENTAGRO also be taken up on the same day. The CENTAGRO had published an advertisement in the *Business Line* on the report of the department of community medicine of the Kozhikode Medical College inviting the attention of the then Chief Justice of the Supreme Court who previously headed the bench hearing the endosulfan case. The DYFI filed a contempt of court petition against the CENTAGRO against the advertisement.

The Supreme Court heard the counsel of the DYFI for well over three hours on February 19, 2013. Though several dates were fixed for hearing the pesticide industry, the date was adjourned and the pesticide industry was yet to be heard by the Supreme Court as part of the final hearing of the case.

20

ENDOSULFAN : LESSONS TO LEARN

The endosulfan controversy which had its origin in a nondescript village in Kasargod in Kerala and which attracted the media limelight all over the country and across the globe, holds some important lessons for the country and particularly for Kerala.

First, it has exposed the lack of serious scientific debate on the issue in the country as a whole. The controversy on endosulfan in Kasargod was basically an issue which concerned science. But far from taking a positive role, scientists shied away from the scene conceding space to political parties which turned it into a political issue. For environmental NGOs, it became an issue of finding medical treatment and rehabilitation for hundreds of alleged victims of the pesticide spray seeking money from international donors for the purpose. It would have become an issue concerning science if only the scientists had shown the courage to assert against the blatant scientific fraud. Not to be left behind, the media projected it as a great man-made tragedy. Therefore, the issue lost its focus.

On a wider canvas, the endosulfan controversy symbolised the modern trade war in which the European Union wanted to eliminate endosulfan, a generic pesticide from India and other tropical countries. European Union is the largest manufacturer of pesticide in the world. However, India is emerging as the sixth leading producer of pesticides. The EU, therefore, wanted to continue its monopoly in the field of pesticide manufacturing by manipulating the Multilateral Environmental Agreements involving chemicals in all the ensuing Stockholm conventions. Most probably, India's Environmental NGOs would be used as tools in the game being played out on the international turf in the coming years. Interestingly, the European Union used the Communist Party of India (Marxist) and the DYFI, its youth organisation, in the anti-pesticide agitation and also in the effort to ban endosulfan in the country.

The endosulfan controversy in India also strayed into the legal arena with the ad-interim ban on the pesticide by the Supreme Court following a writ petition filed by the DYFI. Significantly, the Supreme Court is yet to deliver the final judgement though it was more than three years since the court slapped the interim ban on May 13, 2011.

(But according to the pesticide industry, it was not keen to revive the case in the Supreme Court to get the ad-interim ban on endosulfan revoked since the industry had already incurred heavy losses as the raw materials for manufacturing the pesticide as well as the existing stock of endosulfan had already expired.

It was but natural that political parties would not let go a good opportunity before them. They used the opportunity to activate their cadres by organising agitations and even used the event for electoral politics. And that was what they had exactly done in organising a series of agitations or moving the court.

An important lesson to be learnt in this regard is that even in the age of development of science and technology in the country, science can still be manipulated to favour some powerful vested interests. And that is the cardinal lesson that scientists have to learn from the endosulfan issue. It has exposed the low quality of research being undertaken in the prestigious scientific institutions in the country.

Scientists can be made to fall in line with the thinking of the environmental NGOs. Pesticide manufacturers have alleged dry-labbing by a few scientists working in the prestigious scientific institutions of the country. Collecting samples of food and beverages from the market they can conduct any research. Nobody in the research institute would review the study which would be made known to the public only through the media causing much panic among the people.

Again, scientists should have exerted themselves when influential persons held media conference and made public statements that human beings can carry more than 100 ppm of pesticide residues in their blood and can still be hale and hearty. It was a finding which made fun of the basic principles of science. Instead of coming out against the mockery, scientists kept quiet. They thought that it was a local issue confined to a remote corner of Kerala. But they had no inkling that the endosulfan controversy was only a harbinger of the things to come if science continues to be manipulated in the country.

The discussion on endosulfan and the diseases it had allegedly caused in Kasargod had also come up in the visual media. But the focus of most participants including scientists was negative since the topic of discussion in television programme itself was negative. There would not be any discussion on 'nectar on our plate' when the topic was all about 'poison in our plate'.

But even when some scientists dared to tell the truth in academic forums they were heckled by activists who were planted at the venue of the discussion by interested groups. There was some discussion at the academic level in Kasargod on the endosulfan issue, but the discussions were marred by shouting and heckling.

Unfortunately, scientists as a whole remained lethargic as if they had no opinion of their own in the endosulfan controversy. They very carefully avoided any discussion since they knew that the endosulfan issue has already been co-opted by political leaders.

Doctors who said that they noticed no unusual diseases in the sprayed area were frowned upon. But there was a silver lining in the all pervading gloom when some doctors and scientists came forward to expose the string of lies.

There had been no genuine and serious debate in the internet and the social media on the endosulfan controversy except cramming of campaign materials in cyber space which was increasingly used for propaganda rather than for any serious debate.

In the absence of professional teams it was a free for all in the sprayed area. Scores of surveys were conducted by NGOs and other organisations which all said that there were unusual diseases in the area since that was the only way for them to collect money from foreign and local sources.

There are no laws in the country to punish the erring scientists. The pesticide manufacturers wrote letters to the Prime Minister to make arrangement to prove the unscientific claims of the Centre for Science and Environment, CSE, that people can carry more than 100 ppm of endosulfan in their blood! But nothing materialised.

The reporting of endosulfan controversy by the media can be a case study for journalists. The reporting by the media left much to be desired. Journalists could have discussed it among themselves and suggested measures to extricate the media from the quagmire of disinformation and false reporting in which it had fallen.

Except for a few, the media failed to bring out the truth. Media persons may be under pressure as editors normally demand more and more stories. The endosulfan controversy and the way in which they had reported have afforded an opportunity for journalists to evaluate their work professionally, free from any pressure from environmental NGOs.

Another lesson to be drawn is the role of the NGOs. Various NGOs receiving foreign money scuttle the development of the country. The endosulfan controversy underlined the need to reign in the NGOs trying to scuttle various development projects on behalf of foreign countries which pump money into their bank accounts.

Most often the NGOs functioning in the country with huge foreign funds work against the economic interest of the country. Through the social media network and internet they work against the interest of their own country with impunity. Unfortunately, there is no mechanism in the country to pull up and reign in their activities. While the Union government exposed the conspiracy at the POPRC in Geneva on the endosulfan issue by presenting dissenting notes, the Environmental NGOs were working against the government stand.

The worst affected by the ill motivated propaganda by the NGOs was the horticulture export in India. With an annual production of 75 million tonnes of fruits and 145 million tonnes of vegetables, India ranked one of the major producers of horticulture in the world. Because of the relentless propaganda carried on by Environmental NGOs through internet and the social media, the Indian food products were not finding steady markets in the western countries especially in the European Union.

Following the widespread propaganda of high endosulfan residues in vegetable and horticultural products, started by the NGOs, Indian food products were regarded as highly toxic in most of the foreign countries.

The NGOs wield clout in the domain of policy-making in the country. With hundreds of crores of rupees being pumped annually from foreign sources, the NGOs have become a powerful force in the country. Top scientists of the country working in the prestigious scientific institutions would be roped in to carry on fraudulent research to serve the interest of the NGOs.

Journalists fall easy victims to the Environmental NGOs which would give them tips of newsbreak to entice them. This would make journalists to depend on a single source for their reports resulting in the flouting of all journalistic norms and ethics.

The World Federation of Trade Unions had dubbed NGOs as tools of multinational capitalism. According to it, NGOs were the most dangerous weapons in the hands of multinational capitalism. The NGOs funded by capitalist groups had been engaged in diluting the working class ideology across the globe. The international monetary agencies had deputed hundreds of such organisations particularly in Asian and African countries.

Raising pro-people and catchy slogans on all issues, these NGOs engaged in fostering an ideological ambience suitable for popularising policies of transnational capitalism. True, the NGOs raised pro-people and catchy slogans on the endosulfan issue. The endosulfan issue was a multi-dimensional story. It involved frauds committed by NGOs in the first place using willing scientists to do their work. It was a case which badly reflected journalistic ethics and morality. When majority of media persons were roped in to project the fraudulent scientific research, the media ethics was scattered to the wind with readers permanently kept in the dark. The readers were treated to all sorts of untruths in the name of news stories.

Over a dozen crucial infrastructure projects worth billions of rupees were struck in India because of the silly objections and road blocks raised by various NGOs in the country. All of them were working in the area of environment, health and child welfare. They were all receiving money from abroad and misusing these funds for the purpose of blocking development activities. NGOs have, therefore, become the most powerful pressure groups in the country. They thrive on natural calamities and deprivation. The number of NGOs has risen by 100 per cent in the country over the past decade and the funds they were receiving rose by leaps and bounds.

Kerala has a lot to learn from the endosulfan controversy. It pointed to the need to reign in the so-called environmental activists. Kerala is a highly-politicised state dominated by communal and caste politics. With its favourable climate and resources Kerala should have towered above all other states in the country in terms of development. The economy of the state is buoyant mainly because of its expatriate workforce which remits back millions of dollars a year to keep the state afloat.

When the Gulf countries where majority of the state expatriates are working make any labour rules there, or if there are wars in the Gulf, it would send a shiver down the spine of Kerala fearing that lakhs of people employed in the Gulf countries would have to return home. But the state has no jobs to offer for the expatriates who may come from the Gulf countries in an exodus.

Agriculture was neglected despite the infrastructure facilities in the state and the favourable climate. Now Kerala depends on neighbouring states for all consumer goods including vegetables.

According to a study conducted by the Delhi-based Consortium of Indian Farmers Association, in spite of a plethora of government-run institutions and huge budgetary allocations, Kerala is dependent on other states to feed its burgeoning population. With 22 lakh hectares of land under cultivation in the state, it should have been a leading player in agriculture production in the country. Besides, the state is bestowed with 44 rivers and 2,700 mm average rainfall a year. Further, with more than 100 research stations under the Kerala Agriculture University, agriculture department and the Union government, a very favourable condition existed in the state for agriculture growth. But its performance was rather dismal.

Between 2005-2006 and 2009-2010, the agriculture income of the state declined from ₹ 18,042 crore to ₹ 16,681 crore. Rice production declined from 13 lakh tonnes in 2009-2010 to 6 lakh tonnes. The total requirement of the state is 40 lakh tonnes and the shortage was met from outside the state. Every farm crop in the state showed a drastic declining trend including tapioca, cashew nut, pepper, coconut and milk products.

The state is still in the midst of chronic power shortage resulting in frequent power outages and load shedding. It is dependent on hydro projects and the supply of power from the central power grid for its daily needs in the absence of nuclear plants.

Way back in 1990s, there was a proposal to set up a nuclear power plant in Peringom in north Malabar, but the project was abandoned in the wake of agitation by environmental activists. The proposal for Peringom nuclear plant in Kerala and the Kaiga nuclear plant in Karnataka was made by the Union government simultaneously. While the Kaiga nuclear plant was commissioned, the proposal for Peringom nuclear plant was abandoned in the face of strong opposition from environmental groups in the state. The state periodically organised investors' meet in which industrialists, both non-resident Indians and foreign players pledged crores of rupees for development projects. But the pity was that the state has no adequate power to meet its development needs.

Kerala has a plethora of environmental activists supported by Environmental NGOs getting foreign funds. A proposal was hanging fire for a coal-based thermal power plant in Kasargod district. As soon as the government made the announcement, all anti-endosulfan agitators in Kasargod and from other places made a bee-line to the proposed site of the thermal plant. They created panic among the local people that a thermal power plant would cause severe environmental pollution in the area endangering their lives. No wonder, many educated families are leaving Kerala and settling in other states.

REFERENCES/DOCUMENTS

1. Jayakrishnan T., Prabhakumari C. and Thomas Bina. Part 1 report of the community based 'epidemiological study of health status of population in Kasargod district, Kerala'. Part 2 report of the 'epidemiological study of health effects of endosulfan among adolescent population of Kasargod district in Kerala'. Part 3 report of the estimation of endosulfan residues in human blood in Kasargod, Kerala 2010-11.
2. Letter Ref. E 6/3428/2012/MCC from the Principal of the Kozhikode Medical College to the secretary of the Plantation Corporation Samrakshana Samithi on the epidemiological studies related to health in endosulfan affected areas at Kasargod district.
3. Letter No. 3095/2012/EC1 from State Public Information Officer, Endosulfan Cell, Kasargod to the secretary of the Plantation Corporation Samrakshana Samithi.
4. A critique of the epidemiological studies on health in allegedly endosulfan-affected areas in Kasargod district, published in Current Science, Vol. 104, January 2013 by K.M. Sreekumar and K.D. Prathapan.
5. Media, a bilingual monthly journal of the Kerala Press Academy, issue dated October, 2012.
6. Centre for Science and Environment, New Delhi, Pesticide Residue Monitoring Study CSE/PRM-1/2001.
7. Writ petition No. 10940/2011 on endosulfan filed in the Supreme Court and the recommendation dated 31/12/2010 of the National Human Rights Commission.

8. Original writ petition filed in the Supreme Court of India by the Democratic Youth Federation of India Vs the Union of India.
9. The list of 4,182 persons compiled by the Endosulfan Nodal Cell in two volumes.
10. Affidavit filed by the Democratic Youth Federation of India in the Supreme Court in reply to the response of the expanded joint expert committee appointed by the Supreme Court.
11. Letter no.11/21022(01)2009-FCRA-1 from the Ministry of Home Affairs, Government of India on the foreign contribution received by the Centre for Science and Environment, New Delhi.
12. Reply affidavit filed by the Pesticide Manufacturers and Formulators Association in the Supreme Court.
13. The joint paper presented by Dr K.M. Sreekumar and Dr K.D. Prathapan titled 'endosulfan prasnam—sasthram evide' at the Swadeshi Science Congress at CPCRI, Kasargod on November 7, 2012.
14. Legal notice served on Kerala Chief Secretary under section 80 of the Civil Procedure code by the secretary of the Plantation Corporation Samrakshana Samithi.
15. Response of the Expanded Joint Expert Committee on endosulfan to the Supreme Court.
16. Various orders of the Supreme Court on the endosulfan issue of Kasargod.
17. Writ petition filed by Plantation Corporation Samrakshana Samithi in the Kerala High Court.
18. Submission made by the Centre for Environment and Agrochemicals, CENTAGRO, to the Supreme Court appointed expert committee on endosulfan.
19. Report on pesticide residues prepared by the All India Network Project on Pesticide Residues, New Delhi.

20. The document relating to help given to endosulfan victims of Kasargod district by the state public information officer, Kasargod.
21. Print out from the official website of the Global Green Grants, US, allowing 1,150 dollar to Dr Mohammed Asheel to attend the Stockholm convention. Details of fund given to Thanal, an NGO based in Thiruvananthapuram by the Global Green Grants.
22. Letter no. 57567/2009/G4 from the Public Information Officer on the 486 persons died by endosulfan disaster.
23. Letter from the Public Information Officer to Plantation Corporation Samrakshna Samithi on the number of endosulfan victims in 11 gram pachayats in the district.
24. Colour poster issued by the Pesticide Action Network Asia and Pacific calling for ban on endosulfan.
25. India File, a book on India by Trevor Fishlock.
26. Study by Chengal Reddy, Secretary General of the Consortium of India Farmers Association on 'Regress of Kerala Agriculture'.
27. 'A dodgy game', report on foreign contribution to Thanal and the CSE by Sridhar in the wordpress.
28. Report on official trip to Geneva by Dr Mohammed Asheel, New Indian Express dated 30-4-2011.
29. Press release by the Centre for Science and Environment dated 28/6/2002 captioned 'An industry of death wins'.
30. Census of India 2001- The First report on disability in India-Census report 2001.
31. Report of expert group on endosulfan by Dr O.P. Dubey, Assistant Director General of the ICAR.
32. Order No. MS34/12 dated 21/122012 from the state department of agriculture exempting Plantation Corporation of Kerala from paying compensation to endosulfan victims.

33. Appeal issued by the Endosulfan Victims Relief and Remediation Cell seeking monetary help from the global community.
34. Report on endosulfan (JMPR) evaluations 1998 part II toxicology.
35. Report of the Australian Pesticides and Veterinary Medicines Authority dated 26/3/2010 on 'why endosulfan and carbendazim are still registered in Australia?
36. Review article on assessment of the developmental, reproductive and neurotoxicity on endosulfan by Marin H. Silva and Derek Gammon, department of pesticide regulation, California Environmental Protection Agency, California.
37. Report of the office of Chemical Safety and Pollution Prevention of the United States Environmental Protection Agency, Washington DC on 'Endosulfan: The health effect Divisions Human Risk Assessment'.
38. Book-Endosulfan: Promoted myths Vs proven facts.
39. Book-Chemistry of a scientific fraud on Sunita Narain's scientific scandal in analysing endosulfan residues, published by the CENTAGRO.
40. Book-Erring scientist in an eminent educational institute' exposing the scandal of Dr Padma S. Vankar, scientist of the IIT, Kanpur.
41. Draft discussion papers presented at the national work-shop on comprehensive rehabilitation of endosulfan victims held in Kasargod on July 21-22, 2012.
42. Document on the comprehensive health rehabilitation of endosulfan victims drawn up at the national workshop held in Kasargod.
43. Documents of the Persistent Organic Pollutants Review Committee, POPRC 4 and 5 meet.
44. Documents on Kerala High Court verdict banning endosulfan in Kerala.

45. 'Endosulfan-the Kerala story' published by the department of Health and Family Welfare.
46. OPEN weekly-issue dated 3rd June, 2013.
47. India Today magazine dated 23/6/2001.
48. Hindustan Times dated 16/11/2010.
49. Status report on endosulfan filed in the Supreme Court.
50. The executive summary of the report on endosulfan effect in Padre conducted by the STED.
51. Reply affidavit filed by the Pesticide Manufacturers and Formulators Association in the Supreme Court.
52. Report of the National Institute of Occupational Health, NIOH.
53. Report in the Daily News Analysis, DNA, 'on European Union uses NGOs to push for Endosulfan ban' dated 7/12/2009.
54. Study on endosulfan in Cotton soil under sub-tropical conditions by S. Kathpal, Punjab University.
55. Letter by the Indian Chemical Council to the Prime Minister dated 26/10/2010.
56. Report of the US-based Environ International criticising the epidemiological study of the National Institute of Occupational Health.

Index

N

O

P